Transnational Pakistani Connections

Since restrictions on commonwealth labour immigration to Britain in the 1960s, marriage has been the dominant form of migration between Pakistan and the UK. Most transnational Pakistani marriages are between cousins or other more distant relatives, lending a particular texture to this transnational social field. Based on research in Britain and Pakistan, this book provides a rounded portrayal incorporating the emotional motivations for, and content of, these transnational unions.

The book explores the experiences of families and individuals involved, including the neglected experiences of migrant husbands, and charts the management of the risks of contracting transnational marriages, as well as examining the consequences in cases when marriages run into conflict. Equally, however, the book explores the attractions of marrying 'back home', and the role of transnational marriage in maintaining bonds between people and places. Marriage emerges as a crucial, but dynamic and contested, element of Pakistani transnational connections.

This book is of interest to students and scholars in the fields of migration studies, kinship/the family and South Asian studies, as well as social work, family law and immigration.

Katharine Charsley is Senior Lecturer in Sociology at the University of Bristol, UK. Her research interests are in gender, kinship and migration, with a particular specialism in marriage-related migration. Her edited volume *Transnational Marriage* was published by Routledge in 2012.

Routledge/Edinburgh South Asian Studies Series
Series Editor:
Crispin Bates and the Editorial Committee of the Centre for South Asian Studies, Edinburgh University, UK.

The *Routledge/Edinburgh South Asian Studies Series* is published in association with the Centre for South Asian Studies, Edinburgh University – one of the leading centres for South Asian Studies in the UK, with a strong interdisciplinary focus. This series presents research monographs and high-quality edited volumes as well as textbooks on topics concerning the Indian subcontinent from the modern period to contemporary times. It aims to advance understanding of the key issues in the study of South Asia, and contributions include works by experts in the social sciences and the humanities. In accordance with the academic traditions of Edinburgh, we particularly welcome submissions which emphasise the social in South Asian history, politics, sociology and anthropology, based upon thick description of empirical reality, generalised to provide original and broadly applicable conclusions.

The series welcomes new submissions from young researchers as well as established scholars working on South Asia, from any disciplinary perspective.

Gender and Sexuality in India
Selling sex in Chennai
Salla Sariola

Savagery and Colonialism in the Indian Ocean
Power, pleasure and the Andaman Islanders
Satadru Sen

Sovereignty and Social Reform in India
British colonialism and the campaign against Sati, 1830–60
Andrea Major

Empire, Nationalism and the Postcolonial World
Rabindranath Tagore's writings on history, politics and society
Michael Collins

The Guru in South Asia
New interdisciplinary perspectives
Jacob Copeman and Aya Ikeman

Princely India Re-imagined
A historical anthropology of Mysore
Aya Ikegame

Empire, Industry and Class
The imperial nexus of Jute, 1840–1940
Anthony Cox

Violence, Torture and Memory in Sri Lanka
Life after terror
Dhana Hughes

Transnational Pakistani Connections
Marrying 'back home'
Katharine Charsley

Transnational Pakistani Connections

Marrying 'back home'

Katharine Charsley

LONDON AND NEW YORK

First published 2013
by Routledge
2 Park Square, Milton Park, Abingdon, Oxon OX14 4RN

and by Routledge
711 Third Avenue, New York, NY 10017

Routledge is an imprint of the Taylor & Francis Group, an informa business

© 2013 Katharine Charsley

The right of Katharine Charsley to be identified as author of this work has been asserted by her in accordance with sections 77 and 78 of the Copyright, Designs and Patents Act 1988.

All rights reserved. No part of this book may be reprinted or reproduced or utilised in any form or by any electronic, mechanical, or other means, now known or hereafter invented, including photocopying and recording, or in any information storage or retrieval system, without permission in writing from the publishers.

Trademark notice: Product or corporate names may be trademarks or registered trademarks, and are used only for identification and explanation without intent to infringe.

British Library Cataloguing in Publication Data
A catalogue record for this book is available from the British Library

Library of Congress Cataloging in Publication Data
Charsley, Katharine.
 Transnational Pakistani connections : marrying back home / Katharine Charsley.
  p. cm. – (Routledge/edinburgh south asian studies series)
 Includes bibliographical references and index.
 1. Intercountry marriage. 2. Intercountry marriage–Great Britain. 3. Transnationalism. I. Title.
 HQ1032.C444 2013
 306.84'5–dc23
            2013021546

ISBN: 978-0-415-66066-2 (hbk)
ISBN: 978-1-315-88643-5 (ebk)

Typeset in Times New Roman
by Taylor & Francis Books

Printed and bound by CPI Group (UK) Ltd, Croydon, CR0 4YY

Contents

List of illustrations		viii
Acknowledgements		ix
Introduction		1
1	Weddings	25
2	British Pakistanis and transnationalism	48
3	*Zarurat rishta*: making and maintaining connections	61
4	Close kin marriage: reducing and reproducing risk	86
5	Married but not married: the divisibility of weddings and the protection of women	114
6	Conflicting interests: rifts, concealment, *izzat* and emotion	134
7	Migrant *mangeters*: masculinity, marriage and migration	157
8	Gender, emotion and balancing the picture	183
	Bibliography	190
	Index	205

Illustrations

I.1 Pakistani spouses and fiancés granted entry clearance to the UK, 1990–2000   8
I.2 Pakistani spouses granted settlement in the UK, 2000–09   8

Acknowledgements

This book would not have been possible without the help and support of many people. Foremost are those who took part in the research, offering their time and, in many cases, their friendship. Acknowledging the contributions of participants to ethnographic research without undermining anonymity is difficult, but I wish to express my deep gratitude to you all. In addition, I am grateful to Fatima Jinnah Women's University (Rawalpindi), Aisha Gul Siddiqqi and family, Dr Humala Khalid and family, and Dr Humera and Sabih Rehman, for their help and hospitality in Pakistan, and to Russell and Cabeiri for their support. In Bristol, particular thanks are due to Dhek Bhal, the Bristol Pakistani Community Welfare Organisation (formerly the Bristol Pakistani Women's Organisation) and Aisha Ghauri (for research assistance).

At the University of Edinburgh, Prof. Patricia Jeffery and Prof. Janet Carsten provided thoughtful and inspiring doctoral supervision, and Prof. Tony Good was an excellent postdoctoral mentor. Staff and students in Edinburgh, Oxford and Bristol have provided productive and supportive environments in which to work. Doctoral funding was provided by the ESRC and an RAI/Sutasoma Award. Further research was enabled by the generosity of the Institute of Social and Cultural Anthropology at the University of Oxford, and the award of a University Research Fellowship from the Institute for Advanced Studies, University of Bristol enabled the final push to bring the book together. I am also grateful to Crispin Bates, the editor of this series, for his encouragement and attention to detail. Parveen Akhtar and the anonymous reviewers for Routledge gave useful comments on drafts. My father, mother and brother have given me invaluable moral, intellectual (and financial) support throughout. Finally, of course, thank you to Jerry, and to Lewis who has provided additional inspiration in the last six years.

Parts of my original doctoral thesis were published as articles. Further research for this book means that most have been revised and updated. I am grateful to the journals for permission to reuse the sections that remain unchanged. These publications are:

Charsley, K. (2005) 'Unhappy Husbands: Masculinity and Migration in Transnational Pakistani Marriages', *Journal of the Royal Anthropological Institute* (N.S.) 11: 85–105.

——(2005) 'Vulnerable Brides and Transnational Ghar Damad: Gender, Risk and "Adjustment" among Pakistani Marriage Migrants to Britain', *Indian Journal of Gender Studies* 12(2): 381–406.
——(2006) 'Risk and Ritual: The Protection of British Pakistani Women in Transnational Marriage', *Journal of Ethnic and Migration Studies* 32(7): 1169–88.
——(2007) 'Risk, Trust, Gender and Transnational Cousin Marriage among British Pakistanis', *Ethnic and Racial Studies* 30(6): 1117–31.
Shaw, A. and K. Charsley (2006) 'Rishtas: Adding Emotion to Strategy in Understanding British Pakistani Transnational Marriages', *Global Networks* 6 (4): 405–21.

Introduction

Marriage is increasingly on the immigration policy agenda in Europe. As states seek to control the volume of non-European immigration, the fact that marriage is the route for a substantial proportion of settlement migration from these sources (Kofman 2004) has not escaped notice. The intra-ethnic marriages of ethnic minority populations have received particular attention. These are often represented in policy and media discourse as presenting barriers to integration (a first generation in every generation), or as symptomatic of unequal gender and generational relationships exemplified by the figure of the young European-raised woman forced by her parents into marriage overseas. Such marriages are, moreover, represented as risky even for those willingly involved, carrying the danger that a citizen's trust will be misused by a foreign spouse more interested in migration than in the marital relationship.

Those who take a cynical view of governmental discourses of protection and risk point to the fact that thanks to the European Convention on Human Rights duty to 'respect the right to family life', marriage is a link in chains of migration that has proven particularly difficult to disrupt. As marriage has become one of the few widely available routes for migration into Europe, contracting transnational marriages has thus been represented as a strategy for continuing immigration, with marriage-migrants seen as creative 'border artistes' (Beck-Gernsheim 2011). The intention of this book is to provide a more rounded and balanced portrayal of transnational marriages which incorporates issues of risk and the incentives of immigration, but does not reduce these marriages to matters of power and strategy alone, instead leaving room for the emotional lives and relationships of those involved. In doing so, I hope to provide more pieces of the answer to a puzzle with which many contemporary researchers have grappled (e.g. Beck-Gernsheim 2007; González-Ferrer 2006; Shaw 2001): Why do so many young people marry 'back home' – i.e. with a spouse from their parental or grandparental homeland – when the 'home' in which they have been raised is located in a European country?

The book cannot hope, however, to provide a complete answer, not least because it deals with just one of the ethnic groups involved. The particularities of migration histories and marriage preferences are among the factors influencing motivations for and experiences of marrying transnationally. A significant proportion of Pakistani marriages, for example, take place between cousins or other relatives. Marriage patterns are likely to be more varied among the Indian spouses who also migrate in significant numbers to Britain: kin group endogamy (marriage within the group) is usually avoided by north Indian Hindus and Sikhs, whilst preferences for consanguineous (literally: 'of the same blood', a term used to refer to people descended from the same ancestor) marriage are found in some south Indian populations.[1] A quarter of transnational unions among the Turkish minority in France are apparently consanguineous (Milewski and Hamel 2010), but the proportion is much higher among Pakistanis – over 90% of transnational marriages in one study carried out in Oxford were between kin (Shaw 2001). The patterns and significance of transnational marriages vary, in part at least, because of such differences (Ballard 1990; Charsley and Shaw 2006). Kin marriage lends transnational unions a particular enduring significance for Pakistanis. Their lasting appeal has been demonstrated most clearly under Denmark's exceptionally restrictive marriage immigration regime, which has made it all but impossible for young people from migrant backgrounds to import a spouse from outside Europe (Jørgensen 2012). Despite this, some Danish Pakistanis still marry transnationally, moving across the border to Sweden in order to be reunited with their spouse (Rytter 2011; Schmidt et al. 2009).

In Britain, where the immigration regime has (as yet) not been so restrictive, Pakistanis have long been the largest nationality group of marriage migrants,[2] making them a particularly important subject for research. In addition to exploring motivations for British Pakistanis marrying Pakistani nationals, the aim of this book is to provide insight into the processes of transnational marriage arrangements, and the hopes, fears and experiences of settled and migrant spouses and their families. Whilst previous studies of Pakistani marriage practices have stressed strategic motivations for partner choice, and the literature on Pakistani kinship and marriage will be reviewed at greater length in later chapters, a main strand of my argument is the need for attention to the emotional logics of marrying across borders, but (often) within the extended family. In this, it joins recent scholarship that challenges rigid, unemotional models of South Asian marriage (e.g. Grover 2009; Parry 2001; Mody 2002b).

Emotion, migration and transnationalism

Research for this book took place in two phases. In 2000–01, I spent six months in the Pakistani Punjab, followed by a year in the city of Bristol in south-west England. In 2007–08, I carried out a second round of fieldwork in Bristol, catching up with some of those with whom I had worked earlier, and interviewing new contacts. After my first 18 months of research, I returned to my native Scotland. A few weeks later, a Pakistani friend from Bristol phoned to say that she was missing me. In Urdu, she told me that she felt as if her younger sister had got married. This touching statement encapsulates much about both the product of my research, and my engagement with the topic and with those who helped me reach these understandings.

Unless married into the same household, Pakistani sisters are normally separated by marriage as they leave the natal home they shared as children to live with their husbands and (commonly) her in-laws.[3] Migration is thus part of the conventional experience of most Pakistani women, who may not migrate internationally as the subjects of this study have done, but migrate for marriage nevertheless. It is in this context that it is enough for my friend to mention a sister's marriage to evoke her leaving. Migration, this book will contend, is both a gendered and an emotional matter. My friend's simile, after all, presents the separation of sisters by marriage as an archetype of sadness at the loss of female friendship. In contemporary transnational marriages, however, comparable numbers of men and women migrate.

The emotional content of my friend's phonecall conjures up other compelling factors in this research. Marriage and migration are sensitive matters, not only in the political sense, but also in terms of emotion. Whilst much of my fieldwork passed without drama or intensity, there were points at which the strength of the sentiments of those with whom I worked made a powerful impact on me. At least one interview ended in tears and hugs. Perhaps as a result of this property of the topic – its intimacy – my original fieldwork led to some friendships with women that I value highly. Returning to Bristol after the birth of my son in 2007 provided an opportunity both to update my research and renew some friendships – although family life and employment introduced limitations on my time which had been absent in the earlier phase of research. Nevertheless, these experiences and relationships led to a determination to give an account of these transnational marriages that does not sacrifice such women's (or men's) feelings to a structural or strategic interpretation of marriage, but one which gives emotion a central place in both my evocation of experience and explanation of practice. In this, the study joins an emergent literature exploring emotion, mobility and transnationalism (see Boehm and Swank 2011; Skrbiš 2008; Svašek 2008, 2010 for useful overviews of this body of work). Migration experiences can produce profound emotions, both positive (e.g. in response to the liberatory potential much debated in the gender and migration scholarship) and negative (e.g. loss of loved people and places, rejection through discrimination) (Espin 1997). Incorporating emotion into ethnographic accounts of migration can therefore give greater depth to understanding, 'allowing us to explore the phenomenological, experiential dimensions ... more fully than we would otherwise be able to do' (Maschio 1998: 97). As Skrbiš (2008) has argued, however, emotion is also constitutive of migration experience. Emotions, quite simply, are crucial to any exploration of how people make sense of events, providing us with a 'fuller view of *what is at stake* for people in everyday life' (Lutz and White 1986: 431). In other words, incorporating emotion improves the accuracy of our interpretations of people's motivations for decisions or actions: 'To know what is considered dangerous, a thing worth having, or a loss is crucial for understanding the

4 *Introduction*

motivational basis for all aspects of participation in social life' (Lutz and White 1986: 428).

Emotion can enhance not only understandings of migration, but of the content and experience of relatedness (cf. Abu-Lughod 1988; Jeffery and Jeffery 1996; Lambert 2000a, 2000b; Parkes 2000; Raheja and Gold 1994; Trawick 1990), both central to this exploration of Pakistani marriage migration. Hence, throughout the book the emotional aspects of key concepts concerning Pakistani kin relations, such as *rishta* (proposal/relationship) and *izzat* (honour), are explored as they interweave with migration and transnationalism. Seen in this way, emotions are a 'constitutive part of the transnational family experience' (Skrbiš 2008: 242).

In their exploration of cross-cousin marriages between south India and Singapore, Velayutham and Wise (2005) suggest a 'regime of affect' policed by translocal co-villagers through guilt, shame and fear of ostracism if the expectation of endogamy is not respected. Equally, however, more positive affective ties may underlie the 'emotional labour' (Hochschild 1983) and 'kin work' (di Leonardo 1987; Gardner 2006) in which migrants engage to maintain connections across distance, through visiting, gifting, communication and, here, the arrangement of marriages (Baldassar 2007; Svašek 2010). Transnationalism, moreover, is a complex, disjunctive condition (cf. Appadurai 1990) characterised by inequalities and disruptions (Carling 2008) as much as connection and simultaneity (Levitt and Glick Schiller 2004), so that 'simultaneous transnational ties and disruptions result in complex emotional expressions', in which emotion 'shapes, negotiates and mediates connectedness and disconnectedness' (Boehm and Swank 2011: 1–3). The tracing of these ties and tensions is a central theme of this book. This approach not only helps to 'reanimate the sometimes robotic image of humans which social science has purveyed' (Lutz and White 1986: 431) – a problem that is certainly encountered in studies of migration 'flows' in which migrants as people with emotional lives are not always visible (Turton 2003) – but casts light on processes underlying migration trends. Barbalet (1998, 2002) suggests that as fear of unemployment leading to the establishment of the trade union movements, a social group's 'emotional climate' can lead directly to large-scale social and institutional change. Emotion, it follows, can enhance our understandings of processes not just at an individual level, but as an explanatory factor in wider trends, such as the transnational marriages that are the subject of this book. Contemporary transnational marriages between Britain and Pakistan must also, however, be understood in the context of the history of Pakistani migration. The following sections of this introduction therefore set issues of emotion to one side to provide a brief sketch of this historical and political context.

Pakistani migration

The state of Pakistan was itself born of massive migrations. Between what is called Independence from a Pakistani perspective, or Partition from the point of view of India, and the closing of the border in 1951, 14 million people moved between the two countries. These migrants formed nearly a quarter of the Pakistani population by 1951, and almost half of the inhabitants of the new nation's largest cities (Burki 1988: 11–13). Migration has continuing significance for Pakistan, both in the form of rural–urban movement, and in the large numbers of Pakistani international labour migrants. Migrant remittances make a substantial contribution to Pakistan's economy, and as such are the focus of much government concern and investigation – for example into the informal 'Hundi' money-sending schemes which by-pass state control (OPF n.d.). Much of this movement has been to the Middle East and Gulf states as a consequence of the oil 'boom' of the 1970s and subsequent development. This migration has tended to be temporary, cyclical and overwhelmingly male, due to a combination of socio-cultural, economic and legal factors, with most workers on temporary contracts (Azam 1995) – although increasing Pakistani settlement in the Gulf is reported (Kalra 2009). In the 1960s and 1970s, the building by multinational companies of the massive Mangla and Tarbela dams provided opportunities for construction work. The projects were completed at about the same time as the oil boom, and many Pakistani workers moved to new jobs for the same companies in the Middle East (Azam 1995). Throughout this period, unskilled workers were encouraged to migrate, and in the financial year ending 1976, remittances from the Middle East formed nearly a third of Pakistan's total foreign exchange earnings. Simultaneously, however, there was concern over the numbers of trained physicians leaving Pakistan for the Middle East, to the extent that in 1973, martial law regulations were introduced intended to block this 'brain drain' (Noman 1990).

Migration to Britain from what is now Pakistan pre-dates the creation of the Pakistani state (Anwar 1979; Shaw 1988), but increased in the post-war period as workers needed to rebuild the British economy were recruited from the Commonwealth and Pakistan. Pressure on land and unemployment contributed a 'push' to add to this economic 'pull', but at the beginning of the 1960s, factors in both countries created further spurs to migration. Dam construction in Pakistan once again played a significant role. During the 1960s, 100,000 Mirpuris were displaced by the construction of the Mangla dam.[4] Some moved elsewhere within the country, whilst others used their compensation to start a new life in the UK. Policy changes in both Britain and Pakistan encouraged migration in the form of a 'beat the ban' rush preceding British immigration reforms in 1962 (Anwar 1979: 24): in 1961, Pakistan removed restrictions on emigration in order to promote the migration of 5,000 people as compensation to villagers dispossessed by the Mangla dam, whilst in the UK, the Commonwealth Immigrants Act of 1962 was about to remove the right of Pakistanis to settle in Britain. Thereafter, access was restricted to those with 'vouchers' granted on the basis of employment in Britain, specific skills, or service in the Second World War, and to the dependants of those already living in Britain. This reinforced patterns of chain migration from certain regions of Pakistan to specific areas of the UK (Shaw 1988: 25–26). Most initial migrants came with the intention of earning money and returning to Pakistan after a few years. The major areas of settlement in the UK – West Yorkshire and the West Midlands – reflect the industrial labour shortages drawing such workers to Britain. These male labour migrants left their wives and children in Pakistan and often lived in crowded accommodation shared with other Pakistani men. After the immigration reforms of the 1960s, however, wives and families started to arrive from Pakistan (Shaw 1988), and over the years, as children have been born and grown up here, the 'myth of return' (Anwar 1979) has tended to fade – although Bolognani (2007) suggests experiences of Islamophobia may have reinvigorated ideas of 'ethnic return' migration amongst younger generations of British Pakistanis. Some initial migrants also still harbour dreams of retirement 'back home', but accurate figures on migration from Britain to Pakistan are difficult to obtain.[5]

The Ministry of Overseas Pakistanis (a government department) estimates the number of Pakistanis living in the UK at 1.2 million.[6] The population has been growing rapidly – between the 1991 and 2001 censuses the number of people living in Great Britain giving Pakistani as their ethnic group grew from 494,973 to 727,727.[7] Most of this growth can be accounted for by children born in Britain – the population is disproportionately young, and family sizes tend to be larger than for other ethnic groups (Modood *et al.* 1997), but migration had continued to make a substantial contribution to the growth of the British Pakistani population. In 2000, for example, 11,270 grants of entry for settlement in Britain (subject to a probationary period) were given to applicants from Pakistan (as well as 58,670 grants of entry clearance for temporary purposes). In the same year, 11,010 applications for settlement by Pakistani nationals were accepted, representing almost 10% of the total for the UK.[8] Contemporary Pakistani migration is diverse, including students, irregular migrants and work permit holders, but the majority of settlement migration in recent decades has been through marriage: in 2000, 4,720 husbands and fiancés and 5,560 wives and fiancées in Pakistan obtained entry clearance (Home Office 2001).

Whilst Britain is home to the largest diasporic Pakistani population outside the Gulf, there are significant Pakistani presences in Scandinavia and Germany, smaller populations in other European countries such as Italy and Greece, and North America is an increasingly popular destination (Ballard 1990; Rana 2009; Ahmad 2009). Migrants and their children often retain networks of linkages between various sites in the diaspora, and may even relocate once more. As long ago as 1976, Patricia Jeffery (1976a: 67) documented instances of onward migration from Britain to Canada, and within the global Pakistani community migration continues, not only for work, but also for marriage.

A few cases from my fieldwork will illustrate these global networks and movement. The daughter of a friend in Pakistan, for example, married an engineer in Saudi Arabia. The couple have since moved between Pakistan and the Gulf, where they now look likely to settle for at least the medium term. A few years ago, it seemed more likely that she would follow in the footsteps of her mother's sister and marry in Britain. Two of this aunt's British children have married other cousins from Pakistan. Another woman in Bristol told me that after her daughter is married to a father's brother's son from Pakistan, the young man hopes to gain employment in computing in America, where they will join other close relatives. The bride's mother wondered whether she and her husband may eventually take advantage of the opportunity this could offer to move to the USA, where she considers that her relatives enjoy a better quality of life. A third woman informant in Bristol grew up in Denmark and had come to the UK after marrying a British cousin in a ceremony held in Pakistan, where other close relatives still live.[9]

Marriage migration to Britain

No national figures are available on the proportions of British Pakistanis marrying transnationally. Figures for Bradford in 1992–94 report that 57.6% of Pakistani marriages were to spouses from Pakistan, whilst a survey in Oxford found that 71% of marriages were with spouses from Pakistan, predominantly relatives (Shaw 2001: 327). A review of the Labour Force Surveys from 1992–2005 suggests that 57% of adult UK-born Pakistani women, and 48% of UK-born Pakistani men, had a spouse who migrated to the UK over the age of 18 (Dale 2008), whilst a longer review of the same survey from 1979–2006 found that 68.8% of Pakistani men and 61.1% of Pakistani women born in the UK, or who came to the UK as children, had a spouse who had migrated to Britain after the age of 18 (Georgiadis and Manning 2011). Comparing earlier (born in the 1960s) and later (born from the 1970s) cohorts, Georgiadis and Manning (2011: 555) observe that the proportions married to migrants have remained relatively stable. During my initial fieldwork in Bristol, transnational marriage was the norm to such an extent that on hearing of a school class-fellow's engagement, one young woman informant immediately asked about the future husband's immigration and was surprised to hear that the fiancé was in fact from Bristol.[10]

The numbers of spouses entering Britain from Pakistan rose during the 1990s (see Figure I.1), so that the total number of husbands and wives granted entry clearance more than doubled, from 4,390 in 1990 to 10,280 in 2000. Statistics for spousal entry clearance by nationality were no longer available after 2000, but those for settlement (grants of permanent residence) in 2000–09 are shown in Figure I.2. A dramatic fall in numbers granted settlement in 2003–04 is probably attributable to the closure of consular services in Pakistan for a period after the terrorist attacks of 11 September 2001 (9/11). It is as yet too early to tell whether the figure of 13,035 grants of spousal settlement in 2009 represents a sustained increase in numbers, after the previous decline since 2003.[11] The settlement figures include spouses of migrants, and migrants marrying in the UK, as well as those of British Pakistanis, so this increase does not necessarily reflect renewed popularity of transnational marriages among the 'British-born'.

8 Introduction

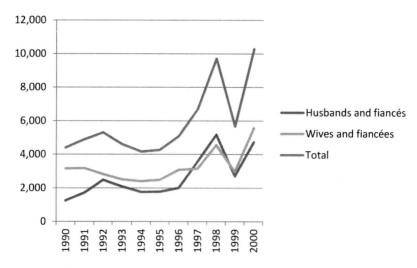

Figure I.1 Pakistani spouses and fiancés granted entry clearance to the UK, 1990–2000

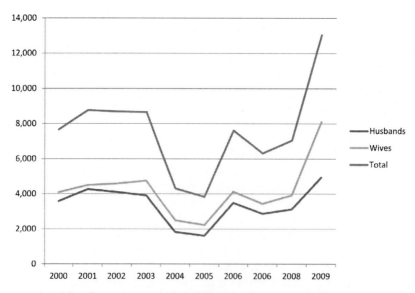

Figure I.2 Pakistani spouses granted settlement in the UK, 2000–09

The changing policy context and fluctuating rates of refusals of applications for spousal visas further complicate the statistical picture. Wray (2011) has provided a valuably detailed account of the regulation of spousal migration to Britain, so I will restrict what follows to highlighting some of the more significant developments.

The 'Primary Purpose Rule' (hereafter PPR), in force between 1980 and 1997, required applicants to prove that the 'primary purpose' of the marriage was not to obtain entry to Britain. This piece of legislation was widely seen as an attempt to limit South Asian immigration in particular (Menski 1999), as part of a broader approach based on a hierarchy of acceptable marriages (Wray 2011). Not only was the requirement hard to fulfil for many partners to arranged marriages, who lacked a romantic history to evince other motivations, but the rule affected male marriage migrants disproportionately, given that migrant husbands were moving against a cultural norm of virilocality, and assumptions that women were less likely to have economic motivations (Gardner and Shukur 1994: 156). In the mid-1990s, more applications for entry clearance by husbands and fiancés from the subcontinent were being initially refused than granted, whilst more than twice as many wives and fiancées were given visas as were refused. The abolition of the PPR in 1997 led to a steep increase in grants of entry clearance to Pakistanis – particularly to husbands and fiancés (from 2,000 in 1996, to 5,160 the year after the abolition) (Home Office 2001).

In the early years of the New Labour government, there was thus a more favourable climate for transnational marriage migration, and efforts were made to clear the backlog of immigration applications. Under 'fast track' schemes in place in 1999 and 2000, the first few applicants on a particular day who could demonstrate adequate documentation and income in the UK would be seen and issued visas on the same day. These initiatives reduced average waiting times to first interview at the Islamabad High Commission from $9^{3}/_{4}$ months for spouses, and 11 months for fiancés (Home Office 1999) to $4^{1}/_{4}$ months for spouses and $5^{1}/_{4}$ for fiancés (Home Office 2001). This scheme was very popular, and several of those I interviewed had benefited from it, whilst another family was very disappointed to discover that the 'fast-track' programme was over, as the daughter had planned to bring her new husband home with her when she returned from her wedding in Pakistan.

The post-1997 period saw a broader shift towards a more positive view of the potential impacts of immigration, and a move towards 'managed migration' in order to maximise the numbers of highly skilled or educational migrants, whilst controlling the influx of other groups considered less desirable. This latter category increasingly, however, included family migrants. European concerns with the 'failure of multiculturalism' and problems of 'integration' or 'social cohesion' soon saw a renewed political problematisation of the transnational marriage practices of British South Asians (Wray 2011; Gedalof 2007). A section of the 2002 immigration White Paper *Secure Borders, Safe Haven* which attracted considerable controversy and protest from members of Britain's South Asian population set out the government's position:

> As time goes on, we expect the number of arranged marriages between UK children and those living abroad to decline. Instead, parents will seek

to choose a suitable partner for their children from among their own communities in this country.

(Home Office 2002: 99)

Not only did some commentators suggest that these inter-ethnic, cross-border marriages promoted segregation and hindered integration (Migration Watch UK 2004, 2005; Kurtz 2007a, 2007b), but there was an increasing focus on the problems of 'sham' marriages (marriages of convenience for immigration purposes) (Wray 2006a) and forced marriage. After the high-profile rescue by the MP Mohammed Sarwar of two Glaswegian-Pakistani girls forced into marriage in Pakistan in 1996 (*The Guardian* 1999), and a number of legal cases involving South Asian women appeared in the British press (Alibhai-Brown 1998a, 1998b, 1998c, 1999), the Home Office set up a working group on the issue, which published its report *A Choice by Right* in June 2000 (Home Office 2000). Although the report takes pains to point out that forced marriages are encountered in many ethnic groups, the issue is generally thought of as a South Asian (and particularly Muslim) problem, as witnessed by the government commissioning a report on 'community perceptions' of forced marriage among Pakistani and Bangladeshi populations in Britain (Samad and Eade 2002).

When I visited the Islamabad British High Commission in 2000, staff complained that since the abolition of the PPR it had been difficult to make a strong case for the rejection of a spouse when they felt that the application was, in the Home Office's terminology, 'bogus'. I was told that even if a British citizen reported in the visa interview that they had been forced to marry and requested that the spouse be refused entry to the UK, it could be difficult to ensure that this did indeed happen. An entry clearance officer (ECO) told me that they had to be extremely careful in such cases, as any hint that the applicant was being rejected on primary purpose grounds would be used in case of appeal. An ECO may refuse the application on the grounds of doubts over the intention of the couple to live together permanently as man and wife, but the visa would be likely to be granted on appeal unless the young person was prepared to stand up in court and say that they did not want their spouse to be allowed into Britain. As pressure from or fear of family members was often the reason that they went through with the marriage in the first place, perhaps assuming that they would be able to scupper the immigration process later on, many were unwilling to take the step of public testimony.[12] Critics, however, have argued that the minority practice of forced marriage has been used to justify restrictions motivated more by immigration concerns than protecting vulnerable young people (Menski 1999; Wilson 2007).

This triple problematisation of marriage migration, as associated with integration problems, forced marriage and immigration fraud, has been used to justify tightening the immigration rules in several ways (for parallel European developments see Bonjour 2010; Bredal 2005; Jørgensen 2012; Schmidt 2011). The probationary period before settlement was increased from one to two years in 2003, and to five years in 2012. Minimum ages for both sponsoring and migrant spouses were increased from 16 to 18 (in 2003–04) and then to 21 (in 2008). The Certificates of Approval scheme introduced in 2005 required migrants to apply for permission from the Home Office before marrying in the UK (permission would be denied to those with less than six months remaining on their visa), and in 2010 the new Coalition government introduced pre-entry English language testing for spouses. In 2011, it was reported that a ministerial authorisation had permitted discriminating against visa applications from countries deemed to be 'high risk' in terms of immigration fraud,[13] whilst 2012 saw the introduction of higher minimum income requirements for those sponsoring the immigration of a spouse.

In retrospect, the late 1990s and turn of the new century, when many of the marriages described in this research took place, was a period in which marital mobility from Pakistan to Britain was relatively unrestricted. Concerns over the encounter with the immigration authorities were still present in my research – one young man told me how advice on the formal presentation of documentation and statements was passed down from family members, whilst Chapter 5 discusses mechanisms by which British Pakistani families may seek to protect daughters against the eventuality that a husband is denied a visa. However, the number of refusals I encountered was relatively low, and negotiating immigration requirements was not a major theme of my interviews.

Returning to the field in 2007–08, my impression was that the popularity of transnational marriages had declined somewhat since my initial fieldwork. Talk of an increasing number of divorces among transnationally married couples was common, and the discourse of forced marriage seemed to have been more widely adopted.[14] Whilst I had come across a couple of cases described as forced in my initial fieldwork, I heard the term more frequently in 2008. One woman told me that there were degrees of force, on a continuum that included, to her mind, more subtle pressure from families to agree to a marriage. By this definition, she said she had several friends who had been forced to marry in Pakistan. When she asked another friend, engaged to a migrant, whether she knew her marriage was forced, the friend replied that she did, but that she was going to go through with it anyway. This same friend, however, told me that divorce was becoming much more acceptable, so women know that if they are not happy with a marriage they don't have to live with the person for ever, suggesting she may have had one eye on the possibility of exit. Another woman who had not described her marriage as forced in 2000 told me later that she had not wanted to marry the Pakistani cousin her parents had selected, and had only agreed so that she could stay living near her mother. Her increasing trust in me after several years' acquaintance may have played a role in the change in her narrative, but the statement was made in front of a group of other women, and reflects a wider shift among many of those with whom I worked in evaluating the nature of parental influence in marital choices, although as this example shows, this does not necessarily entail conflictual inter-generational relationships. The transnational marriages described in this book should therefore not be viewed as an unchanging cultural norm, but as a particular point – although perhaps given the legal and demographic context, a particularly interesting point – in a dynamic process of negotiating relationships between marriage and migration (cf. Rytter 2012).

The Bristol Pakistani community

The study is also based on fieldwork carried out in particular places, with distinct social characteristics.

Bristol is a city in the south-west of England of just over 380,000 people. The 2001 census (the most recent available at the time of writing, and that most relevant to the period in which the research was conducted) gives Bristol population figures for self-ascribed ethnicity of 5,585 black Caribbeans, 4,595 Indians and 4,050 Pakistanis, the latter accounting for 1.06% of the inhabitants of the city. Bristolians tend to have a clear conceptual map of ethnic minority residential concentration in the city, with St Pauls near the city centre thought of as the 'black' area, and Easton, a little further east, talked of as the main 'Asian' area. Ethnic minority households can of course be found in most areas, including the most affluent, and many Pakistanis live in St Pauls, and Afro-Caribbeans in Easton. Indeed, Patricia Jeffery reports that the majority of initial Pakistani migrants to the city in the 1950s and 1960s settled in St Pauls, attracted like those from the Caribbean and Ireland before them by the cheap but dilapidated housing in this depopulated inner-city area. By the time of her research in the early 1970s, some had moved north to Montpelier, east to Easton, or south of the river to Totterdown and Bedminster (Jeffery 1976a).[15]

There is, however, some truth to the simplistic model of an 'Asian' area of Bristol. Easton has become a centre for Muslim and South Asian services, with food and cloth shops, mosques and community centres, and has a large Pakistani population. To give a rough idea of the ethnic geography of the city around the time of my initial fieldwork, Easton could be thought of as the centre of a wedge of east Bristol in which Pakistanis were concentrated, from the tip in St Pauls, expanding through Easton, Barton Hill and St George's, and out to Eastville and Fishponds. To a certain extent this outward movement corresponded to affluence, as St Paul's, Easton and Barton Hill are areas of deprivation, smaller housing and social problems, with larger properties and more leafy areas found in Eastville and Fishponds. A second, smaller concentration is found in the south of the city in Totterdown, Bedminster and Windmill Hill. Again, this area had a mosque, but fewer Asian shops, and again some families were living in generally more expensive properties a little further out in Knowle. Social networks tended to be more dense within these areas than between them, and Easton and Totterdown also feature as centres in Bristol Pakistanis' own conceptualisation of the local community. Azra, for example, told me that she was unusual in knowing both the Easton and the Totterdown 'posse', as her family had originally lived in the south of the city before moving to Easton.

The pattern of highly concentrated residential settlement is not restricted to the city of Bristol. The 1994 PSI survey (Modood *et al.* 1997) found that out of all minority ethnic groups sampled, Pakistanis were most likely to live in wards with a high density of residents of their own ethnic group, and to express a preference to reside in an area with a greater proportion of their own ethnic group than others. Although the majority were in owner-occupied accommodation, Pakistani homes were often of poor standard, featuring levels of overcrowding second only to Bangladeshis. Assessing these figures against household size and income, the authors concluded that overcrowding was a result of the lack of housing appropriate for larger families. Migration may also have played a part in perpetuating these conditions through a migrant ethos of saving by reducing living expenses.

Several families in Bristol with whose housing history I am familiar moved from the ethnic 'centres' of Easton or Totterdown to larger properties in the more desirable areas further out along these corridors, but others who could perhaps afford to move prefer to stay close to the facilities that an area like Easton provides. One woman in Easton, for example, told me that she could find a larger house in another area to accommodate a household consisting of herself, her three children (two now adult) and one daughter's husband and child. She did not want to move, however, as she would miss the convenience of being able to take her son to the mosque's Quranic classes after school, shop locally, visit friends and walk to work. Assessments of socio-economic status are further complicated by the fact that many families living in modest conditions have invested in other properties – whether houses to rent out in Bristol, or land and property in Pakistan (Erdal 2011). By 2008, two families involved in this research had decided not to postpone enjoyment of the fruits of their investment further, and sold a number of properties in order to purchase larger homes in affluent areas of Bristol, away from the traditional areas of Pakistani settlement.

As elsewhere in Britain, Pakistanis use the English word 'community' frequently and to mean various groupings, including aspects of religious affiliation (Shaw 2000a: 10; Werbner 2002b: 29–31). Probably the most common usage in my experience in Bristol is to denote the Pakistani community as an ethnic group. This distinction is made in Urdu as between *ham log / apne log / hamāre log* (we people / one's own people / our people) and *gore log* (white people). People expect to know of other Pakistanis in Bristol – I was frequently quizzed about those I mentioned until they were correctly identified. At one wedding I attended, a woman whose family tries not to 'mix with the community' was approached by other young women who wanted to know where she was from, not believing she could be from Bristol as they had not seen her before.

Although many Pakistanis in Bristol enjoy participating in, and benefit from, the multiple social ties that constitute the local 'community',

'community' is at the same time largely talked about as something external, often with negative characteristics: scrutinising, gossiping and critical, with the effect of limiting people's freedom of action through worry over what the community would say (cf. Bolognani 2009a).[16] It is seen as essentially conservative – frowning on such things as divorce or new styles of dress or marriage party, and jealous of individual families' achievements. So one informant said she would not like to do any kind of work that brought her into too much contact with the community, whilst a community worker said she tends not to visit any of the clients' homes for fear of causing jealousy and conflict. When one of the families mentioned above moved out of an 'Asian' area, there was apparently gossip that they did so in order to conceal their daughters' 'scandalous' behaviour. Another told me that she chose to live in an area outside the main concentration of Asian households to avoid scrutiny from the community, whilst another did not divorce her violent husband for 10 years until her parents had died, for fear of the effect on their reputation. Being involved with 'the community' by living in the ethnic centres or running important 'ethnic' services can also increase social obligations in terms of reciprocating invitations to family weddings, and *salami* money gifts: one wedding with an estimated 900 guests ('and that's without the Mirpuris') was in a family where the mother was involved in community groups, while the father had run a *halal* meat shop and so came into frequent contact with even more Pakistanis.

'Community' may refer to the whole Pakistani population of the city – the Bristol community as opposed to those of other cities – or sometimes only to that of Totterdown or Easton.[17] The idea of a community as a bounded social reality has been subject to academic criticism, and ways in which community is imagined or symbolised have been explored (Anderson 1983; Cohen 1985). In common with many writers on South Asians in Britain, I will make use of the term to reflect its usage by my informants. In doing so, however, I do not wish to imply acceptance of the much-criticised implications of the concept, such as homogeneity or boundedness (Anthias 1998). Indeed, I would argue that my informants are themselves aware that within the Bristol Pakistani community there is great heterogeneity, and that any boundaries are inevitably artificial, as their own social and kinship networks do not map onto this imagined unit. 'Community', both for them and this project, serves as a convenient shorthand to facilitate communication in a complex social reality, whilst reflecting and creating a cognitive schema for mapping and dividing the social world.

In addition to current residence within Bristol, place of origin in Pakistan plays a role in Bristol Pakistanis' self- and mutual identification. As Alison Shaw notes, data on area of origin are hard to come by as they are seldom mentioned in public records. Evidence from Birmingham and Bradford, however, suggests four main regions of origin for Pakistanis in Britain: Mirpur district in Azad Kashmir; Attock district; an area of Peshawar; and some Punjabi villages in Rawalpindi, Jhelum, Gujrat and Faisalabad districts.

The presence of these groups varies in different British cities. Some of those with the largest Pakistani populations in Britain such as Bradford and Birmingham are predominantly Mirpuri (Shaw 2000a: 15–16). In Bristol, the two main groups are Mirpuri and Punjabi, the latter including some from cities such as Rawalpindi and Lahore (Jeffery 1976a; Shaw 2000a).

Two final inter-related social distinctions stem from this variation in origin: the rural–urban divide, and that between Mirpuris and non-Mirpuris. As Shaw points out, almost all Pakistanis in Britain are city dwellers now, but the connotations of being from a city or a village still underlie local prejudice, with city dwellers thought to be superior and villagers denigrated as 'uneducated, ill mannered, crude and short tempered'. Whilst Shaw reports urban-origin Pakistanis in Oxford distancing themselves from other Pakistanis through negative evaluations of villagers as *jangli* (wild, uncultivated – from the same root as jungle) (2000a: 20), amongst my informants in Bristol, the equivalent derogatory term is *pindu*, a Punjabi word literally meaning from the village (*pind*), with all of the preceding connotations. With respect to marriage, villagers were described to me as more inclined to be strict about close kin marriage and marriage within the *zat* (caste), and to have higher levels of transnational marriage. This book, however, provides plenty of evidence for these practices among 'urban' Punjabis.

For city-origin Pakistanis, there is an overlap in the prejudices against villagers and Mirpuris. Mirpuris are often described as *pindu*, in addition to the specific derogatory term 'M.P.s', which I frequently heard young people use in 2000–01 to refer to people of Mirpuri descent. One woman whose family is from a town near Rawalpindi compared the English north–south divide with that between Punjabis and Mirpuris. Mirpur is like the Yorkshire of Pakistan, she said, so Mirpuris from places like Bradford are doubly backward, a statement that humorously combines southern English and Punjabi prejudices. There is some blurring of the geographical boundaries in this geography of stereotypes: I have heard of the villages around Gujrat in eastern Punjab being lumped in with Mirpuris as being 'all the same kind of people'. Although the social divide between Mirpuris and non-Mirpuris is porous, and many of the private judgements of others as 'backward' do not necessarily preclude friendships between the two categories, marriage can be a different case. One woman I interviewed had a love marriage vetoed by her family on the grounds that the boy was a Mirpuri:

> Because when my father came to the country he came across some real like – what can I say – the worst you can think of. Like poo-ing in the garden and things like that ... We're from the city, we just can't accept them.

She eventually married this man against her family's wishes, and sees her Mirpuri in-laws as 'innocent', moderating the damning description above. This (often submerged) ambivalence is reflected in other commentaries by my British Pakistani informants on villagers as 'simple', an attribute that is

16 *Introduction*

valued, particularly in women.[18] Mirpur, moreover, lies within Azad Kashmir, and whilst Mirpuris may be the subject of negative stereotypes, Kashmiri women are often represented as fair skinned (and sometimes pale eyed) beauties. The term *desi* provides a further positive evaluation of the rural, linking authenticity and autochthony with the provinces rather than the urban centres in its meaning: 'of or belonging to a country, native, indigenous; home-made; local; provincial'; or as a noun: 'native of a country' (Platts 2000 [1884]). Free-range eggs, associated with the village and valued over battery versions, are described as *desi ande*, and the term *desi* has been used in celebration of ethnic identity in some British Asian popular music.[19]

Urban families, by contrast with Pakistanis (and British Pakistanis) whose families come from rural areas, may be viewed as overly 'modern' by those they themselves deride as *pindu*. This morally dubious modernity is evinced by women working, going about without covering their heads and 'doing fashion'. A community worker from Rawalpindi told me that her Mirpuri clients are always surprised that she prays and considers religion important as they assume that she has 'forgotten Allah' because she doesn't wear the *hijab*, and has a short hairstyle. The woman married to a Mirpuri above explained that it had taken her a while to convince her in-laws to like her:

> These *pindus* [laughs] ... they don't like to give girls out of the family or take girls out of the family [in marriage]. And my husband was the first person to bring me, an outsider. And the respect I get from them now! They think they must have been mad not to consider girls like us ... They think we're big headed and really full of ourselves, no manners, and I think I've proved them wrong ... And because we're modern and I don't wear a *hijab* – they're all into *hijabs* and things. They have this thing that we're modern and we're ... probably bad basically because outgoing girls for them are bad.

Individual family histories not infrequently cross these geographical divides. Households may have moved from villages to cities in recent generations, or combine members from different regions or, indeed, continents. Geographically based presentations of identities may elide or draw attention to such differences. In one conversation, for example, two migrant wives – one brought up in Pakistan and the other in a mainland European country – agreed that they were both 'proper Lahoris', unlike others they knew whose parents or grandparents had moved to Lahore from elsewhere in Pakistan.

A further shorthand that will be used throughout the book, but which necessitates qualification is the analytical distinction between Pakistanis and British Pakistanis. The complicated and ongoing history of migration from Pakistan to Britain often muddles these neat divisions. How, for example, should one label Bushra, a woman in her forties who was born in Pakistan but came to Britain as a young child and was schooled here? Or Humera, who came when she was a little older, and might on the surface seem more

'Pakistani' as she did not go to school in the UK and is still self-conscious about her English even decades later. Nevertheless, when her husband arrived from Pakistan, she perceived strong cultural differences and her seeming English-ness proved difficult for her husband to accept. Or how about Tahir, born in London but brought up in Pakistan, now returned to live in Britain as the husband of a cousin who was born and spent her whole life in Bristol? Another of this couple's relatives migrated to Britain and had a child with a white British woman. When the marriage broke down he took the young child back to Pakistan where she was brought up and lived until she married a Pakistani national and her dual citizenship enabled them to settle in the UK. The categories of Pakistani and British Pakistani belie this complexity, to the point of being meaningless in some cases. In this book I will attempt to reserve the description 'British Pakistani' for people born and brought up in Britain, and 'Pakistani' for those whose lives up until migration were spent in Pakistan. Occasionally, however, when considering migration and transnational marriage they will be used as descriptors for those who have spent most of their lives in the relevant nation, or to signify that the greatest part of the individual's socialisation has taken place in that country, for the purposes of discussing what my informants call 'culture clash'.

A similar difficulty is encountered when writing of 'generation'. The literature on ethnic minorities is peppered with references to the 'first', 'second', 'third' or even '1.5' generation (e.g. Levitt and Waters 2002; Narayan 2002) – in other words, those who migrated to the country, their British-born children and grandchildren, and those who migrated as children. Given that Pakistani migration to Britain has continued across the years since the initial migrants arrived, however, these distinctions are artificial (cf. Gardner and Shukur 1994). Particularly with significant levels of transnational marriage, many households contain newly arrived migrant members. If they have married a 'second-generation' British-born Pakistani, will their children be second generation as the offspring of an immigrant, or third generation by virtue of their other parent being born in Britain? Even ignoring transnational marriage, similar difficulties would be encountered within the 'settled' UK Pakistani population, given that initial immigrants arrived at different times, so that in a couple of the same age, one might be second and one third generation. Hence, although the concept of generations was used by some of my informants to evoke cultural change, in contrast to the other two problematic categories outlined above, I do not find it either descriptively or analytically helpful in this study of transnational marriages.[20]

Methods

My fieldwork on transnational marriages was itself transnational, involving research in both Britain and Pakistan. During an initial period in Pakistan, I focused on language learning and general cultural acclimatisation, planning a second trip to conduct more structured fieldwork at the end of my time in

Bristol. The aftermath of 9/11 intervened, however, as my funder considered security risks in Pakistan too great for me to return. With new family and work commitments to negotiate, my 2007–08 research was restricted to the UK context. More of the research for this book was therefore carried out in Britain than in Pakistan. All 'multi-sited ethnographies' may, however, inevitably be 'the product of knowledge bases of varying intensities and qualities' (Marcus 1995: 100). Having previously worked and established Pakistani contacts in Bristol provided me with a 'head start' in local knowledge, access and personal acclimatisation (cf. Altorki and el-Sohl 1988), which I lacked in Pakistan where my Urdu was limited and language learning occupied much of my time. Nevertheless, my time in Pakistan gave me some contextual knowledge, in particular of wedding customs, kinship and perceptions of Britain and British Pakistanis, thanks to the extraordinary generosity and hospitality of so many of those with whom I came into contact. I was initially based at a women's university in Rawalpindi, where I lived in a hostel with students, all young women of marriageable age. They were kind enough to spend endless hours conversing, answering questions, helping me with my Urdu, advising me on clothing and showing me around. One young woman in particular, Aisha, deserves special thanks for taking me away from the city to spend weekends with her family, and offering constant and valuable advice, including patiently instructing me on how to wear my shawl appropriately. Several members of staff were good enough to spend time talking with me, and one in particular welcomed me into her home and family life on many weekends and holidays. After two months I moved out of the hostel to stay at the home of another member of staff. She and her husband were extremely welcoming and helpful, and took me to several weddings. I was also fortunate enough to be able to spend time with four groups of British Pakistanis on their visits to relatives in Pakistan and at weddings, and I am very grateful to them and their relatives for allowing me an insight into the experiences of such visits.

The initial period in Pakistan proved invaluable for my Bristol fieldwork, enriching my understanding and providing me with areas of inquiry that might not have been obvious without this 'off-stage' knowledge. Like Patricia Jeffery (1976a) almost 30 years before, I found that it also made a great difference in terms of access, evincing to potential participants that my interest was genuine and grounded in a certain amount of knowledge. By the time I reached Bristol, some local Pakistanis had even seen footage of me in a wedding video shot a few months before in Pakistan, all of which helped create interest in both me and my project. Existing contacts, families of people I had met in Pakistan, and voluntary work with two community organisations provided me with starting points for 'snowballing' contacts and opportunities for informal discussion and participant observation. I arranged more formal semi-structured interviews with participants in transnational marriages (including sponsoring and migrant spouses, and family members) whenever the opportunity arose.

The quotations from interviews presented in this book are, unless specified, in the original English. I present data gathered in Urdu/Punjabi either by quoting the Urdu with appropriate translation, or by giving information in English without presenting it as a direct quotation. Given the sensitive nature of some of the material presented here, and as is conventional practice, all names have been changed. Re-naming is a responsibility: names have meanings, associations and fashions of their own. A white British teenager is currently unlikely to be called Dorothy, or an octogenarian to answer to Kylie. I have taken advice on names appropriate for men and women of different age groups and employed my own judgements of naming trends (for example, in the recent trend towards names considered to be more purely Muslim than Pakistani), in an attempt to avoid inappropriate choices. It may be that names have particular regional or class connotations outside the scope of my knowledge. I can only apologise for any misjudgements. In addition to changing names, some features of people's lives such as their employment or details of their family have been omitted or (in a very few cases) altered in an attempt to protect their identity.

Having made an effort to learn Urdu was appreciated, as something that very few *gore log* attempt. I made some contacts after simply starting conversations in Urdu (in shops or taxis, for example), prompting pleased surprise and curiosity. Even in interviews with young British Pakistanis conducted in English, being able to use the Urdu term for a wedding ritual, for example, could lead to a more detailed discussion than might otherwise have been the case, as they sometimes shifted descriptive registers, having gathered that I knew more than the average non-Pakistani. My Urdu was of course not fluent, but I could understand much of what was said, and at least towards the end of my fieldwork, I could conduct interviews in Urdu. Many Pakistanis in Bristol speak one of several dialects of Punjabi, but I was advised to learn Urdu rather than Punjabi as so many at least understand the language. Urdu is considered by many to be a more educated, respectful and beautiful language, and when I had asked Pakistani women to teach me Punjabi phrases during a previous research project, I was repeatedly told that Urdu was the 'proper' language for me to learn. Urdu and Punjabi are closely related, so I was often able to understand the gist of Punjabi conversations.

My travel to Pakistan, previous connections in Bristol, voluntary work and attempts to learn Urdu all helped develop relationships that were remarkably resilient during the difficult months after 9/11. Increased tension was apparent: 'Osama bin Laden' became an insult shouted at visibly Muslim men in the street; I was told of a woman who had her scarf pulled off and beer poured on her head, whilst another reported a stone thrown through her window. In this context, one woman seeing me for the first time at a community group asked another worker suspiciously who this *gori* (white woman/girl – often used derogatively) was. Reassuring her, my friend replied: '*Gori hay – lekin hamari gori hay*' (She's a *gori*, but she's *our gori*), leading to embarrassed laughter when the woman realised I could understand the conversation.

Although I did not physically accompany spouses in their migration, in one case I was able to attend a marriage in Pakistan and then meet the couple again in Bristol some months later, as the immigration process had been completed within the timescale of my research. More often, however, I visited individuals and families in either Pakistan or Britain, and gathered other kinds of information in the sites from which they migrated, or to which they intend to migrate. This constitutes 'off-stage' information for a 'foreshortened' version of multi-sited ethnography ('the strategically situated [single-site] ethnography'), with other sites and a sense of the wider system evoked through knowledge of what happens to the subjects in other places (Marcus 1995: 110). Further 'off-stage' information was often available in the form of participants' wedding videos (a term I'll treat as encompassing DVD technology) and photographs, which in addition provided fertile ground for enriching and expanding discussions. Having attended many weddings in Pakistan, I was able to surmise to an extent the practices and contexts of the production of these artefacts (another layer of this time literally 'off-stage' information), aiding interpretation.

The location of my Pakistani fieldwork had implications for the constituency of the Bristol section of my study. Most of the people I worked with in Bristol are Punjabis. A small number are from Sindh province, but all of these have strong family ties to the Punjab. A few of my informants are Mirpuri. My social networks developed in this way partly because of the connections I had established in Pakistan, including one very large extended family with many branches in Bristol. In addition, both of the voluntary organisations I worked with were run and staffed primarily by Punjabis, further emphasising the geographical bias of my study. For the same reasons, my informants are probably disproportionately from urban backgrounds. Although this may make this study less representative of Pakistanis in Britain as a whole, no single community could really claim to be representative of the geographically varied British Pakistani population. Moreover, a focus on non-Mirpuri and urban-background Pakistanis may help to balance the overwhelming interest in recent years on the predominantly Mirpuri communities of northern and central England, particularly in the context of increased concern with inter-ethnic relations in these areas following the 2001 riots.

A final issue in my fieldwork was that of gender. Ardener (1975: 3) famously wrote that 'The fact is that no one could come back from an ethnographic study of "the X", having talked only *to* women and *about* men'. As a female researcher in a Muslim context, the danger was that I might end up in just such a situation, although as Carsten (1997) points out, this does not mean an ethnography of the world of women, but the world of men and women from the perspective of women. Women researchers in Muslim societies may learn more about men's worlds than a man would about the lives of women (Abu-Lughod 1988), whilst the question of whether non-Muslim Western women researchers may transcend gender norms has also been debated (Jeffery 1976a; Papanek 1964; Pastner 1982).

'[O]ne is never just a man or a woman' (Callaway 1992: 34), and numerous attributes may affect interactions in the field (cf. Altorki and el-Sohl 1988). We may manage to talk to men and women of 'the X', but how they talk to us, and what they talk about, depends on how they 'read' us (Crick 1992: 180). Caplan, for example, found that the wife of a key informant talked to her more freely on a return research trip, considering her finally to have 'grown up' by marrying and having children (Caplan 1992). As a young, unmarried woman during my first fieldwork, I faced similar issues. Many of my 'key informants' were other young women, and progressing to interview older members of their families was not straightforward as I was associated with the daughters of the household. In other relationships, however, my first contact was with the mother, some of whom 'volunteered' their children to help me with my research.

Women researchers have often sought to influence the way they are perceived through clothing. While Papanek (1964: 161) writes that Western dress permitted access to ceremonies that local women could not attend, Pastner (1982: 262) found veiling necessary in Pakistan to avoid public chastisement. In Pakistan I wore *shalwar qamis*, whilst in Bristol I often wore non-revealing 'Western' clothes in environments where I considered this would make me less, rather than more, conspicuous, reserving my Pakistani clothes for functions and social occasions. My interest in Pakistani fashion was a topic of mutual interest in conversations with many women. Nonetheless, caution is required in taking advice on the most appropriate attire. During Greek fieldwork, Kenna's attempts to seek advice on clothing misfired. Older women reported idealised standards from their youth, with the result that:

> ... I turned myself into an anachronism without realising it and was then held up to young island women as a shining example. No wonder that many of them were shy with me and unwilling to confide.
> (Kenna 1992: 153)

In Pakistan I encountered the opposite problem. On arriving in Rawalpindi, I asked some of the young women I met to advise me on clothing, and ended up with some fashionable but (unbeknown to me) slightly daring outfits, including suits with slim-fitting trousers featuring small side-splits. Whilst some hostel mates borrowed these objects of desire to have them copied, others may have disapproved.

I was prepared for accessing men to constitute a challenge. In addition to the issues discussed above, many Pakistani men in Bristol work long hours or night shifts, creating difficulties in finding appropriate times for research. I included interviews in my methodological design for this reason, hoping men would be willing to arrange more formal appointments. Interviewing has been recommended as a tool for urban kinship research (Barnard and Good 1984), and in previous urban fieldwork I had found that it provided a reason for making contact, established a relationship in which questions can be asked, and often led to further interactions or invitations. Of course, the nature of information given in interviews differs from that gathered during participant observation, so I combined these data with other statements and observations (cf. Passaro 1997; Hannerz 1980). Whilst my participant observation predominantly took place in mainly female environments such as community groups and people's back sitting rooms (see Shaw 2000a for the gendered division of space in British Pakistani homes), this was supplemented with interviews and conversations with men wherever possible. My altered status during my later fieldwork – as a less youthful, married woman and mother – and a change of tactic to recruiting male contacts through taxi companies (rather than through families and community groups) were probably behind the greater ease with which I was able to arrange interviews with men.

The structure of the book

In constructing this work, I have employed several lengthy excerpts from interviews. In doing so, I hope not only to give 'voice' to my informants, but also to give a flavour of the nature of my fieldwork. These interviews were all, however, conducted in Bristol. Most of the weddings of British Pakistanis to Pakistani nationals, on the other hand, take place in Pakistan, which was also the starting point for my ethnographic journey. For all these reasons, Chapter 1 is built around a description of the first wedding I attended in Pakistan, between a British Pakistani woman and a Pakistani national who later came to join her in Bristol. This is followed in Chapter 2 by a discussion of transnationalism, including British Pakistanis' varying engagements with the transnational, influenced by factors including gender and lifecourse. I then go on to address how some young people negotiate these engagements during visits and wedding celebrations in Pakistan. Chapter 3 describes the process of looking for a potential partner, and suggests that the Pakistani term for a 'match', *rishta*, reintroduces elements of emotional connection between family members absent in some strategic accounts of South Asian spouse selection. These two facets are highlighted in transnational arrangements where both the gains to be had from a marriage and the weakening of valued relationships through migration are heightened. For siblings separated by their own emigration, a marriage between their children can be an opportunity to re-establish these connections across continents.

Chapter 4 looks at reasons for the popularity of close kin marriage. Again, a model based on maximising benefits, such as the retention of family assets, is revised through the inclusion of emotion to reflect better the understandings and motivations of participants. Close kin marriage, I will suggest, is part of the ways in which people seek to reduce risk (treated as a gendered emotional discourse) in arranging marriage. It is often hoped in particular that similarity, kinship morality and family pressure will deter the mistreatment of a valued daughter by her husband or in-laws. Chapter 5 suggests another way in which risks are managed, in the disaggregation of marriage ceremonies to delay consummation, a development that takes advantage of the legal pluralism inherent in transnational marriage. The extended narrative from Yasmin, a young Bristolian woman, which opens Chapter 6 illustrates both this extended form of marriage ceremony and the dangers that families hope to avoid. It also features disagreements and factions forming within the kin group over the marriage. Yasmin's father's response to the failure of his daughter's marriage is explored, introducing the concept of *izzat* and offering several interpretations for his behaviour, based on different models of honour, before concluding with an argument for the contextual eliding of *izzat* and emotion. Chapter 7 explores the position of migrant husbands. For some, the experience of marriage migration can be profoundly frustrating, in conflict with ideals of masculinity, and analogous to the derided Pakistani position of *ghar damad* (house son-in-law). Counter-examples show how other husbands have fared better in their marriage migration experience. The chapter ends with a return to the complexity of *izzat*, illustrated by a narrative from Junaid, a divorced former migrant husband. In concluding the volume, I argue for both the ethnographic utility and political necessity of an approach incorporating emotion in order to reveal a more rounded account of the motivations for, and experiences of, transnational marriages. In the context of a political climate that is increasingly critical of such marriages, and tightening spousal immigration regimes across Europe, such understandings of the human face of transnational marriage are sorely needed.

Notes

1 See Shaw (2009) for a review of the literature on cousin marriage, which is common in many parts of South Asia and the Middle East, often with a preference for unions between more specific categories of relatives.
2 See Charsley *et al.* (2012) for an overview of the diversity of marriage-related migration to Britain.
3 i.e. a virilocal (residence with or near the husband's family) rather than uxorilocal (residence with or near the wife's family) norm.
4 Mirpur is a district of Azad (Free) Kashmir, one of the main areas of origin of Pakistani migrants to Britain, although this is a disputed territory in ongoing troubles between India and Pakistan.
5 The International Passenger Survey provides estimates of the number of people who state on arrival that they intend to stay in the country of destination for a year or more, but contacts a mere 0.2%–5% of passengers, depending on season. Its figure of 900 people (mostly female and all Pakistan-born Pakistani citizens) migrating from Britain to Pakistan in 1998, is thus based on surveying only three actual passengers (ONS 1998).
6 See: www.moops.gov.pk (accessed 07/02/2012).
7 See: www.ethnicity.ac.uk/census/869_CCSR_Bulletin_How_has_ethnic_diversity_grown_v4NW.pdf (accessed 15/08/2013).
8 South Asians overall accounted for 20% of the total applications for settlement in 2000.
9 In 2001, there were an estimated 3,000 UK British Pakistanis living in Denmark, suggesting that marriage migration also takes place in the opposite direction (Hussain 2001).

24   *Introduction*

10 The ways in which British Pakistanis locate suitable partners within the UK, and how those marriages are negotiated and experienced are not the focus of this book.
11 Statistics from the Control of Immigration Statistics United Kingdom reports for the relevant years (the relevant data are found in supplementary table 4c in the 2008 and 2009 reports), webarchive.nationalarchives.gov.uk.
12 Consul officials also said that they thought many did not think through all the implications of agreeing to an unwanted marriage, and in particular that they would be expected to consummate the marriage.
13 See: www.freemovement.org.uk/2011/05/31/secret-race-discrimination/ (accessed 31/01/2012). Further proposals to restrict marriage-related immigration and settlement were also made during this period (see Wray 2011 for details).
14 For discussion of increasing rates of divorce and single parenthood among British Pakistanis (and other South Asian groups), in contrast to frequent portrayals of unchanging 'traditional' family forms, see Qureshi *et al.* (2012).
15 See Brettell (2003) on the importance of city structures in the development of ethnic neighbourhoods.
16 In the context of the ethnography of an English town, Edwards and Strathern (2000: 151) note that although locals recognise the negative side of community, this aspect is often missing in academic commentary.
17 'Community' sits happily alongside another flexible term, *baraderi* (patrilineage or kin group), which will be discussed in a later chapter.
18 They use the English word 'simple'. See Chapter 4 for a lengthier discussion of the simple–modern contrast.
19 Cf. Kurin's Pakistani informants' contrasts between city and village dwellers. The former are seen as both noble and sophisticated, but also as cunning plotters, whilst the latter are wild savages, but straightforward and innocent (Kurin 1988). Also see Gardner (1995: 120) on the consumption of *deshi* produce by overseas Bangladeshis as a 'social statement of the spirituality of the *desh*'.
20 I am also dubious about the applicability of Fouron and Glick Schiller's suggestion that the 'second generation' be expanded to encompass 'the entire generation in both homeland and new land who grow up within transnational social fields' (Fouron and Glick Schiller 2002: 193) to this context. Whilst appreciating the potential significance of transnational connections for both, the extension of an already problematic concept risks obscuring the importance of 'particularities of location within the transnational terrain' (Fouron and Glick Schiller 2002: 198).

1 Weddings

Most weddings between British Pakistanis and spouses from Pakistan take place in Pakistan,[1] although there may also be a function held in Britain to celebrate the arrival of the immigrant spouse. In addition to the difficulty of obtaining visas for fiancé(e)s to come to Britain from Pakistan, this arrangement allows relatives still living in Pakistan to attend. Moreover, given price differentials and the ready availability of marriage goods, services and facilities, a far more lavish function can be held than would be the case in Britain. The event I will describe consisted of the three conventional main days, the *mehndi*, *barat* and *walima* (although weddings may be as long as five days or as short as one). Narrating each in turn will act as an introduction to the Pakistani marriage customs that will feature in discussions throughout the book. Iram's wedding was in many ways at the traditional end of the spectrum of marriage styles, but styles of functions are subject to change and debate in Pakistan and the diaspora. This chapter is therefore intended to provide a snapshot of the dynamic and contested nature of practices and discourses that exist in both my field sites. It also introduces some vignettes of transnational experience, as British Pakistanis are seen in the process of marrying abroad.

Before Iram's wedding

I arrived at the small village in south-western Punjab the day before the marriage. Iram was 22, from Bristol and happy with the match with Hamid, her maternal grandfather's younger brother's son, who lived in another village. Her sister Shabanna had come from Bristol four months earlier to spend time in their ancestral home, and her mother Shanaz had arrived a few weeks ago, when preparations for the wedding really got under way. Earlier in the day they had sent furniture including a double bed to Iram's future in-laws' house as part of the *jahez* (dowry). The extended family – including several others from Bristol – gathered for an evening meal in the house of another relative in the village. Iram turned to her mother and asked, 'Am I supposed to be here?'

In the 15 days preceding her marriage a bride is conventionally meant to stay at home, refrain from wearing make-up, and undertake beauty treatments such as the removal of body hair and application of *ubtan*, a paste that is yellow with turmeric, to make the skin 'clean' and beautiful for her wedding day. The extent to which these conventions are followed varies – Iram had been out to the beauty parlour in the nearest town, and although she told me that she 'wasn't supposed' to have contact with her fiancé, he had telephoned a few days earlier to wish her a happy Eid. Restriction on contact between engaged couples is relaxed further in some families, with telephone calls, emails, or accompanied visits permitted. One young couple I interviewed in 2008, for example, emailed, texted and phoned each other so frequently during the time between their engagement and marriage in Pakistan that the British fiancé ran up a £600 phone bill in one month. Whilst his mother chastised him for wasting money, she also described the story as 'romantic'. Her daughter-in-law thought that the prohibition on engaged couples talking was dying out among middle-class Lahori families like her own, saying:

> There are still a few cities where they don't allow the groom and the bride – they don't talk until and unless they get *nikah* (Islamic marriage contract) done before *barat* and all that. But still, we live in Lahore, that's like the biggest city of the Pakistan and obviously our parents are not that conservative. I'm a working woman ... I was a working woman ... and [husband was British], so they were quite broad minded and didn't mind if we were talking. Obviously we are going to spend the whole life together – we have to know about each other.

Even where families are not in favour of contact between the couple, technology may allow them to find ways to communicate – a student I met in Pakistan, for example, carried out a secret email correspondence with a fiancé she had never met, while another woman reminisced about how her fiancé would telephone hoping she would answer, and she would pretend to be talking to a girlfriend.

Iram's *mehndi*

The evening of the day I arrived was to be Iram's *mehndi* celebration. I showed Shanaz the clothes I had brought with me and she told me to wear a green velvet *shalwar qamis*, as green was the colour of *mehndi*. *Mehndi* literally means henna, which is a greenish-brown colour in its paste form, and green and yellow feature prominently in the clothes worn to *mehndi* celebrations – in women's outfits and in the yellow scarves that the groom's male friends and relatives may wear round their necks and hold aloft in exuberant dances.[2]

I was taken upstairs to a room above the internal courtyard where Shabanna and her maternal cousin from Bristol were getting themselves ready in velvet outfits, costume jewellery and make-up. Iram wore a green and yellow *shalwar qamis* sent by the groom's family. She wore no make-up, but said she felt naked without jewellery and so was wearing a bit of gold. This was my first Pakistani wedding, so I asked the young women what was going to happen. They said they didn't know – all the *mehndis* they'd attended had been in Britain – but there was usually singing and playing the *dholki* (small double-ended drum). Shabanna put some bhangra-style music on the cassette player. 'I'll have to dance to this later', she said. However, there was to be no dancing, drumming or singing. The family's trip to Pakistan not only coincided with Eid, a popular time for weddings when families are gathered after the fasting of *Ramazan*, but was also the first anniversary of Iram's father's death. His body had been repatriated and buried in the family graveyard in the village, and they were also in Pakistan to mark the anniversary. Shanaz, the bride's mother, had told the women from the groom's family not to 'bring *mehndi*' (*mehndi lekar ana*) with its accompanying joyful/teasing singing and drumming to the house on such a sad occasion, so they stayed at home to celebrate the groom's *mehndi*.

Girls from the village came upstairs and joined us, sitting on the other side of the room. The video cameraman was late, so we sat waiting for several hours, the Bristol group talking in English between themselves, and changing tapes of bhangra and Hindi film music now and then. Eventually, Shabanna put on some aggressive hip-hop. 'It'll be all f***, f***', she said, 'but they [gesturing to the village girls] won't understand it anyway!'

Eventually the video man arrived, and I and some of the bride's younger female relatives were handed plates decorated with silver foil on which lumps of *mehndi* bore lit candles. We carried them outside to re-enter the house slowly and ceremoniously for the cameras. 'The whole of Bristol's going to see this', whispered Shabanna. We put the plates on the floor in front of a sofa that had been brought out into the courtyard – at other *mehndis* I have attended the *mehndi*-bearers sing on their entrance, and sisters of the bride or groom dance round the plates on the floor. Then Iram, head bowed and covered, garlanded with roses, was brought down to the courtyard under a red and gold *dupatta* shawl held aloft by female relatives – Shanaz pushed me forward to join them. The bride was seated on the sofa, her sister on one side and her cousin on the other, and filmed under bright lights for a while. I strained to get a view past the barrage of lights, cameramen, and relatives coming forward to take pictures. People came forward to hand-feed *mithai* (sweetmeats) to the bride and her companions, and place money and small lumps of *mehndi* paste on Iram's outstretched hand, the professionally applied patterns on her palm protected from henna stains by bank notes.[3]

When the guests finally dispersed, Iram's elder brother, his friend from Bristol and another British male cousin who had been looking sheepish in front of the cameras all day were gathered round the plates of *mehndi* left on the floor. One of them pushed a plate with his foot: 'I don't understand this. It's just mud, innit', he said, adding that putting it on banknotes was a waste of good money. The young men smiled at his irreverence. Later that night they were given guns to fire in the air.[4]

Making the bride beautiful

The *mehndi* is the culmination of the ceremonies that precede a marriage. It is traditionally the occasion on which the bride's hands, feet and sometimes arms are decorated with intricate henna patterns, the colours of which deepen to anything from a rich orange to dark brown by her wedding day. In practice, as for Iram, the designs are often applied separately by a professional or skilled relative or friend. More than the other days of a wedding, the *mehndi* is eagerly anticipated as an occasion for women to gather, play the *dholki*, dance and sing. Women from the other 'side' (i.e. the groom or bride's relatives) come to the celebration bringing trays of *mehndi*, and the singing and dancing can become quite competitive, with songs that ridicule the groom and his family, and the bride and groom's sisters striving to perform the best dances. It is often combined with the *tel* rite, when oil is poured into the hair of the bride or groom, and is then known as a *tel-mehndi*. Henna and mustard oil used are both 'cooling' substances, and these rituals have been interpreted as part of a process of heating and cooling that socialises the dangerous sexual heat implicit in the marriage union (Werbner 1990).[5] Participants' exegeses, however, invariably stress the beautifying properties of these substances. *Ubtan* is supposed to render the skin clean and glowing, while women in Pakistan often oil their hair before washing it to make it strong and shiny, and young girls practice wielding cones of henna to effect the latest designs, for occasions such as *chand-rat* (moon night) when the much anticipated new moon marks the end of *Ramazan* fasting.

By the day of her wedding the bride's beauty is the culmination of the work, care and affection of her family who have secluded her, ensured her skin and hair will shine, embellished her hands and feet with *mehndi* designs, dressed her in beautiful, costly clothes and lavished gold upon her, spending hard-earned savings or melting down the precious items mothers were given by their own parents when they left their natal homes. The bride in her wedding finery comes close to being what Mauss (1924) called a total prestation, embodying her family's wealth and standing, and the parental care and duties which are being transferred in the marriage. As such, her beauty can have important implications for her standing in her new family, as a lack of effort may be perceived as a lack of regard on the part of her parents, implying that the girl is poorly supported and therefore vulnerable. One woman on a visit to Britain from Pakistan who had a taste for subdued colours, for example, was pitied by a neighbour who asked if her parents had stopped sending her good clothes after only a few years of marriage.

The beautification of the bride should not, however, be understood as merely economic or symbolic. It is often part of the experiential aesthetic of romance and affection in the lives of Pakistani women. As Kohn (1998: 72–73) writes of Nepal, 'The interest women have in gold is, on the one hand, a material one, for gold jewellery often represents a rural family's entire life savings. On the other hand it is also an interest in the romance intrinsic to the act of giving gold and bestowing beauty on new wives'. It is in this light that I understand Iram's mother Shanaz's words about a heavy gold coin she showed me before the wedding. She said that she could have had it melted down and made into a new set for Iram, but her late husband had given it to her, so she had decided to keep it just the way it was. The allure of gold seems not to fade: Bushra, another women in her forties, had been collecting gold to make her daughter's wedding jewellery in a few years' time. After a visit to Pakistan, however, she reappeared wearing a solid-looking gold heart on a thick chain, saying her husband had said she should have something made for herself in the meantime. Although the gender politics of dowry as practised in South Asia have been criticised (Menski 1998; Sharma 1984; Srinivas 1984), parents and daughters can understand it as bound up with the affection and care demonstrated in the bride's beauty. The gold she wears is a central part of her *jahez*, and Mody (2002b) describes the sadness of a man whose daughter eloped and so denied him the opportunity of lavishing gold on her in a demonstration of his fatherly love.[6]

A romantic aesthetic is often missing from descriptions of South Asian arranged marriages. Kohn (1998: 77) argues that an 'archaic but ever-present focus on function and structure imposes a hierarchy of motivation for marriage' that ignores love and romance. For the bride, although she may be apprehensive, her wedding day represents the pinnacle of her beauty, as never before has she worn such lavish and costly clothes, and shone with so much gold. Most women took pride in showing me photographs of themselves on their wedding day. One 19 year old in Bristol was already planning the design for gold sets based on ones she has seen at other weddings, although it would be several years before she is married. Of course, for those coerced into marriage, their wedding is not a happy occasion, but the romance and beauty of weddings is widely celebrated. Bollywood movies glorify romantic images of weddings and brides, and the wedding videos I watched during my fieldwork often featured images of the bride set into romantic backgrounds – at the centre of a rose, for example. Another common feature depicted layers of the same image of the bride (and often other attractive young women in attendance) peeling off, like rose petals, while soundtracks feature romantic songs.

Pakistani brides conventionally look downcast on their wedding days – it would not be seemly to be looking forward to their departure from their parental home, let alone their wedding night – but this does not necessarily mean that they do not enjoy the occasion of the wedding. Watching one recent wedding video in 2008, I was surprised to see the bride smiling happily, and it seems this is still rather unusual. The groom's mother in Bristol reported that her young niece's playful impressions of the expression she will wear on her wedding day have changed (from glum to smiling) since this event, and joked that the bride couldn't cry after her family spent 20,000 rupees on her bridal make-up.

With their opportunities for dressing up and socialising, weddings are among the most exciting occasions in the lives of many women both in Pakistan and the UK. Where young South Asian men can turn to sport for culturally sanctioned enjoyment, 'wedding culture' has been suggested as women's primary 'fun space' (Werbner 1996). Although Werbner describes weddings as a source of female enjoyment, the groom is also fêted. Talib from Bristol was surprised by how much he enjoyed his wedding day. A young man with strong religious views, he had been apprehensive about the process, but once he was dressed up and sitting on the stage, he felt, in his words, 'wicked and lush'.[7] Saif, another British groom, said about his wedding day:

> It was fantastic. Honestly, those two days were probably the best time I've ever had. Without a doubt. Well, it's just to see so many family in the same room at the same time – everyone coming up and giving their wishes and the money. And the ceremony, which I was trying to absorb at the same time. I wanted to remember the experience ... I don't think we had dancing at the *mehndi* – on the *barat* we did. Yeah, on the second day we did – which was excellent as well. It was completely different because I don't think we do that on family occasions ... So that was great fun because it was all the boys and I've got the nephews and cousins who come from here, and cousins from America and Manchester and all the different parts of the world – Kuwait, Dubai, Pakistan. They're all in the same place at the same time, all for me, and I thought well, you know, people make that effort then this must be a really special occasion, which made me feel really special.

Religion and tradition

Mehndi functions are traditionally held separately for the bride and groom, with the bride's party (without the bride) travelling to the groom's *mehndi* and then vice versa.[8] In modern urban Pakistani weddings, however, a 'joint' *mehndi* is often held. I was told that this was because city houses are small and those who can afford to often hire a venue for the occasion, either the function rooms of a hotel, or one of the *shadi* (wedding) halls that can be found in any reasonable-sized town. It then makes financial sense for the families to share the cost of one hall rather than rent two separately.

At one hotel *mehndi* I attended in Rawalpindi, the bride and groom were seated beside each other on a sofa in the room designated for women.[9] The bride sat demurely with her head down and covered while the groom was brought in by relatives dancing wildly, with a triumphal air. She remained silent and still while his male friends took the anointing to playful excess, smearing his face lavishly with *ubtan* and henna, and pouring oil into his hair until he looked thoroughly dishevelled. Others later told me that the joviality of the occasion was a marker of bonds of kinship between the two sides – without these ties the rivalry can apparently get out of hand. Fellow guests said that this couple had probably signed the *nikah-nama* (Islamic marriage contract) before the *mehndi*, or their sitting together might have been a minor scandal, breaching the conventional taboo against contact between an unmarried man and woman. In 2008, however, I watched a film of a recent Bristol 'love marriage' between young people raised in Britain, at which the couple sat together at the *mehndi* without having signed their *nikah-nama*, suggesting once more that such practices vary over space and time.

Not only is opinion divided on whether the couple should sit together, but the desirability of *mehndis* themselves is subject to divergent views, and not every wedding includes this function. Some Pakistani Muslims view the *mehndi* as an un-Islamic Hindu accretion, an example of the bad habits picked up from generations living side by side with Hindus in India.[10] A wedding in Bristol provided a clear illustration of the coexistence of divergent opinions. Whilst one woman lamented to me that *mehndis* in Britain were not as much fun as in Pakistan, with less money, dancing and singing, when I relayed this comment to Azra, a married woman in her mid-twenties who wears the *hijab*, she replied, 'Yes – it's much better here'. Leyla, who is 19, Bristolian and engaged to a cousin, is keen to ask her elderly relatives about old traditions she can incorporate into her wedding, but others try to pare down their marriages to purify them of 'tradition' or 'custom', leaving them purely 'religious'. Tahira told me that her wedding in Bristol to her paternal grandfather's brother's son (a migrant from Pakistan) was 'quite simple, because my family they're quite religious and they don't want anything too grand'. The *nikah* was done at home, and a couple of days later they had a single function for around 200 people in a hall in Bristol. There was no *mehndi* or wedding day, the function being the *walima*, the celebration given by the groom's side once the bride has been taken to her new home. According to *sunnat*, the sayings of the prophet, the *nikah* and *walima* are the essential elements of a Muslim wedding. Tahira commented about Pakistani wedding traditions: 'my dad was saying a lot of this stuff is derived from Hinduism. You know – custom'. Her husband elaborated:

> It's not of religion, because it came from our culture. We came from Hindu culture – we became Muslims from Hindus ... A lot of people say this [but] when they do [it] themselves they don't mind it, they just keep doing it [i.e. they know it's not religiously correct but carry on with these traditions].

Of course, a simple religious ceremony with limited celebrations is also much less costly, particularly for the bride's family, as the *walima* is conventionally the responsibility of the groom's side (although many of my informants reported that the wealthier British side had shouldered the majority of wedding expenses, regardless of whether they were the family of the bride or groom). Fatima from Bristol, however, described her campaign for a simple, inexpensive wedding when she fell in love with a cousin in Azad Kashmir as motivated not by economic or religious concerns, but simply because she 'wanted the marriage not the wedding'. Later, when she admitted feeling some jealousy on seeing her cousin's fancy wedding, complete with ornate, flower-bedecked wedding night bedstead, her husband sprinkled rose petals on their own marital bed.

Iram's wedding day

The women from the beauty parlour were late. The *barat* (groom's party) were due to arrive at 11.00, but by 12.00 there was still no sign of the women who were to dress Iram's hair, do her make-up, and help arrange her wedding clothes and jewellery. Her sister and cousin got themselves ready, Shabanna struggling with safety pins to ensure that her sari didn't show any skin around her waist. She hadn't worn a sari before, but luckily the innovation of stitching the pleats onto a belt, which gave it a fashionable slim-fit, eliminated the need for skilful folding. Shanaz had lent me a red and gold *lehnga* (skirt with a tunic top) bought in Britain for £45 but which all three girls had rejected, preferring to buy much more elaborate and up-to-date outfits locally. Iram set about painting her own nails in the burgundy colour of her wedding *lehnga,* applying gold transfers to the varnish.

Eventually the beauticians arrived, and I went downstairs to defrost my toes. It was a crisp winter day and they were turning white in my thin *lehnga* and wedding *kusse*.[11] Unfortunately this meant that I missed the arrival of the *nikah-nama*, which Iram signed without reading.[12] Some guests arrived, and women surged up the stairs to try to get a look at the bride, to cries of 'Don't let them in!' Iram's aunt and I squeezed past them and were admitted to find Iram transformed in her heavily beaded red and gold *lehnga*, gold necklaces and rings, heavy make-up, and the final touches of gold glitter being sprayed onto her elaborate rolled hair-style. 'This isn't me', she said, playing with the rings – family had given so much jewellery that she had two rings to a finger, and her mother had kept some of the money sent by relatives in Europe to buy gold for future purchases of household items when the groom came to England.

The girls grumbled that they were hungry – there were supposed to be *samosas* (savoury filled pastries) when the *barat* arrived, and the wedding was, as is often the case, running several hours late. Then word came that the *barat* were on their way. Along with the other women, I was given a plate of rose petals, many from the garlands of the previous night, and we made our way to the entrance to the village. The groom, with his uncle by his side (his father, who would normally have played this role, had also died) came walking down the village street from their coach and cars, followed by the rest of his relatives and friends. Shabanna, her cousin from Bristol and another female cousin of a similar age from the village approached the groom and his uncle. In a small space in front of the cameras, with people crowding round trying for a view, Shabanna offered Hamid a sip from a cup decorated with silver foil and sequins[13] and Hamid's uncle gave the girls some money. This done, the *barat* came forwards, women from their side embracing women from ours, and men doing the same. As we made our way back to the house one of the girls told me excitedly, 'I got fifteen hundred rupees – that's like a hundred and thirty pounds!'

The female guests gathered inside the courtyard to watch the display of the *burri* (Urdu) or *vurri* (Punjabi) gifts of clothes, jewellery and accessories from the groom's family to the bride. Outfit after embroidered outfit was held aloft to be inspected by the audience, followed by shoes in the latest platform styles, beauty cases and gold jewellery. The display of Iram's *burri* was followed by a meal, served to women and men separately in *shamiyanas* (decorated marquees) outside the house.

Finally we returned to the courtyard to witness the couple sitting together as man and wife. Guests approached to put *salami* money gifts into the hands of bride and groom, and some sat beside the couple to be filmed by the camera, which once again had the best view. The day is generally understood to be arduous for the bride, with the weight of her jewellery and heavily bead-worked *lehnga* under the hot lights. She sat unsmiling, with her head modestly down.

Eventually it was time for the *rukhsati*, when the bride is sent to her husband's home. She is normally taken out surrounded by female relatives weeping at her departure, although she will return for a short stay at her natal home the following day if her husband's home is not too distant. This time the tears were particularly numerous as the women of the family remembered that her father could not be there to see her married. When she had been escorted to the waiting car, the *barat* drove off.

Traditions of opposition

Numerous traditions, which may or may not be performed at any individual wedding, take the form of the groom paying his bride's sister in order to progress with the marriage. If the bride has no or few sisters, then other female relatives will perform this role, and at the marriage of an American woman with no suitable kin, those demanding payment were her female friends. Fines paid to the relatives of the bride and other attempts to delay the progress of the groom's party through the marriage are seen by many commentators as a kind of symbolic battle between the two sides. For Bloch (1992), these traditions are part of the 'rebounding violence' found in all ritual, but in weddings such practices have been seen as expressing tensions and differences between the families of the bride and groom: see Campbell

(1964: 132–35) on Sarakatsani, and Carsten (1997: 209) on Malay marriage ceremonies. In both cases, affines (relatives through marriage) are potentially dangerous outsiders, and the challenge of a marriage is to manage this difference and create bonds of kinship or cooperation. In Pakistani weddings, however, the two 'sides' are often already closely related. For guests equally related to both the bride and groom, it can be difficult to say whether they should arrive with the *barat*, or be there to welcome them. Patricia Jeffery reports a jovial celebration of a marriage between Muslim first cousins in north India during which 'joking turned on the double roles which everyone could play'. The bride's mother, in her role as the groom's aunt, visited her own daughter to 'see the bride's face', and the bride's brother insisted that he should arrive and be feted with the groom, his 'cousin-brother' (Jeffery 1979: 173). Nevertheless, Pakistani wedding customs are 'structured around the cultural fiction of an alliance between distinct kindreds' (Werbner 1990). The elements of mock fighting at Pakistani weddings – the bribing of the bride's sisters, or the triumphal dancing of the groom's party on the *mehndi* – can be viewed as part of the way in which this distinction is created. For Pakistanis engaged in close kin marriages, such customs help to create the distance needed for affinity, so that a bride is not kept within the family (which would imply incest) but given to another.[14]

Money may be required before the groom can enter the marriage venue, and one particularly popular ritual, *jute* (shoes), involves the sisters of the bride seizing one of the groom's shoes and holding it to ransom until a sufficient sum is offered. The women are being compensated for the loss of their sister, and the amounts involved can be substantial, but the playful nature of many of these practices also refers to the temporary state of joking and licensed behaviour permitted between a man and his bride's sisters (Werbner 1990: 278–79). Although Werbner writes of this as signalling the temporary incorporation of the groom into the bride's family, a phase that ends once the marriage has been consummated, during another wedding described to me, this behaviour carried on during the *walima*:

> At the end they thought, 'Oh yeah – your brother-in-law has to sit on your lap'. It's a custom or something. [I said] 'Yeah, but you haven't got no brothers', and all his cousins come over … All of them got something [money] – they were begging for it, from me … I think the youngest one has to sit on your lap, but he was too shy – he was a little baby. He's about four years old … So all of them, they start massaging my legs, saying, 'We're doing something for you!' … Some of them were men! I thought, 'Don't touch me, just have some money!' I gave them my purse – 'Just have what you want!' We had lots of fun.
>
> (Asma)

In most cases, the demands for money are playful, as befits the artificial and temporary creation of opposing sides from mutual kin, but marriages can sometimes reveal underlying tensions between participants (cf. Werbner 1990: 252–53). The low 'price' eventually given for a shoe at one function was accepted with only a little good-natured teasing, although one guest commented that this was mean considering that the groom was gaining the opportunity to go abroad through this marriage, with the implication that he would soon be earning far more and so could have afforded to be generous. In one wedding video I was shown, however, the haggling turned into a fairly heated argument between relatives from each side.

If there are two bridal outfits, one for the *barat* day and the other for the *walima*, one will normally be provided by the bride's family and the other by the groom's side. The bride is equipped with many sets of fancy clothes by her own family as part of her *jahez*, and is expected to appear in all her finery at dinner invitations and functions in the weeks following her marriage. This display brings prestige to her husband's family by showing that their new member is beautiful, and has brought wealth with her, and by demonstrating the expense that they themselves have lavished on her. Hence, when I met Iram at a wedding a fortnight after her marriage and admired the many sets of gold jewellery she was wearing, she explained that she didn't really want to wear all of it, but had been told that she should.

While the beautification of the bride embodies the care and status of the family who give her in marriage, the *burri*, which may be equal in value to the *jahez* (Fischer 1991), demonstrates the effort, care and investment that is also put into the new bride by her in-laws. In her discussion of Pakistani marriages Pnina Werbner quotes a Hindu hymn about the transfer of the bride cited by Lévi-Strauss, 'Love has given; love has received. Love has filled the ocean', saying that 'for Pakistanis a wedding is about a transfer of love, nurture and authority' (Werbner 1990: 259), but the mutual investment of the two families in the bride's splendour is a meeting between the 'two loves'.

Werbner and Lévi-Strauss describe this as only a momentary joining on the occasion of marriage, after which the bride is transferred to her in-law's family. The bride's relationship with her parents does indeed become more circumscribed after marriage. One imported husband in Bristol, for example, limited his wife's daily visits to eat at her mother's house, saying that it 'didn't look nice'. Not only should her duties now lie with her husband, but providing for her is his responsibility. North Indian and Pakistani families no longer take food from their daughter after she has married, signalling that she has become part of another household as a gift, for which nothing should be accepted in return (Jeffery *et al.* 1989: 53). For north Indian Hindus, the bride is *kanya dan*, the gift of a virgin (Fruzzetti 1982; Raheja and Gold 1994). *Dan* is a type of gift that removes inauspiciousness from the donor and therefore should not be reciprocated (Raheja 1988; Raheja and Gold 1994: 74–92; Parry 1986). This religious connotation is absent for Muslims, but the expectation of non-reciprocity is similar, although less strictly observed where marriages are between close kin. Sisters whose children are husband and wife, for example, may continue to give each other gifts.

Women married into Britain may find ways of sharing the financial benefits of their migration with relatives in Pakistan. Some migrant wives who worked in factories reportedly made secret arrangements to send some of their wages home. More recently I have been told of women remitting their child benefit payments, or in one case the allowance received from the government for caring for her disabled husband. Money has commonly been sent through the unofficial 'Hundi' system in which local agents take deposits and relatives can collect the money from an agent in Pakistan, saving time and bank charges (OPF n.d.), and without the need for villagers to open bank accounts. It is rumoured that one man involved in the 'money business' in Bristol took advantage of the secrecy to start affairs with his clients. Part of the reason for the clandestine nature of these arrangements is of course simply that the women are siphoning off a portion of the household's income for their own purposes, but it also reflects the strength of the social expectation that women's parents will not receive monies or goods from their daughter after she is married.

The wedding meal

At Iram's wedding, food was served before the couple sat together, but at other functions I attended, the serving of food was normally left until after the marriage ceremonies, when the bride and groom are seated together. Many guests leave directly after eating, with only closer family and friends staying to witness the departure of the bride to her new home (the *rukhsati*). One guide to Pakistan gives the following warning to foreign visitors attending Pakistani weddings:

> Some time during these proceedings dinner will be announced. The news spreads like wild fire and everyone abandons the bridal couple and moves towards the food. Don't be shocked at the jostling, shoving and pushing that you will experience at the dinner table, which is usually a buffet. Everyone attacks the food table as if it is the last meal he is going to get and in a matter of minutes the food has disappeared from the table. A team of harangued waiters clears up the mess. The bridal couple gets a dinner table set up before them on the stage.
>
> (Mittman and Ihsan 1991)

As part of political attempts to control expenditure on weddings, the serving of meals at marriages was banned in 1997, but the 2003 Punjab Marriage Functions Act[15] permits one main dish to be served at the Walima function. In addition to economic control, this legislation may be viewed as part of the trend to 'purify' Islam. Ostentatious expenditure is sometimes seen as a Hindu characteristic, contrasting with Islamic values of frugality and simplicity. During my Pakistani fieldwork, a few raids in which food was confiscated made the papers, but function halls (known as *shadi* halls) sometimes got away with providing a meal by failing to mention that the event was a wedding – I have seen notices on announcement boards for 'X family function', for example. Nevertheless, during my stay in Pakistan I got into the habit of eating a snack before going to a wedding in order to stave off hunger, as on occasion the anticipated meal turned out to be limited to *kashmiri chai* (a pink, milky tea), or soup served in a tea cup (drinks were permitted under the ban). The restrictions could be avoided in village weddings, or those held at home rather than in *shadi* halls. While most of those I spoke to in Pakistan agreed that curbing excessive spending was an admirable goal, few were prepared to forgo serving a meal, saying that if guests have come from a distance, it is impossible to send them away without feeding them. Weddings are part of the exchanges between kin and friends that form both an important social obligation and a source of prestige, so the legislation intended to curtail expenditure on hospitality at weddings was widely flouted.

Weddings in Britain and Pakistan alike generally involve a lot of sitting around waiting. In addition to the excitement for the women of dressing up and seeing the bride's clothes, or commenting on how well matched the couple may or may not be, the food is the highlight and most discussed aspect of the event: whether it was served too late; what was served; and who it was served by. It is traditionally the duty of the men of the family to serve the wedding food, a function performed by waiters at hotel/*shadi* hall weddings. Some people with strong religious views, however, object to women being served by men. At Iram's *walima* I was warned to be careful of the men serving, but on the *barat*, the wedding day, a buffet-style meal meant that the involvement of the men was minimal.

Wedding styles

Some of the different styles of functions have been mentioned already: village/home versus halls, joint/separate *mehndis*, and the issue of religious purity against local marriage traditions. This last aspect was of particular interest to participants in Bristol, who talked about some functions as 'religious weddings'. As mentioned above, these may involve the segregation of men and women, and the absence of music and dancing, but may also mean limiting or excluding filming and photography.

At most weddings I attended in Pakistan, the video camera was a marked presence with its attendant scrum of lights, lighting operators and cameramen. Nothing could be done until it was in place, it monopolised the best viewpoints of the couple and ceremony, and as is evident from Iram's wedding, determined the pace of the event. Even when guests were eating, the camera pursued them, something many women find embarrassing. Copies of videos are dispersed to relatives, sometimes across the globe, including those who could not attend. They are watched and re-watched to the accompaniment of reminiscences, and commentaries on women's dress or eating habits. As time goes by they provide opportunities to revisit the images of relatives who have since died, so that on a visit to his daughter in Britain, one elderly man asked to be shown a family wedding video in which a recently deceased relative could be seen. It is just this dispersal, however, that makes some people object to videoing on religious grounds, as unrelated (*gair mehram*) men may see the faces and wedding finery of the women in attendance. While some 'religious weddings' do without a video camera, however, few can resist altogether having some photographic record of the day, so when Rashida in Bristol asked me to take photographs of a function to celebrate her daughter-in-law's arrival in Britain, she said that while filming and photographing were wrong in Islamic terms, it would still be 'nice to have a few snaps'.

At another wedding in Bristol, I became aware that there was a third element to moral assessments of wedding styles. While some marriage celebrations are seen as 'traditional' and others 'religious', this function was seen by some as scandalously 'modern'. It was a sit-down affair with named table settings held at a city-centre hotel, and incorporated some elements of ethnic British wedding styles – the bride and groom joined hands to cut a tiered wedding cake, there was a band (an out-of-town Asian ensemble performing *filmi* songs), and the couple danced the first close dance together. However, the seemingly British style held particular Pakistani significance. Zaynab, seated at my table, was scathing about the dancing. Women may dance in front of other women at *mehndis*, and men may do a bhangra in front of a mixed audience, but it is neither traditional nor religious convention for a husband and wife to touch each other, let alone dance together, in public. To make matters worse for Zaynab, the bride's sisters and their husbands started dancing, and then swapped partners so that men were dancing with women who were not their wives. One of the sisters' husbands is from the Middle East, and Zaynab said that this behaviour was all right for him because it was the tradition of his country, but she disapproved of it for Pakistanis. All the weddings in Birmingham, she told me, have dancing these days. Her nephew in Birmingham, of whom she is extremely fond, told her that she must dance at his wedding, but she replied that if there was dancing, she wouldn't attend.

Polarised attitudes to cities such as Birmingham and London, with larger Pakistani communities and considered far more 'modern' than Bristol, mirror those towards other things considered 'modern', from some styles of weddings to educated working women or the latest fashions in *shalwar qamis*. Some, like Zaynab, disapprove and talk about the moral degeneracy of these 'modern' spaces, such as badly behaved city boys who cruise around in their cars making comments at girls. Others, and particularly the young, dismissed Bristol as 'backwards' and craved the opportunity of the big cities. However, just as most Bristol Pakistanis jump at the opportunity for a shopping trip to Birmingham, most incorporate some elements that might be considered 'modern' into their lives and marriages, whether that be a woman developing a career, 'doing fashion' or holding a joint *mehndi*, and the terms are understood here as my informant's, rather than analytic, categories. As Fauzia Ahmad has commented of her research on British South Asian Muslim women's participation in higher education, things '"colloquialised" as either "traditional" or "modern/Westernised" were often overlapping, suggesting their inadequacy and rigidity as descriptive concepts' (Ahmad 2001: 139). Apparently 'traditional' transnational marriages, as will be seen, may serve 'modern' ends.

Nonetheless, the tripartite classification of 'religion', 'tradition' and 'modernity' present important sets of oppositions for my informants in Bristol. The English words 'religion', 'tradition' and 'modern' are used by many of my informants in Bristol. I also use them in this context to gloss terms such as *rasm* (custom), and more specific references to Islam or, for example, *sunnat*. The Introduction mentioned the use of such categories in mutual evaluations of Mirpuris and urban Punjabis, and subsequent chapters will show how these characteristics are involved in decisions on marriage partners. As is apparent from this present discussion of modernity, however, the moral evaluation attached to each attribute may be reversed according to the standpoint of the speaker. While some condemn wedding traditions as both 'backwards' and against religion, others value them as an enjoyable part of their cultural heritage. I have never, on the other hand, heard religion criticised by a (British) Pakistani Muslim, but I have occasionally encountered the pejorative term 'fundamentalism' employed to contest practices and attitudes that the practitioners themselves view as 'religious'.

A political economy of British Pakistani wedding styles

As noted above, a 'religious' wedding is almost by definition a less costly affair, but this is not the only factor in the political economy of wedding styles. When Bushra's brother Saif's wife arrived from Pakistan, the family decided to hold a function to celebrate. This would allow British relatives and friends who had not attended the marriage in Pakistan to participate, and such events are often referred to as weddings (*shadi*). Bushra and Saif explained the implications of and reasons for their choice of venue and the size of the function.

Saif, a 'modern' young man, wanted to hire a hotel function suite, with a sit-down meal, and even considered the stylish setting of Ashton Court mansion, just outside the city. There were three major problems with this aspiration. First, most establishments expect to provide the food themselves, while most Pakistanis would like to have the function catered for by a reputable Pakistani source, both to ensure that the meal is appropriate to Pakistani tastes and dietary requirements, and because it can be significantly cheaper.[16] At the time Saif's party was being organised, there was a shortage of hotels in the city willing to accept this arrangement. Although choice had expanded by 2008,[17] the willingness of wedding venues to accommodate Pakistani requirements was still an issue – one woman spoke longingly of the manor house that had eventually agreed to outside caterers for her son's wedding, only to find that the caterers could not comply with the venue's list of conditions for use. The second drawback was that this type of function is extremely expensive. Finally, if there is to be a seated table plan, the number of people who can be invited must be curtailed and monitored. Even if expense were not an issue, the number of people such a venue could hold are usually limited to 200 or 300, while I attended a function in a school hall with three sittings to eat at canteen tables where the hosts estimated that 900 guests were in attendance.

Bushra explained the political implications of decisions over the style and thus scale of weddings. Failure to reciprocate previous wedding invitations with an invitation when there is a marriage in your family can be taken as an insult (*besti*[18]). However, invitations can be understood to apply to the whole household or even the extended family, making limiting numbers difficult. One Bristol bride told me that they gave out 300 cards, expecting 700 attendees, but on the day they estimated 1,500 had turned up. Another woman told me that she considered which invitations to accept very carefully, bearing in mind that her children were coming up to marriageable age and that acceptances would increase the numbers of guests she would have to invite to their weddings. Obligations can span the years. Humera told me that when she attended Farida's wedding in 1975, her family was small – just Humera and her sister Zaynab – but when her own daughter marries she will have to invite Farida's whole family, grown large in the intervening years. Bushra and Saif jokingly complained about one particularly large family in their area: 'You invite one [family name] and they all come!' Having a seating plan, and so needing to control numbers precisely, can thus be controversial. Equally, however, it may be that such arrangements are desired precisely in order to have a mechanism to control numbers and censor who can attend.

Saif was also, however, tempted by the idea of a large hall, and several of Bristol's school assembly halls were popular venues. The advantage of this style of wedding, he explained, was that room hire costs are low, and if a large number of guests is invited, the returns in the form of *salami* (money gifts) can be high. *Salami* is given to the bride or groom, or both, depending to which side the giver is related or otherwise connected. The amount depends on the closeness of the relationship. My enquiries and observations in 2001 suggest that £20 was a fairly standard amount, with £10 the minimum acceptable. By 2008, one informant told me £20 was the expected minimum, as £10 'didn't look nice'. A close friend or relative might give £50 or even £100. Again, the large family mentioned above were given as an example of a problem with this scheme: as *salami* is generally given on behalf of a household (*ghar*), a large family who only give one *salami* but bring many members to be fed can be an expensive proposition, although some account of this may be taken in the amount given. While Saif was obviously enticed by the prospect of so much cash, and it can undoubtedly be of great assistance in bearing the expense of functions, the money will in effect be repaid as a return *salami* gift on the next wedding in the giver's family. Thus Shanaz saw some of the larger amounts of *salami* given to Iram as a burden. Some of Iram's friends, she complained, had given £100, which meant that at some time in the near future, she was going to have to find £100 for each of them. At most weddings, a relative will be delegated to make note of who gives what, although the process seemed to have been made more straightforward at functions I attended in Bristol by the widespread giving of *salami* inside a greeting card in which the giver's name is written.

Some literature on north Indian and Pakistani gifting reports that return gifts should be of a slightly greater value than that received, in order to continue the gifting relationship, while a gift of the same value will be understood as closing the exchange (e.g. Shaw 2000a: 236–37). Werbner writes that a pound note would sometimes be added to the sum to represent the ongoing relationship (Werbner 1990: 251), and figures of 101 or 1,001 rupees occur in the subcontinent. During my fieldwork, however, neither of these appeared to be the case. My informants reported that they would give an equal amount of *salami* to that given. An explanation for this may lie in changes in British currency from one pound notes to coins – when I asked why they wouldn't give gifts of say £11, one woman told me that coins are never given as they 'look cheap'.[19] The same practical difference between Pakistan and England probably accounts for the fact that money *har* (garlands) seem less common at British functions. In Pakistan, the groom often sports impressive garlands made from low-denomination notes, which I am told may be un-stitched, or taken back to the manufacturer who will exchange the money minus a small amount for labour. In England, however, with a minimum note value of £5, such *har* would be extremely expensive, and even imported ones made from one-rupee notes sold for £20 and more in Birmingham in 2001, many times their face value.

Cash is once more a prominent feature in Pakistani weddings when the groom arrives for the *mehndi* accompanied by yellow-clad drummers who can be found waiting for business on certain streets in the cities. His male friends and family rotate notes above his head ('for luck'; cf. Raheja and Gold 1994) and flinging them into the air for the drummers to gather as payment. As neither drummers nor low-denomination notes are available in Bristol, this exuberant display is absent. As much of this would suggest, and contrary to the project of 'purifying' Islam in the subcontinent, conspicuous consumption and display of wealth is a prominent feature of most Pakistani weddings, so that at Rubina's wedding her grandfather displayed a cheque for a million rupees as a wedding gift. The cheque was destroyed later, having been 'just for the show at the time'.

Determining wedding styles

In Britain, then, wedding styles are partially determined by the local environment – the types of venues, materials and services available. These have expanded significantly in recent years, along with the popularity of Asian bridal magazines and even specialist Asian bridal shows. As Mand (2012) notes of Sikh weddings, there may be an increasing desire to stamp the event with individual taste or 'distinction' – holding events in different kinds of venues to the traditional school hall, for example. In addition, there is great regional variation within Pakistan, and between British families who hail from these different regions. On one occasion my questions about wedding customs led two women into a discussion in which each was constantly surprised by the practices of the other. One described a tradition in which the women of the groom's family carry a water pot on their head. The other said she had only ever seen this done on videos. Beyond these determinants, however, the wedding may still not turn out as the bride or groom have envisioned it. Saif, who wanted a posh, modern function in Bristol, eventually accepted his father and elder brothers' decision to opt for a school hall at the lower end of the price range. However, parents and those financing the wedding will not always have the final say. Azra religiously avoids being photographed, and she and her mother were determined to have a wedding without videos or photography. On the day, however, other relatives brought video cameras. Azra's mother managed to stop them filming, but they were unable to resist pressure to have photographs taken.

Brides may not choose what they will wear on their wedding day. While I was in Pakistan, for example, I went on several shopping trips with Mariam from London, who had been commissioned to buy all the clothes for her sister's wedding in England. Some arrive in Pakistan to find that mothers or sisters who were able to leave earlier have selected their wedding *lehnga* and other fancy outfits. Luckily, close relatives are often good at judging the other's tastes:

> I'm sure by the time [of my marriage] I'll just forget it and let everyone else get on with it. I trust everyone else in the family, that's the thing. I trust they'd get the right outfit and they'd get the right jewellery and everything, because they're quite modern. They're quite in with the times.
> (Leyla)

One wedding outfit and many sets of fancy clothes to be worn after the wedding will normally be provided by the groom's side, and choices made by those who do not know the bride so well may be less successful. Raisa, for example, keeps her wedding photographs hidden so as not to be reminded of the awful (from her perspective) clothes and make-up she had to wear.

Decisions on how the wedding will proceed may also be criticised by more distant relatives. Asma's husband's family did not ask for *jahez* (dowry) as the couple were going to live in Britain, and Asma's father provided household goods for them when they set up house independently in Bristol. One of Asma's aunts from a village background, however, goaded Asma's mother about the decision saying, 'Oh, don't you want to give anything to them? Like a bed or some cupboards?' The family stood their ground, but in other cases people may bow to pressure from relatives so that, for example, *mehndis* may be held for young men and women who do not believe in them.

The style of a wedding thus becomes a corporate decision, and family styles develop over time. People often explain the presence or absence of particular practices in their marriages by what 'we' as a family do or do not do. There can, however, be differences between even close relatives: on a marriage between first cousins, one side may hold a *mehndi* while the other does not. When Tahir married Asma, he was keen to sit beside his fiancée on their *mehndi*, but his attempts to have a romantic night were foiled:

> I asked, 'Can we sit together?' My mother also asked, 'Let them sit together', but their side didn't let us ... That's a relatively new style. Some people do it that way – quite a few changes coming in now ... I wanted to sit close to her! One thing I did was I got her a rose, one of my friends got a rose. I went quietly over the hall – she was in [a] separate room – and tried to enter ... She's got a big aunt. She's quite big and fat and she came in the way ... [Boys in Pakistan are] quite romantic, they are, most of them. I don't know why but most of them think that way about girls – maybe the frustration or something!

Iram's *walima*

The next day we boarded a coach hired for the occasion and set off for Hamid's village. When we arrived, we were shown straight into a room where Iram was sitting in a gold *lehnga* on the double bed sent by her family, which was decorated with strings of multicoloured tinsel. I followed as her relatives went up one by one to embrace her, and then took their seats or went outside to the courtyard where more chairs had been laid out. Some whispered something to her; Shanaz asked if she had taken a bath,[20] while the younger Bristol women had other concerns: as Shabanna sat down, her cousin asked, 'Did she have a good night?'

Shanaz pushed her youngest son forward, 'Go and *mil* your sister' she instructed (*milna* is the verb to meet). Shanaz was wearing her gold jewellery and make-up today – yesterday she had worn neither, and had never taken off the black shawl covering the beautiful blue *shalwar qamis* she had had made for this special occasion. She had spent the wedding day stressed and avoiding the cameras, but now that her responsibilities were discharged and the wedding had passed off smoothly she was able to relax. All that was left now was the visa to bring Hamid to Bristol. After a meal, the guests departed.

Seeing the bride

I have never accompanied the *barat* as they take the bride home or to her husband's home or wedding night hotel, but am told she is seated on the bed in which she will spend the first night with her husband. People may visit to view her. When the couple are left alone together, it is traditional for the groom to persuade his shy young bride to lift her veil and show her face by giving her a gift, usually of a ring. This is called the *munh-dikhai*, which literally means 'face showing'. Of course, these days most couples have seen each other before, and one young woman from Bristol told me of her wedding night in a way which contradicts the image of the shy new wife, as she playfully argued over the lifting of her veil:

> It was our *munh-dikhai* time and my husband actually ordered me a ring but it wasn't ready for our wedding day ... so he gave me a thousand rupees ... [but she said] 'When you've brought my ring, [then] you can pull my scarf up!' And he said to me, 'What can I give you?' ... And he took his watch off and he took his ring off, and he said, 'You keep this. I promise you I've got your thing. You keep hold of this, you don't have to give it back to me ... I promise you sure I've got this for you and we'll go tomorrow, we'll go see that man' ... And I said to him, 'This isn't really enough!' ... He was a bit nervous [saying] 'Oh my God what shall I do!' And he took his watch off and his ring and said you have this. And I said, 'I suppose it will have to do!'
>
> (Shareen)

In light of the intimacy of the *munh-dikhai*, a startling feature of many wedding albums is the intrusion of the camera into this moment. The bride may be photographed sitting on the decorated wedding bed, veiled and with her skirts spread out around her. In some photo-shoots I have seen, the camera mimics the new husband's view in a close-up as the young woman lifts the scarf covering her face. Women I have talked to about this say they find it embarrassing to be photographed on the bed in this way. I can only surmise that this might not be the only change that photographic technology has brought to Pakistani weddings. As evinced in the description of Iram's wedding, the video and stills cameras are given pride of place at weddings to the extent that guests struggle to get a view of the proceedings. Interestingly, there are hints that it is not only at the *munh-dikhai* that the camera seems to undermine the traditional practices of modesty of the bride. At another wedding, for example, the bride's head was originally covered with a modest brown embroidered shawl, which had to be removed so that the camera could capture the beauty of the intricately beaded fabric of the wedding outfit. I have been told that in earlier times when the couple was seated together for the first time as man and wife, the bride's head was completely covered, and a mirror might be placed between them so that they could glimpse each other's faces. The importance of the *munh-dikhai* as the first viewing in private is highlighted under such circumstances, but it may be that the demands of the camera helped to advance the viewing of the bride's face so that it is now uncovered on the wedding day itself. Undermining the significance of *munh-dikhai* is taken further by the intrusion of the camera into the marital bedroom. As will be seen in a later chapter, some confusion and lack of knowledge of the practice now seems to exist among young people in both Britain and Pakistan.

Not only the camera, but the camera operator or operators can be an intrusive presence. To satisfy the demands of the lens, the private celebration of the *mehndi* is exposed to the gaze of a male outsider – all the camera operators I have seen have been men. I have often heard young women at weddings refer to the cameraman as 'video uncle'. The English word 'uncle' is often used by young British Pakistanis as a term of respect for older men, but here may moderate the undesirability of an unrelated man intruding into the predominantly female space of the *mehndi*. I am tempted to speculate that the tradition of women singing irreverent songs to each other at *mehndi*s may come under threat from the exposure of the event to a wider audience, through self-censorship of behaviour that some might view as less than respectable.[21]

Brides complain that the heat of lights and constant scrutiny add to the burden of maintaining their composure under the weight of both expectation and the elaborate wedding dress. My field notes from Iram's wedding note how struck I was by the intrusiveness of the cameras, which inevitably obscure the view of guests:

> The groom is grinding his teeth. The camera is very close. The bride is brought down by her sisters, with her head lowered, and sits on the sofa beside the groom. They are filmed and photographed by successive people – lights bright in their faces as different relatives from both sides sit on the chairs and sofa beside them ... This goes on for a long time – I move around a bit to try to get views – I'm not the only one standing on chairs and things. They both [the couple] look rigid.

The dominant presence of the camera reflects the importance of images of the wedding. The professional video team may be joined by relatives with their own still or video cameras. Videos and photographs are kept as mementos by the bride and groom and their families, and may circulate locally and globally, allowing many more people to participate, at least in terms of imagination, in the event. In this way, they aid in the maintenance of relations between kin and friends, and between Pakistan and the diaspora (cf. Mand 2012). They document the splendour of the occasion and thus are a testimony to the status families hope to display at such events, and the affection lavished upon the bride. Guests are filmed, charting the relatives, friends and acquaintances in attendance. For this reason, videos may even present an opportunity for viewers to spot potential spouses for themselves or their relatives. Videos and photographs may not only be sent over great distances, but are also durable. As time goes by they can become a cherished record not only of events, but of relationships (cf. Mand 2012) – an experience in which I shared in 2007–08 as I watched videos featuring those I had known in Pakistan. All these factors

46 *Weddings*

contribute to the value of such media in the long-term maintenance of relationships across continents.

Later chapters of this book focus on the arrangement of transnational marriages, and the subsequent experiences of both migrant and resident spouses. Several themes that have emerged in this chapter will continue to underlie the discussion, including gendered experience; the contrasts between religion, tradition and modernity; and the interplay of legislation, strategy, kinship and emotion in producing dynamic practices. In this chapter we have also started to explore some of the experiences of British Pakistani visitors to Pakistan in the context of their own and their relatives' marriages. Humour, enjoyment and uncertainty have all been present in their words and actions. The following chapter will attempt to site this ethnography within the broader processes and literature of transnationalism, and will end by returning to Iram's brothers at the *walima* as they '*mil*' their newly married sister. A review of the actions and narratives that have been presented in this chapter, in combination with further ethnographic material, will then allow an exploration of the individual and characteristic forms of transnationalism presented by these young people.

Notes

1. A Home Office report states 96% of the marriages of Pakistani applicants for UK spousal visas took place in Pakistan, indicating a very low proportion of marriages registered as taking place in Britain (Home Office 2011: 13).
2. See Werbner 1990 for a symbolic analysis of colours in Pakistani weddings.
3. When I showed the photographs to a Pakistani friend she pointed to this use of money as an example of British Pakistani ostentation – her family use tissue paper or a leaf.
4. Firing guns on a wedding night appears also to occur in neighbouring Afghanistan, leading to a tragic attack on a wedding party by Western coalition forces who believed they were under attack. Several young British men I met relished the opportunity to hold and shoot firearms in Pakistan. In light of the contemporary political situation, however, Saif from Bristol joked that it was perhaps just as well that he hadn't managed to fulfil his ambition of returning with photographs of himself, a young Muslim, firing a Kalashnikov.
5. As is common across South Asia, Pakistanis commonly view substances such as foodstuffs as being hot or cold.
6. Some brides now apparently wear costume jewellery matching their outfit, rather than their *jahez* gold (P. Akhtar, personal communication).
7. 'Wicked': great (contemporary British slang); 'lush': lovely (Bristolian).
8. In a 2002 Channel 4 documentary called 'Marrying a Stranger', a groom from Birmingham is shown sneaking into his Pakistani bride-to-be's *mehndi* celebration among his relatives, in an attempt to catch his first glimpse of the woman he has agreed to marry.
9. Weddings are often segregated, either with men in one room/*shamiyana* tent and women in another, or with one room divided by a screen. The bride or couple are then seated in the women's section.
10. This folk model belies the fact that many Muslims in the subcontinent may be descendants of converts from Hinduism; Jeffery *et al.* (2004) note that improving literature for Muslim girls and young women in north India produced by reformist movements stresses the importance of purging such traditions from religious practice.

11 Traditional decorated leather shoes made to a single pattern which must be worn to mould them to fit left and right feet. The male version worn by the groom often have long, extravagantly curled toes.
12 At the women's university where I stayed, teachers entreated the female students to be sure to read their *nikah-nama*. Not only does it specify the amount of the *mahr* payment to the wife, but sections are sometimes crossed out to remove the woman's right to divorce (cf. Shah-Kazemi 2001, on Islamic divorce).
13 The *dudh-wali* or milk cup, but nowadays sometimes filled with cola.
14 Similarity, kinship and affinity are discussed further in Chapter 4.
15 See: www.commonlii.org/pk/legis/pj/consol_act/pmfa2003255/ (accessed 10/10/2012).
16 One popular caterer was referred to as the Cardiff-*wala*, the man from Cardiff.
17 Ashton Court had started accepting outside caterers.
18 A contraction of *be-izzati* (dishonour) – discussed in Chapter 6.
19 I was not, however, able to ascertain whether this had been the custom before the switch to notes.
20 For Muslims, sexual intercourse causes a state of impurity to be removed by washing (see Shaw 2000a: 213).
21 Mand (2012) describes the impact of filming, including the minimisation of similar women's events, in Sikh wedding videos.

2 British Pakistanis and transnationalism

Ethnic groups and transnational boundaries

When I first started working with South Asian organisations in Bristol in the late 1990s, there was already a substantial academic literature on these well-established ethnic groups. Much sociological work in the 1980s and 1990s grew out of an earlier 'race-relations' framework (Bates 2001: 9), and was concerned with inequalities of various kinds (Rex 1997: 206), including health (Donnovan 1986; Nazroo 1997), housing (Smith 1989) and socio-economic position (Modood *et al.* 1997), regarding ethnic minorities as a whole, and more specifically South Asian groups (Williams *et al.* 1998). Existing anthropological research (e.g. Ballard 1994; Clarke *et al.* 1990a; Bhachu 1986), often took the form of a community study set in a single British town or city (Anwar 1979; Jeffery 1976a; Shaw 1988; Werbner 1990). Much of the earlier literature on South Asian populations in Britain featured a Barthian focus on social institutions, ethnic identities and boundary maintenance (Gardner 1995: 6–7). The term 'enclave' had been used to describe the Pakistani community (Werbner 1987), and attempts to maintain ethnic boundaries vis-à-vis the majority white population were seen in various phenomena, from the 'myth of return' to resurgent Islamic identities (Anwar 1979; Jeffery 1976a; Shaw 1994).

Having delved into this substantial and valuable literature, when I started fieldwork in Bristol I was surprised by the extent and immediacy of connections to Pakistan, or indeed other sites in the Pakistani diaspora, amongst many of those with whom I was working. Arriving at a community group where I was volunteering one day, I asked a co-worker how her weekend had been. 'Terrible', she replied, 'my son's been ill, and my cousin was kidnapped'. I was startled by the second part of her statement, but it later became apparent that the cousin in question was in Pakistan. Both events were narrated with equal emotion, collapsing the affective distance between continents. After this conversation, I became increasingly aware of other cross-border connections, particularly in the form of transnational marriages. The research on which this book is based grew out of these experiences. It would be incorrect, however, to suggest that ongoing ties between South Asian migrants and their countries of origin had not been noticed by earlier researchers. Writing in 1976, Patricia

Jeffery criticised what would later come to be known as 'methodological nationalism' (Wimmer and Glick Schiller 2002) in British studies of ethnic minorities, noting that 'the geographical base in Britain is assumed to be important, and there is little attempt to take seriously the links which extend outside Britain to the sending country' (Jeffery 1976a: 3).[1] As long ago as 1990, the term 'transcontinental families' was used of Indian Gujaratis (Kelly 1990). A focus on transnational marriages, however, necessitates placing greater emphasis on these networks.

The transnational turn in migration studies (Basch *et al.* 1994) has influenced the increasing volume of research focused on South Asian cross-border networks and activities. Recent writers on South Asian diaspora have discussed issues from global political and religious formations (Werbner 2002a, 2002b), to transnational rituals (Gardner 2002a; Mand 2002) and (ethnic) return migration (Bolognani 2007; Ramji 2006). Whilst much early work on transnationalism focused on political or economic aspects, interest in the 'transnational domestic sphere' (Gardner and Grillo 2002: 179) has been increasing. Work on transnational kinship connections in particular casts valuable light on the experiential bases of global and local relations, including insights into the ways in which transnationalism is gendered (Salih 2003). Hence, this study joins a by-now healthy body of literature on transnational household and ritual (Gardner and Grillo 2002), transnational families (e.g. Bryceson and Vuorela 2002; Chamberlain and Leydesdorff 2004; Parreñas 2005) and, increasingly, on transnational marriage in particular (e.g. Beck-Gernsheim 2007; Charsley 2012; Constable 2005; Shaw and Charsley 2006).[2]

One danger in the transition from an ethnic minorities to a transnational perspective, however, is that the previous model of ethnic groups, criticised for implying homogeneity and boundedness, may be replaced by a similar construction merely stretched across geographical distance (Wimmer and Glick Schiller 2003; cf. Anthias 1998). Some scholars of transnationalism, for example, have framed their research in terms of 'transnational communities' (e.g. Hirsch 1999; Portes 1998). Whilst 'community' may, as I assert in the Introduction, be employed without such implications, and many of my informants in Bristol use the term to refer to local Pakistanis, they do not use it in this expanded transnational sense. Of course, analytic usage need not mirror 'lay' parlance, but this reflects a qualitative difference in patterns of relationships. Within Bristol, interactions with other Pakistanis in mosques, at weddings or other functions, and in the context of neighbourhood shops and services allow for the development of a sense of being part of a community, all of whose members are potentially knowable. Transnational connections, on the other hand, take place primarily through networks of families and friends. Some such networks overlap, particularly where families knew each other in Pakistan, or came to know each other in the UK after migration, and particularly where inter-marriage takes place, but in general this broader sense of multiple, community-like connections is lacking. This situation is very different to that described by Levitt (2001b) in which co-villagers from the Dominican

Republic reside in a particular neighbourhood in Boston – a situation with such a density of ties that she writes of a 'transnational village'.[3]

Among the alternative conceptualisations of border-crossing social formations, probably the most widely adopted has been that of 'transnational social fields' (Levitt and Glick Schiller 2004) – networks of networks which may include both migrant and non-migrants. When operationalised, however, such concepts have usually translated into the study of populations sharing an ethnic identity, leading to the suggestion that whilst the transnational turn has responded to the problem of 'methodological nationalism', it has tended to reproduce 'methodological ethnicity' (Glick Schiller 2008). Combined with the critique of 'groupism' (Brubaker 2002), such observations have led to calls for the de-ethnicisation of research designs (Glick Schiller *et al.* 2006; Wimmer 2004, 2007). Whilst there is undoubted value in de-privileging ethnicity in migration studies, there are still areas where mono-ethnic research designs remain valid. As Wimmer observes, there is no reason 'why a study design should not start by taking individuals from a particular country (or countries) of origin [or ethnic group] as the unit of observation', but care should be taken not to assume 'communitarian closure, cultural difference, and strong identities' (Wimmer 2007: 28). The high level of transnational marriages, and particularly consanguineous transnational marriages, involving British Pakistanis, is a research problem that demands an ethnically based sample. In focusing on transnational marriages, however, attention is necessarily directed away from inter-ethnic marital and other relationships, and from those 'lost to the group' (Wimmer 2007: 28). This should be taken as pragmatic research design, rather than reflecting assumptions about the ethnic cohesiveness of British Pakistanis, or the uniformity of their transnational involvement. The following section of this chapter will illustrate some of the variation that exists in British Pakistanis' orientation towards Pakistan.

Varying transnational engagements

Transnational engagements vary considerably. As Portes (1998: 16) notes as a corrective to over-use of the term transnationalism, 'not all immigrants are involved in transnational activities'. Guarnizo distinguishes between 'core' and 'expanded' transnationalism according to the centrality and frequency of transnational activities, whilst Levitt (2001b) observes that individuals can participate in transnational social fields in various ways and to varying degrees ('comprehensive' or 'selective'). The nature of transnational activity differs between migrant/ethnic groups, so Ballard and Gardner (n.d.) have pointed to the role of differing marriage practices in producing variation in the extent to which South Asian communities overseas preserve transnational links. Whilst Jullunduri Sikh populations have rapidly 'gone offshore', maintaining exchanges with each other more than with the original 'home base', kin marriage has meant that Mirpuri connections to the homeland have remained stronger.

Gender and age can impact upon forms of transnational engagement, as seen in Werbner's (1996) account of the differing transnational arenas available to British Pakistanis. Whilst older men dominate religious debates and organisations, young men follow sport, and women participate in 'wedding culture'.[4] Katy Gardner (2002a) documents how gender influences Bangladeshi women's ability to travel and participate in transnational ritual, leading many to experience additional grief when they cannot attend their husbands' funerals in Bangladesh. Much debate has concerned the role of generation in transnationalism – in particular whether transnational activity decreases across the generations after migration (see Levitt and Waters 2002), but relationships to ancestral homelands may change over a lifetime. As Peggy Levitt remarks, '[t]ransnational activities do not remain constant across the lifecycle. Instead, they ebb and flow at different stages, varying with the demands of work, school and family' (Levitt 2002: 139; cf. Smith 2002).

Following participants through transnational marriages demonstrates the role of gender, kinship and 'lifestage' in creating variation in engagement with the transnational, but also suggests a great deal of *individual* variation. Whilst some of those I worked with spoke seamlessly about their lives and families in two (or more) countries, Arif spoke of his difficulties adjusting on his occasional visits to Pakistan, and his feeling that he was a different person in this foreign context. 'It's like a different life', he told me. Others do not travel to Pakistan at all. Personal preference undoubtedly plays a part – two sisters I know consider their Pakistani relatives rude and 'backwards' and so do not want to visit the country again, let alone marry there, whilst their younger brother has actively pursued a match for himself with a cousin in Pakistan. I will, however, argue that lifestage and crucial life events have a major role in producing both variation between individuals, and changes in orientation over the lifecourse. The sisters in question, for example, hold opinions of Pakistan that are in large part a product of unhappy experience with their first, migrant, husbands. The historical changes in pioneer Pakistani migrants' orientation from a 'five-year plan' of return, to gradual acceptance that their settlement was permanent, as children were born and their lives became more and more entangled with their 'host' country, have been well documented. Here I will argue that life events – birth, death and, most importantly, marriage – can have comparable but diverging effects in re-orienting the next generation away from Britain or, on the other hand, in loosening transnational connections.

Marriage, then, is a 'vital conjuncture' – a phrase suggested by Jennifer Johnson-Hanks (2002) to capture her argument that rather than viewing the 'lifecycle' as a series of standardised (cultural) 'lifestages', we should explore major life events such as marriage as 'a nexus of potential social futures':

> ... a socially structured zone of possibility that emerges around specific periods of potential transformation in a life or lives. It is a temporary configuration of possible change, a duration of uncertainty and potential. Although most social life may be thought of as conjunctural, in the sense

that action is conjoined to a particular, temporary manifestation of social structure, vital conjunctures are particularly critical durations when more than usual is in play, when the futures at stake are significant.

(Johnson-Hanks 2002: 871)

I am not the first to use the concept of 'vital conjunctures' in relation to Pakistani marriage. Mikkel Rytter (2012: 3) argues that, 'Danish Pakistanis' choice of a marriage partner ... not only constitutes a public statement of "who they are", but also a projection of "who they want to be"'. He writes that in choosing a love marriage as opposed to their parents' preference for an endogamous match, young people are engaging in 'symbolic mobility', positioning themselves as modern and Danish. Here, however, I wish to suggest the practical, rather than symbolic, consequences of the choice of marriage partner from Pakistan or Britain. Some case studies will serve to illustrate the argument.

Bushra, now in her forties, was brought to Britain as a young child and had all her schooling in the UK. With air travel expensive, she did not visit Pakistan frequently in her childhood and adolescence, although the family did make one mammoth overland trip to the subcontinent. When she married a Pakistani man of her parents' choosing, she thought that she would not have to make such choices for her own children. She assumed that by the time they reached marriageable age, practices would have changed and young people would be finding their own spouses in Britain.

Bushra speaks good Urdu, and during my fieldwork I would sometimes discuss my language learning with her. One day she confessed that she had not always spoken Urdu. As a child, her family had spoken Punjabi, so when she married she spoke only Punjabi and English. Then came her first trip with her husband to visit his family in Pakistan. Since the birth of the nation, Urdu has become increasingly spoken both as a marker of education and of national identity. Families are spoken of as Urdu- or Punjabi-*bolnewale* (speaking), and matrimonial adverts in English language newspapers may specify that the advertiser is looking for a spouse from an Urdu-speaking background. Bushra's husband's family spoke Urdu, so during her first visit she was ashamed to talk and vowed to learn the language. By her next trip to Pakistan, she could communicate happily with her in-laws. The couple keep up close communication with family in Pakistan and Bushra looks forward to the visits that she and her husband make as frequently as they can afford. The most recent of these was to organise and attend the marriage of her younger brother to a Pakistani relative. On another recent trip, a female relative of her husband approached her to suggest marriages between her children and their cousins in Pakistan, to which she happily agreed. At least one of the young couples is likely to settle in America, where other close relatives are prospering.

In her youth, Bushra was thus predominantly oriented towards Britain, and imagined a future for her family here. By contracting a transnational marriage, however, she became involved with networks that inevitably entailed closer engagement with Pakistan by necessitating visits, remittances and involvement in the decisions of a family that now spanned the globe. In motherhood she became the pivotal figure in these transnational ties as future connections between the families were decided – it was, for example, Bushra rather than her husband with whom the Pakistani relative discussed the *rishta* between their children. Her transnational involvement will be broadened and intensified as the families make arrangements to celebrate the marriages, multiply the kinship links between them, and perhaps continue to disperse across further continents.

In contrast, Rasham's transnational involvements have decreased as her life has progressed through crucial junctures. She suffered violence at the hands of her Pakistani migrant husband, and eventually divorced him. As her parents had also died, there was then less to bind her to either Pakistan or to the Pakistani community in Bristol. She now frequently dresses in 'Western' clothes in public, including sleeveless tops often considered risqué, and has a close friend who is both black and male – something that might be viewed as a minor scandal by some. I was not surprised, therefore, to witness tensions come to a head when a heated argument broke out at a community function between Rasham and the mothers of children who had been making critical remarks about her daughters. She does send her children to the mosque to learn the Quran, and to Urdu language lessons. It is unlikely, however, that she will arrange marriages for any of them in Pakistan, and as the years go on, her children may have little reason to visit their ancestral lands.

The power of marriages, above all lifecourse decisions, to ensure ongoing transnational involvement is not lost on parents eager to maintain connections with places and kin they left behind when they themselves migrated. Ghalib, who came to Britain for marriage in the 1970s, hopes that his son's wedding to a relative from Pakistan will facilitate his eventual retirement there. If he does retire to Pakistan and his wife Rashida goes with him, she will have come a long way from the little girl who was the 'only brown face' in her class, and who Ghalib found shockingly British when he arrived in the country to marry. The lives of these older people present the opportunity for viewing outcomes of these 'vital conjunctures' in those who have experienced most of the crucial events of kinship. However, they have also seen great technological changes, and 'being transnational' in whatever sense and to whatever degree is greatly facilitated by improvements in communications and the increasing affordability of travel. Bushra and her children, for example, keep in regular contact with Pakistani relatives by email, live-time chatting is possible at a fraction of the cost of a telephone call, and more frequent (e.g. biennial) visits to Pakistan are now within more people's financial reach. The final section of this chapter looks at some of those who have grown up with these developments. It returns to Iram's wedding, as a starting point for an examination of how some young British Pakistanis, often in collaboration with their parents, manage their transnational experiences. This discussion moves away from the issue of variation in transnational involvement, which I

54 *British Pakistanis and transnationalism*

take as a given. Those discussed here do not represent the universal behaviour of a 'second generation', but merely those with whom I have had the opportunity to spend most time, and I make no claims as to their representativeness.

'Just *mil*ing everybody': language, culture and code-switching

Many of the British Pakistanis I have met mix Punjabi/Urdu and English as Shanaz did at her daughter's Iram's *walima* when she told her son to *mil* his sister. At another family wedding, I heard Iram's sister Shabanna respond to a cousin's enquiries about what she had been doing in Pakistan by saying, 'Nothing, just *mil*ing everybody'. Her answer was particularly striking not only for the Anglicisation of the verb *milna* (to meet),[5] but because the question had been asked in Punjabi, and Shabanna had chosen to respond in English.

In his introduction to the influential 1994 volume *Desh Pardesh*, Roger Ballard focuses on language use to address the ways in which British South Asians navigate their dual cultural environments: the 'ethnic colony' and relationships with the 'indigenous majority' (Ballard 1994: 29). He suggests that while the discourse of cultural and generational conflict epitomised by the title of James Watson's influential *Between Two Cultures* (1977) has been appropriated by young British Asians,[6] it does not reflect the true experience of hybridity. Instead, he uses linguistic theory to draw an analogy between bilingualism and the way people negotiate the demands of multiple cultures. Conflict is avoided, he argues, by code-switching in different environments, or in other words by changing their behaviour, speech, dress and so on as appropriate to varying spaces and encounters. From this perspective, Shabanna's English response is a refusal to code-switch, which Ballard views as a strategic action:

> … advantages can often be gained by those who deliberately code their behaviour inappropriately. For example, young men or women who begin to act in an over-anglicised way at home may well simply be seeking to assert themselves: efforts to resist parental hegemony should not be misread as 'culture conflict'. Exactly the reverse of this process occurs when young people set out to make space for themselves in majority contexts. Hence to switch 'inappropriately' into Urdu or Punjabi speech, to wear a turban or *shalwar kamiz*, to condemn the publication of *The Satanic Verses*, to praise arranged marriages – or indeed to reject any other aspect of Western orthodoxy – is a particularly effective way of re-establishing personal dignity in the face of racial and ethnic denigration.
>
> (Ballard 1994: 33)

Here, however, this interpretation is undermined by the fact that Shabanna's mother Shanaz, who came to Britain for marriage many years ago, herself often uses English with her children, even in 'Pakistani' environments such as the wedding. I have frequently heard the use of English to respond to parents'

Punjabi or Urdu, and the casual nature of many of these responses led me to believe that they are not always part of a strategy of self-assertion. This linguistic mixing may rather be one of the new styles of interaction that Ballard himself suggested young British Asians to be developing among themselves, delighting in 'drawing eclectically on every tradition available to them'. In other words, rather than the conscious forms of hybridity that have the power to shock, this is the genre of unconscious hybridity through which culture evolves and develops (Baktin, as used by Werbner 1997: 4–6).

Friedman (2002) has argued that hybridity is in the eye of the beholder; that researchers label objects or behaviours 'hybrid' when they consider them to be matter out of place, and that this 'hybridity-for-us' does not reflect participants' experience which sees nothing remarkable in the use of what we might see as 'foreign' matter into their practices. I would not go quite that far. Some of the behaviour of young British Pakistanis undoubtedly contains an element of conscious creation of cultural matter out of place. During my fieldwork, even some older Pakistani women with limited English seemed to delight in the political potential of humorous language mixing – one well-received joke from an elderly lady on a community group day trip involved imitating 'modern' young Pakistani women saying 'Hi' (hello), which quickly turned into '*Hai! Hai!*' (a Punjabi/Urdu lamentation) and melodramatic clutching of her chest, poking fun at the 'hybridity' of youth. However, much of the daily, casual mixing of language, dress, music and so on should not be over-interpreted.

For many of my young informants, these behaviours are not just developed among their peers, but are negotiated within the household. I was often surprised at the open relationships many young women had with their mothers, freely discussing subjects such as marriage or their non-Pakistani friends' romantic lives in their presence. It is worth noting at the outset the socio-economic factors that may enable such a situation: the mothers of the young women to whom I am referring are often very different from the stereotype of the uneducated village woman with little English who does not work outside the house, and certainly not outside the ethnic 'enclave'. Whilst some of the women with children of marriageable age involved in this research do come from such backgrounds, many others have or have had paid employment (some in predominantly English environments), are from relatively educated urban backgrounds, or, like Bushra, came to Britain themselves as children and so experienced the British school environment.

Bushra talked to me about the difficulties of bringing up children, particularly girls, in non-Muslim Britain. While she felt she needed to limit what they were allowed to do, she realised this was hard for the children and made sure she discussed the reasons behind rules, and gave them alternative opportunities to enjoy themselves. In several cases I know, young people and their parents have reached amicable agreements about permitted behaviour, removing much of the need for code-switching between home and outside environments. Many young women do change into 'Western' clothes to go to school or work, and back into *shalwar qamis* at home, but this may be partly in order to be accepted by mixed-ethnicity peer groups, rather than just pressure to behave in more 'Asian' ways at home. The arrangements young women make with their mothers about behaviour at home, however, may include agreements about code-switching in other environments, and in the presence of other members of the Pakistani community. So Saika, who has just finished her degree and lives at home in Bristol, says that she wears what she likes within reason, and even goes to the pub with her white friends, as her parents trust her not to drink, but she has an agreement with her mother that she will wear Pakistani clothes in certain situations such as at community functions.

In another example, I was at Nasreen's house one day when her sister and sister-in-law dropped in for a visit, as they do most days. Relatives from London arrived unannounced, sending the girls into a panic: Nasreen was just back from university and was still wearing her 'English' clothes – a long skirt and top; her sister and sister-in-law were in *shalwar qamis*, but had left their *dupatta* scarves at home; and another sister was also *dupatta*-less, but was able to find one quickly in her room. To top it all, there I was – a white friend – resulting in the London relatives questioning Nasreen's family about who this *gori* was. While these young women do not need to change their behaviour at home, their panic when they could not manage to alter their appearance in the presence of more distant relative serves to illustrate that they still expect and are expected to code-switch for certain extra-domestic audiences.

What happens, however, when these young people go to Pakistan? At Iram's wedding there were other examples of young people displaying 'British' behaviour: the hip-hop played on the *mehndi* night, and the young men making fun of the *mehndi* traditions. In other instances, Nasreen's brothers refused to wear Pakistani clothes to their sisters' weddings, and are conspicuous on the wedding videos with their UK street-style ultra-short hair, skinny rap-star beards, tight T-shirts and seemingly confident swagger. Their sister was adamant that she wouldn't let the beauticians lighten her skin for the marriage, as is common practice, as it offended her racial-political sensitivities. When Asma's *ubtan* was applied she was instructed not to shower or change her clothes, but washed and changed the minute she was left alone. I was with another young woman in a fancy clothes shop in Pakistan when she led her cousins in displays of cheering when they finally haggled the price of her sister's wedding *lehnga* down to their target, attracting disapproving stares from other shoppers (such raucous behaviour is not expected of Pakistani women in public). Later, she publicly chastised a tailor for his 'backwardness' in never having spoken to his young fiancée despite a two-year engagement.

I found these assertive refusals to code-switch surprising, particularly as I myself was directing much effort into attempts not to stand out – to dress in local styles, speak in local languages and behave in culturally accepted ways. Why, I wondered, did these young people react so differently? Another example from Iram's wedding may be particularly illuminating in this regard.

When kicking a lump of henna around, one of the young men at Iram's *mehndi* joked, 'I don't understand this', and lack of understanding may be precisely the point. These young people know what to do when code-switching is required of them in a limited number of mainly familiar situations in the UK. In Pakistan, however, they find themselves at a disadvantage in terms of cultural and practical knowledge. Even with their best efforts, they will not know what is expected of them in every situation, and can seldom pass as locals. A young man in Birmingham complained to me that he and people like him didn't fit in anywhere: they are seen as foreign both in Britain and Pakistan.[7] This point is picked up by Katy Gardner writing of British Bangladeshis whose imaginings of 'home' crumble when they visit Bangladesh, leading them to perceive themselves as more British. She describes a young British man's sulking in his ancestral home as 'asserting his Britishness' (Gardner 1993; see also Gardner and Shukur 1994).

Faced with the impossibility of fitting in, of code-switching effectively, it seems that many decide not to try. This can take the form of small retreats to the comfort of the familiar under conditions of heightened stress, as Bushra's daughter Leyla explained of her behaviour during a visit to Pakistan soon after becoming engaged to one of her cousins there:

> I think my Punjabi isn't very good, but think my Urdu is OK. I know when I go there I pick it up really quickly and when I come back to England I forget it really quickly ... Even when I'm in Pakistan I'll say [to relatives] 'Do you want some tea? Do you want some tea?', and I'll speak in Urdu, and then I'll come to him [the fiancé] and I'll say in English – I speak to him in English! I don't know why I do that. I'll speak to everyone in the room in Urdu but when it comes to him I'll speak in English ... I think because I'm not that confident in speaking the other language and I don't want to make a fool of myself in front of him, so I always speak the language I'm comfortable with ... [Is he fluent in English?] I don't really know. He doesn't really speak it back to me ... He speaks Urdu back to me ... Because he doesn't feel comfortable ... I was thinking about that the other day, I was thinking, 'Why do I do that?' But it is because I feel more comfortable ... Every evening I'd have my cup of tea but I made my English tea by diluting the milk and I'd go round everybody and I'd be like, 'Shama – *chai* [the Urdu for tea]?' and she'd say '*ji*' [respectful yes] sort of thing, '[next relative] – *chai*?' and then I'd be like 'Asif [fiancé] – do you want some tea?'!

Whilst this is a familiar phenomenon, a response shared by many language learners, the young men playing with the henna take it further, by actively playing up their difference. As in their case, this is often done with a sense of irony. Irony has been a very fashionable type of humour in contemporary Britain, from 'New Laddism' to kitsch styling, so it may not be the form but rather the fact of the humour that is significant. Joking and poking fun are, of course, classic 'weapons of the weak' (Scott 1985). British visitors to Pakistan are hardly in a weak position financially; indeed, British families often remit substantial sums to support their relatives in Pakistan. However, what they have economically they may lack in cultural terms, and stories abound in Pakistan of wealthy overseas families who are easily taken advantage of by unscrupulous locals, or even their own relatives. Their relative wealth may itself leave them vulnerable: if you are foolish enough to take a taxi more than 100 miles from Islamabad airport to Mirpur, I was told, you're bound to be charged over the odds. In addition, there is the weakness that stems from generational difference and gender, so that young British Pakistanis visiting with their parents may find that they have little authority over what happens to them during their stay as plans are made by their parents, grandparents, aunts and uncles. Even Rashida, a middle-aged mother of adult children, complained that she had no control over many of the arrangements for her son's wedding, as negotiations with (male) caterers and so on had to be done by male relatives.[8]

Weddings compound all these factors. Young British Pakistanis at their own marriage, or that of a close relative, in Pakistan may find themselves on the brink of a life-changing event, in unfamiliar surroundings, unsure of what exactly will happen during the next few days, and with very little control over the process. It is my suggestion that the assertive and often humorous refusals to 'play the game' outlined above, are means by which they may regain some small measure of control. Not only is code-switching problematic – a game they cannot win as they are not, as it were, fluent in the local culture – but by holding fast to a reified British identity, they may provide themselves with some sort of ontological security at a time of profound change and insecurity.

One of the most powerful unified identities a young British Pakistani can adopt is to emphasise religion. The visible sign of Islamic identity that has been most discussed in Britain and elsewhere in Europe in recent years is the *hijab* headscarf worn by some Muslim women (Franks 2000; Watson 1994). The *hijab* has been variously interpreted as denoting oppression, 'postcolonial resistance' against racist denigration, and as influenced by life in the transcultural metropolis (Tarlo 2007). Haw (2010) writes of young women adopting the *hijab* as a way of resolving the felt contradictions of contemporary British and traditional Pakistani moral views; of conflicting experiences of religion, Britishness and Islamophobia. 'In a bid to reconcile these tensions, the answer is to "distil" their choices to an essence' (Haw 2010: 355) by adopting this visibly Muslim form of dress. Apart from acknowledgements of migrant backgrounds, the transnational context appears only fleetingly in such accounts, as a 'backdrop of globalisation' (Haw 2010: 355), or global Islamic movements (Tarlo 2007). They frame the *hijab* as a phenomenon primarily to be understood within the context of British multicultural society. In contrast, Bowen (2004) stresses the importance of Islam as a 'transnational public space' as a context for the recent European controversies over the *hijab*. Here, however, I suggest that a visible Muslim identity may also be effective as a 'distilled' identity in the context of the transnational Pakistani social field, and on visits to Pakistan.

By wearing the *hijab* (women) or growing a beard (men) and following religious practices, they may be able to transcend the need to code-switch, without sacrificing respect either in Pakistan or from the Pakistani community in Britain,[9] and simultaneously symbolising an Islamic identity for wider British society. This makes such statements of religious identity uniquely effective in multiple domains: with regard to the ethnic majority populations in Britain, with co-ethnics (and co-religionists), and for an audience in Pakistan. Thus two very different lifestyle/identity choices made by young Pakistanis in Britain – the Islamic revivalist and the self-assured British urban street style – could be seen as, at least in part, adaptations to the same conundrum posed by adaptation to the multiplied cultural environments necessitated by engaging with transnationalism. The unitary identities that some young Pakistanis in Bristol have negotiated within their peer groups and households to replace earlier code-switching have proven valuable resources with which to withstand the increasingly common experience of marriage in a country that was home to their parents, but often presents all the challenges of a foreign culture to a young person who has grown up in Britain.

Writing on Muslims in Sweden and the USA, Schmidt offers a further explanation for the adoption of a pan-Islamic rather than a regional identity, noting that the young do not have as …

> … direct and deeply felt connection to the country of migration as their parents. 'Back home' may be a country of ideals and longing during childhood, but often short or even extended visits are disappointing. Then dreams and hopes may crumble, leaving only disappointment.
> (Schmidt 2002: 12)

Given that they have not yet gone through many of the important life course events noted above, young people are likely to be 'less' transnational than their parents, or indeed perhaps than their future selves. If they contract a marriage in Pakistan, this may change and new dreams, hopes and transnational involvements emerge. There may also, however, be greater demands on them to adapt their behaviour to accommodate an immigrant spouse used to different social norms. The issue of 'culture clash' (my informants' term) that can arise in this situation will be addressed in later chapters.

This chapter has started to explore British Pakistanis' cross-border connections. Whilst the volume and significance of marriages contracted between British Pakistanis and Pakistani nationals suggests that any understanding of the British Pakistani population merely in terms of the British ethnic and national context would be incomplete, it is clear that transnational engagements vary significantly. Marriage, I have argued, is a particularly critical juncture – a 'vital conjuncture' (Johnson-Hanks 2002). Marrying transnationally may (re)orient British Pakistanis towards greater transnational involvement. There may be impacts for their children, who may be more likely to be taken to Pakistan for visits, and for whom a more significant proportion of their relatives, and potential *baraderi* marriage partners, will probably be located in Pakistan than would have been the case if their parent had married in Britain. In visiting and eventually perhaps marrying in Pakistan, however, they must negotiate issues of identity and power. Some of the young British Pakistanis I have described present an interesting paradox by being assertively local even as they form and perpetuate transnational links through their marriages. The following chapter looks at how such marriages are arranged, and what is sought in a spouse.

Notes

1 Both Jeffery and Shaw (1988) included stays in Pakistan in their research design.
2 For a more extensive review of this literature, see Charsley 2012.
3 It is possible that contexts more comparable to Levitt's 'transnational village' exist in areas such as Bradford with concentrations of migrants from relatively small areas of Pakistan and their descendants.
4 See also Akhtar (forthcoming) on contrasting political engagements between younger and older British Pakistanis.
5 Gardner (2002a) calls such linguistic mixing among British Bangladeshis 'Banglish'.
6 The notion of being 'between two cultures' has also been influential in academic circles – see Hall (2002), or Bradby's (2000) subtle reformulation of Punjabi women's perceptions of their 'dual loyalties' as expressed in geographical metaphors.
7 A 'between two cultures' statement of the type referred to earlier.
8 See also Gardner and Grillo (2002) on gendered difference in involvement in transnational rituals.
9 See Schmidt (2002) for comparative material on the pan-Islamic identity among young Muslims in Sweden and the USA, suggesting that such behaviour can cause conflict with 'co-ethnics'.

3 *Zarurat rishta*
Making and maintaining connections

This chapter explores the search for a good *rishta*, which means a proposal or marriage partner. After discussing what people want in a spouse and how marriages are arranged, I argue that clarifying the connotations of the term *rishta* (plural: *rishte*) leads to a better understanding of what is sought in arranging marriage, and one that resolves some difficulties in the literature on Pakistani marriage preferences. Transnational marriages prove to be a powerful heuristic tool in this exercise, as they exaggerate features present in the local search for a *rishta*. Matchmaking in Pakistan thus serves as a backdrop against which the process of arranging transnational marriages, much of which happens in Pakistan, can be understood.

Zarurat rishta: proposal wanted

In the years since my original fieldwork, internet matchmaking sites aimed at South Asians (e.g. shaadi.com), Muslims (e.g. singlemuslim.com), or Pakistanis in particular (e.g. getrishta.com) have proliferated. India-based shaadi.com was founded in 1996 and now has a global reach, claiming over 20 million members at the time of writing. Most of the marriages discussed in this work took place before the growth in usage of these sites, but matrimonial advertising predates the internet revolution. During my time in Pakistan in 2000–01, English language newspapers carried 'matrimonial' columns, whilst in the Urdu papers, alongside *zarurat plat* (house plot wanted), and other similar titles, was the heading *zarurat rishta* (proposal wanted). The text of English language matrimonial adverts often includes phrases such as 'proposal sought from … ' with a list of the desired characteristics of the prospective spouse and their family. The matrimonial sections of Pakistani papers were, however, much shorter than those I had seen on visits to India, where several pages were often devoted to requests for spouses. An explanation for this difference can be found in the norm of kin-group exogamy amongst Hindus in north India, in contrast to the ideal of *baraderi* endogamy for Pakistani Muslims. Most Pakistani marriages are contracted either with kin or through personal contacts, making matrimonial advertising less popular. In addition, given the desirability for matches to be made through relatives or trusted personal contacts, advertising may be viewed as a somewhat dubious method for finding a spouse. Whilst the number of private advertisers can be low, *zarurat rishta* columns also carried advertisements for the services of matchmakers, such as:

> ISLAMABAD Social Service matrimonial contact parents from educated, cultured families, Mrs Khawaja [telephone number], www.khawaja.bigstep.com.
>
> (*The News*, 14/01/2001)

> Two American national engineer boys, in addition ladies and gentlemen education matric to MA Bachelor, divorcee, widower. International Marriage bureau. [contact details].
>
> (Trans. from Urdu, *Daily Jang*, 08/12/2001)

More people may use such services than would like to admit. One advert from the *Daily Jang*, for example, played on the stigma that can surround the activity, stating that some people do not like to be seen to be going to matchmakers or do not want their parents to know they are using these services, so Begam Hashmi would like to meet parents of potential spouses in her home, or to be invited to theirs (*Daily Jang*, 02/12/2001).

The majority of Pakistani marriages may be arranged without resort to matrimonial adverts or matchmakers, but *zarurat rishta* entries can nevertheless prove useful in exploring what is sought in a *rishta*. In the *Daily Jang*, typical adverts were from marriage brokers simply giving the age, qualifications, *zat* (caste) and employment of men seeking brides. In the English language *The News*, more emphasis seemed to be placed on education, employment or financial background than on caste, for example:

> EDUCATED Family in F-10 [wealthy area of Islamabad] requires suitable match for their son 27 MBA, settled in America, beautiful tall educated girl living in posh area of Islamabad may contact Box No. 364, C/o The News, Rawalpindi.

In Pakistan, I found these adverts to be a convenient tool to stimulate conversations with young women about the search for a spouse. One university student, Naseema, pointed out that adverts about 'boys' never said whether they were handsome, but only gave information that would indicate their income. On the other hand, 'girls' tend to be described as beautiful, humble *and* educated. As this and the examples above suggest, the attributes most desired differ between the sexes. A beautiful bride is valued, with the result that most young women put great effort into making themselves attractive, particularly for occasions such as weddings when they may be spotted as a potential *rishta*. Their family may take an interest, so that one young woman with an acne problem told me despairingly that her father was always on at her to do something about her skin. In Pakistan, as in India, facial lightening creams such as 'Fair and Lovely' have been popular as women try to achieve the 'fair' skin considered to be a sign of beauty. On her wedding day, the bride is normally made up with thick pale foundation, so that she conforms to this ideal of beauty whatever her natural colour. A dark husband is frequently dreaded, and handsome young men's fairness is praised, but the issue is seen as more crucial for the marriageability of women (cf. Jha and Adelman 2009).

As will be clear, Pakistani discourse on the matter of *rishte* tends to focus on the desired qualities of brides rather than husbands, so Wakil notes that 'preferred traits in a male seldom get any mention or scrutiny. An able bodied male – of the right origins – is all that seems to count' (Wakil 1991: 45). 'However', he goes on, 'implied in much talk are the traits of being "responsible" and able to earn a living' (Wakil 1991: 45). The young women and their families whom I met in Pakistan and Bristol certainly seemed to have strong opinions on what makes a good husband. Prominent among these for the students at the university hostel where I initially lodged in Rawalpindi was indeed that he should be financially stable. In the majority of middle-class Pakistani households, men are the main earners, so a potential husband's educational achievements and employment are crucial in determining a woman's standard of living after marriage.

Some attributes are desired by my informants in both men and women. Among these, education is an issue that will recur in discussion of spousal selection throughout this book. As in India, among the middle and aspirant classes, education has become 'fetishised to the point that qualifications are the status symbol par excellence' (Elliot 2002, citing Varma 1999), so that the ideal bride, although she may never be employed, is often expected to be educated. In Bangladesh, Gardner reports, the education of daughters has become an important source of prestige to 'attract better quality husbands, and was crucial if a marriage with a Londoni [someone settled in the UK] was on the cards' (Gardner 1995: 130). In addition, Vatuk notes of urban India that education gives a young woman something to do as a 'socially acceptable way that she can occupy her time, aside from needlecraft and housework, while waiting for a match to be arranged' (Vatuk 1972: 79). For the same reason, some staff at the women's university were cynical about their students' (and the students' parents') commitment to academic work, commenting that the university was used as a kind of finishing school before marriage. In the run-up to exams at the university, I heard one young woman encourage a friend to neglect her revision, saying it didn't matter as they would just get married anyway. Others, however, view educational achievement not as conflicting with the realities of marriage, but as important if they are to teach their own children, and as a fall-back in case they are not married quickly, or fall on hard times later in life.[1] Among the university students in Pakistan, those with ambitions to pursue a career after marriage, however, acknowledged that their husband's consent to go out to work would be crucial. For the families of British Pakistani women pursuing higher education, the significance of distance from 'backwards' families with more patriarchal views which, from this perspective, confuse 'tradition' with 'religion' is a further element of cultural capital to be gained. Too much education may, however, 'price' a daughter out of the intra-ethnic marriage market (Ahmad 2001). Several of my informants in Britain worried about highly educated women being left 'on the shelf' whilst their male counterparts married someone with more modest qualifications in Britain, or chose a wife from Pakistan.

Other forms of capital may be sought in both brides and grooms. As the adverts above suggest, foreign nationality or domicile can be a valuable asset, and entries seeking matches for, or requesting proposals from, Pakistanis settled overseas appeared fairly frequently. The couple I lodged with in Pakistan, for example, received a large number of replies to an advert in *The World* placed following the woman's mother's request for a *rishta* for a son in Britain. A 'good background', 'good family' or 'respectable family' is also commonly required. Not only is this important in a society where much rides on reputation, status and networking – one popular guide to Pakistani culture writes that almost everything is accomplished through friendships and connections (Mittman and Ihsan 1991) – but it is crucial for the prospects of the bride who will normally go to live with her in-laws.

Although I use *zarurat rishta* adverts as a starting point for this discussion, they are not the normal way of finding a spouse, and represent those who are going outside the societal norms of marriage within the kin group or social networks. Many adverts sought partners for divorced or widowed people, or those older than the conventional marriage age, or settled overseas, and so whose ability to find spouses through normal routes may be curtailed. As such, they concentrate on what Donnan (1994: 325) has called the 'personal expectations' of marriage in terms of advantageous characteristics and connections, rather than the conventional cultural or social expectations as to who will be married. This latter category include preferences and obligations to marry within the *zat* and kin group. Such social norms act as 'strategic resources', which can be used to propose, accept or reject a marriage. As such they have the 'double utility of specifying which categories of women are culturally good to marry ... as well as providing the rhetoric or idiom for negotiations where they can be used to enforce claims on others' (Donnan 1994: 325).

For middle-class Pakistanis in both the UK and Pakistan education has become a matter not just of personal, but of social expectation, displaying the characteristics of Donnan's 'strategic resources'. In Bristol, for example, families who fulfilled social conventions of kin marriage by marrying their educated British children to uneducated relatives from Pakistan were often discussed with disapproval. The rhetoric of education is commonly used to justify or reject *rishte*, so a woman married outside the family told me that her mother had refused all *rishte* from uneducated kin on the grounds that she was only looking for educated spouses for her children. In several cases, marriages were refused or delayed on the grounds that the young person had not yet completed their studies, suggesting the acknowledged importance of education. This rhetoric may, however, mask other agendas – I was told that if a really good *rishta* was received, it would usually be accepted no matter what the stage of the young woman's studies. Saba, who came to Bristol from Pakistan in 1999, said her mother initially refused a transnational *rishta* with the son of a friend of the family because Saba had only just started her medical training, and the young man 'can't wait five more years for you to finish your medicine'. The young man in this case was the son of a family friend, and had a good job with a major transnational company. A couple of weeks later, Saba's mother decided to let the couple be introduced after all, so that they could make up their own minds, illustrating the temptation of a good *rishta*. Several students from the university in Rawalpindi had left their courses for matrimony, and a few were married but had stayed on to complete their studies.[2]

The *rishta* as match

Rishta has thus far been translated as 'proposal' or potential spouse, but it carries the additional sense of 'match', as in the English usage connoting a suitable partner (e.g. 'matchmaker'). There is a strong ideal that couples should literally be well matched in terms of background (in terms of socio-economic status, education and often *zat* or caste), character and appearance, a type of preference that has been termed 'homogamy' (Samad and Eade 2002).[3] The ideal is that the couple should be of similar builds and skin colour, and that the husband should be slightly taller and older than his wife. Comments will be made if one is much darker, fatter or taller than the other. Equally, wedding guests and those viewing photos of marriages often comment approvingly if the couple fulfil these criteria. When I asked my host in Rawalpindi what kind of husband he would want for a daughter, he stressed similarity: if she looked beautiful in the framed photographs beside his bed, she should not be standing next to 'a monkey'; if he felt happy talking to her, he should feel the same with her husband. This logic is sometimes used to explain why marriages between people of different castes are undesirable. So one man in Pakistan whose wife was from a different *zat* told me that the two castes were of the same level in terms of social standing and so they could understand each other; he would not like a match with, for example, the grandchild of a cleaner (cf. Fischer and Lyon 2000).

A mis-match in age is one commonly given reason for refusing a *rishta*. In interviews I carried out in Bristol several people who explained that they had married a particular relative because there were no other possible *rishte* in their family turned out to have other cousins of a similar age, but the man was younger by a year or two, making the match impossible. This would again appear to be less a firm rule than part of the rhetoric of refusal and justification of choices. In this excerpt from an interview, Asma from Bristol revises her reliance on this discourse as contradictions from her own family emerged:

> There's no one on my Dad's side, to tell you the truth, because they're all younger than me ... I was the eldest granddaughter. I had a cousin who was a month younger than me [and so was not a match] ... Even though he's married to a twenty-six year old now and he's twenty-four himself ... So I could have married him, but I think because I know him too well – I've lived with him, went to nursery with him, school with him. He's like your brother and you're like, 'Yuck [noise of disgust], I don't want to marry you!'

Saif – a 27 year old from Bristol – was concerned when he learnt that the *rishta* proposed for him was with a 19-year-old girl, and several of his contemporaries were disapproving. Nevertheless he went ahead with the wedding, and now justifies this apparent mis-match by saying that not only did she appear to be particularly mature, but that she looks older than her age while he looks younger, thereby implying that they represent a match in practice.

The value placed on similarity, a 'good match', might be thought to discourage transnational marriages as a husband and wife brought up in different countries are likely to have many significant differences. Indeed, many British Pakistanis disapprovingly relate stories of catastrophic mis-matches – most often an uneducated 'boy' from the village married to an educated British 'girl'. As one women told me, 'if one wheel is high and one wheel is low, the car can't go'. However, wealth, an urban background and education are credited with being able to bridge the differences, particularly if the British spouse is not overly 'Western'. Thus Bushra explained why she had faith in the match between her Bristolian children and her husband's sister's children in Pakistan:

> I think it may have been different if they lived in a village and they weren't so educated – I think they may have had different thoughts. But because they live in quite a modern environment, and they're quite modern as well – as in dress and the way they are. They're sort of pretty well-off as well and they've got mod cons ... They're quite similar to our children here because obviously our children, we keep them a little bit restricted because we're living in a Western environment, Western culture. So I think they feel they've got a lot in common. They seem to get on very well.

Education is once more seen as particularly important, allowing the Pakistani spouse to transcend cultural differences. A lack of education in one of the couple is seen as negating the possibility of the 'mental understanding' the Rawalpindi university students hoped for in a marriage. Amina, who had come to Bristol from Lahore two years previously, told me, 'You can't understand and adjust with an uneducated man – the minds won't go together'.

A lack of similarity between people raised on different continents is an argument often made against transnational marriages: the cultural difference, or 'culture clash' as my informants commonly called it, is simply too great.

Yasmin, for example, reported that her Western tastes in music, films and clothes were a source of tension with her Pakistani husband. Another Bristolian Pakistani woman, an unmarried professional in her mid-thirties, explained that she simply would not consider a potential spouse from Pakistan, as even the most educated of those suggested for her simply had a different outlook on life. This mutual incomprehension is given as a reason why some young women, and some parents, are resisting transnational marriages. 'I mean, I like football, you know?' one young woman explained, using her enjoyment of a conventionally male pursuit to sum up why she didn't want to marry a man from Pakistan who, she assumes, would expect her to conform to Pakistani models of feminine behaviour. While this book concerns the logics and experiences of transnational marriages, it should not therefore be taken to imply consensus on the desirability of such matches, as many British Pakistanis argue strongly against the practice of marrying 'back home'. As one commentator on a website for 'Muslim Youth' wrote under the topic 'I Ain't Marrying No Paki' (a quote from the film *East is East*), 'The way I look at it ... I am "home" so "back home" wouldn't be MY home'.[4] Chapter 4 will discuss the balancing of similarity and difference in the search for a spouse, but for some, the differences between people raised in Britain and Pakistan are considered too great for a successful marriage.

During my fieldwork I was told stories to illustrate the problem of 'culture clash' on several occasions. The typical plot, told as a real story or as an example of what can happen, is of a young man who comes over and sees his wife talking to unrelated men with whom she has studied in school or college. They may call her by her first name, and seem to be overly familiar. The boy does not understand that this is normal behaviour in Britain, and becomes enraged, leading to arguments and perhaps the break-up of the marriage. Here is Ghalib's version:

> There's one article I read here a few years back – you can put it in your book, [it's] very interesting ... A young girl [who had] grown up here, done a degree, had a good job and her parents said we'd like to marry you in our clan. So they went to Pakistan, found a boy – he was absolutely illiterate, never went to school, grown up in a small village somewhere in Pakistan, I don't want to give any name of particular area [enquiries suggested that it was Mirpur, but that he did not want to appear prejudiced] ...
>
> He came up here [to Britain] and the girl went to an airport to collect him. As they were coming out from the departure lounge, the girl – one of her class fellows in university came down, English fellow. And he said to her, traditionally as they say [in Britain], 'Hello Amina, how are you?' And he just go and embrace her in front of her husband and her father and her mother. They [the parents] could understand it – it's just student friends and that's not a problem ... [It was] not a really big embrace, [just a] showbiz kiss, cheek to the cheek, 'Mwa, Mwa' ... She just said, 'I'm fine,

thank you, meet my husband'. And he [the class fellow] just say [to the wife], 'Ok then, nice to see you'. And [they were] talking and looking into each other's eyes and smiling. To a strange man! It's a very new experience for a young man coming from Pakistan. So they went home and all night he could not sleep and next morning he said, 'I don't want to be married with this girl. I don't want to get on with this girl. I want to go home. She's got boyfriends, she's corrupt', and this and that. And he divorced her and he went back to Pakistan.

Now, what exactly went wrong here? ... A very big culture clash. And if the boy was educated or went to school or college in Pakistan, and he came here and he had seen a little bit of this he might have said, 'Oh it's two school friends saying hello to each other'. [Lack of education] and culture clash, two things together made worse. And that's why their marriage has broken. And when I came here it was very, very new for me as well. If somebody had done like this in front of me to my wife, I might well not be far off either ...

Here again, education on the part of the Pakistani spouse is credited with being able to overcome cultural difference. In some couples, however, the differences are not just cultural but also linguistic. Arif, for example, was born in Pakistan but grew up in Britain, only returning for one extended visit during his youth. By the time he married his Pakistani wife he had been living away from home for five years and had, in his words, 'hardly any contact with Asia'. He reports having had great difficulties communicating with his wife in the early days of their marriage, when his Punjabi was 'terrible'. Saba and her husband were another couple who had difficulties communicating: she was Urdu speaking, whilst her English-speaking husband knew only Punjabi. Her account, however, provides an alternative perspective on the class and educational differences between spouses raised in Britain and Pakistan to the hierarchy employed by many British Pakistani informants in which the handicap of being raised in Pakistan may be compensated for by education:

... the generation which was born and bred here – their parents who came so long ago and they weren't that educated, so they came speaking Punjabi. And then the generation which grew up in Pakistan – they were more civilised, more educated and so Urdu became more common.

The forms of cultural capital desirable in a spouse, and assessments of the 'match' in status between a couple, are thus complicated by the transnational context.

Doing *rishte*

'Doing *rishte*', or suggesting matches, is a heavy responsibility involving decisions which can, if things go wrong, cause offence or lead to deep unhappiness. Nevertheless, particularly among the women I have encountered in Britain and Pakistan, the subject can provide an endless topic of conversation and source of enjoyment.

Some *rishte* are settled in the family in childhood. Many would not dream of betrothing their children when they are too young to consent, but the assessment of availability of suitable matches among the kin group inevitably starts early. Opposite-sex cousins of similar ages, or where the boy is a few years older than the girl, are talked about as matches from a young age, and children and adolescents are teased and tease each other about these nascent *rishte*. The pairing may be particularly strong if the two are a good match in other ways, so Azra from Bristol and her Pakistani husband, both slender and strongly religious, were always considered a match even though she was originally inclined towards another cousin. When a match is obvious to the rest of the family, it can take quite some effort to resist. Salma in Islamabad and her cousin in Lahore, both high-achieving, 'modern' young people, were considered such a match that Salma's mother had to announce to relatives that she would not be looking for a *rishta* from within the family.

If a *rishta* is not settled early, or if a childhood match is refused, the search for a husband or wife really takes off as young people approach marriageable age. Parents, aunts, uncles and so on may ask friends and relations if they can think of a good *rishta*, and social gatherings such as weddings provide opportunities to spot potential matches. If they are not well known to the family, enquiries will be made to find out about the background and character of any likely seeming person. The young man's family conventionally takes the initiative (Wakil 1991: 43). In Bristol, one mother of a single woman in her twenties told me that although she would have been able to talk to a sibling about a match between their children, she cannot approach people outside the family to suggest a *rishta*, as the suggestion must come from the 'boy's' side. I did hear from one British Pakistani man that his wife had stood out from the other potential matches he had been shown in Pakistan because of the active role she and her mother took in the early stages of the process, coming at short notice to his house for the initial meeting – something he took, along with the fact that she was in paid employment, and seemed at ease talking directly to him, as a sign of an unusual and attractive lack of traditionality. Among most families I knew in Pakistan, however, the practice was that once a suitable match has been identified, the 'boy's' family will visit the 'girl's' home for snacks or a meal, giving the potential bridegroom and his family a chance to 'view' the young woman and the environment in which she has been brought up. This visit may sometimes take place in the absence of the prospective bride – one young woman I met in Pakistan was away at university when her engagement took place, her fiancé and his family having visited her parents and been shown photographs and a wedding video in which she could be seen.

The groom and his family may visit several homes and consider several different matches before deciding to offer a proposal. Although the woman's side can refuse proposals, and may see a variety of suitors as part of this process, the 'boy's side is generally considered to have the upper hand. If a proposal is accepted, it is often followed by a formal engagement when the groom's family present a ring, money and other gifts for the bride. Sometimes there is no engagement as such, but the marriage is agreed upon by the sides giving their word (*zaban dena*).

Looking for a *rishta* is a delicate process. Timing is crucial: ask too early and you risk being rejected on the grounds that the child is too young or in the middle of their education, but too late and a desirable prospect may already have their *rishta* settled elsewhere. Being 'viewed' and then passed over can be disappointing or insulting – information about the prospective spouse and family has already been exchanged, so it may be assumed that a rejection is a response to personal attributes of family members or the attractiveness of the candidate. Farida in Bristol told me that she hated going to view girls with her son, knowing what a difficult position the family was in, and was glad that her son had liked the first potential match they visited. Here Talib's father Ghalib describes how they went about discreetly looking at the options on a visit to Pakistan:

> So we went to few families, shown few girls. Not like face to face you know, but obviously we went there and sat down and having our food. Then quietly I said to him, 'Look, this is the girl which we would like to see, what do you think about this?' ... He did have little word, like: '*Salaam-alai-kum*, how are you? What are you studying?' things like that. Not letting the family know why we are here – but they do have little bit [of an] idea.

Young people themselves may not be told about all the *rishte* proposed for them, and as in this case, the purpose of these exploratory visits may be concealed. Mumtaza from Jhelum, who came to Bristol in 1984, told me how a matchmaker employed by her future husband had brought him to her house. Mumtaza's mother called her home from an aunt's house, saying her grandmother was ill, and asked her to take a glass of water to the female guest in another room, who was in fact the matchmaker. This allowed the young man accompanying her to see Mumtaza, but he wanted another look, so her mother sent her in with something else, whereupon the matchmaker took her arm and started asking her questions.

Although most families I know do without the services of paid matchmakers, some kind of mediator (perhaps a mutual relative) is usually required unless the match is between very close family or friends: two sisters, for example, may discuss between themselves arranging a marriage between their children. The use of intermediaries in other cases is partly in order to spare the feelings of those involved, or 'save face' in case of rejection (Wakil 1991: 430; see also Das 1976). The use of go-betweens seems to be even more important in the case of 'outside' (*bahar se*, i.e. non-kin) *rishte*, and here has connotations of propriety. Although these matches are considered different from marriages between kin, some connection such as a mutual friend must usually exist for these negotiations to begin. When my host in Pakistan was asked to come up with a *rishta* for his wife's brother, for example, he thought of a young woman he had met through work. As an unrelated man he could not approach her directly on the matter, but after some enquiries, he found a link through mutual friends to the woman's father, whom he could then approach. The need to go through proper channels of mutual connection also applies without the gender barrier. Gafoora in Islamabad related with shock how when a British relative's son pointed out a pretty girl at a wedding, his mother 'went straight over' to the girl's mother and said directly that they wanted to come to their house to talk about it.[5]

The process of finding, assessing and securing *rishte* is obviously complicated in the case of transnational marriages where visiting is curtailed by distance. British families looking for matches for their children often rely on relatives in Pakistan to suggest suitable people. Decision making is assisted by technologies that help bridge the distance: likely candidates may be viewed in photographs and videos of weddings they have attended, while telephone and the internet facilitate discussions between the two sides and the gathering of information from third parties. When Rubina in Bristol was in her late teens, her parents decided to look for a *rishta* for her in Pakistan:

> What they said was, would that be OK if we told one of my mum's brothers? They told him they were looking for a match, and the type of person that they might need, and that sort of thing. I said that's OK … It happened a lot quicker than I expected that they actually had found a match and they told us about it. And my dad asked, 'Are there any other matches?' but my uncle said none that we sort of considered were really good ones. So the in-laws they sent a photo, that sort of thing, and mum and dad liked the look of it.

After being told about the young man by relatives in Pakistan, the engagement was settled over the telephone, and Rubina did not meet her fiancé until she went to Pakistan to get married the following year. Her cousin Jamilah was married at the same time, but she had the choice of a few possible matches:

> Even before we got there, we started scanning a few pictures. I went through a few suggestions from my parents and a few pictures. So I'd already seen his picture before I went to Pakistan. And he's got some family here as well, so people just advised my parents what they thought was appropriate, and they just give you suggestions. And then when I got there, of all the ones that my parents had suggested, this seemed like the best one. Only from picture, mind, it was not from conversation or anything like that.

We had a short meeting, the two of us, but it was accompanied by other people, it wasn't on a one-to-one basis. And that was supposed to help me decide and make the final decision, although I couldn't tell much from it at all. It was very frustrating ... it all felt uncomfortable. And then that was in June, and then in July we got married. So it was all really from one picture and then one visit ... My parents had told me things about him ... The most obvious things were his age, his height, education and just things about him. Things about his family, and little things ... my father doesn't like ... like smoking is a big no-no, so if he'd been all perfect but smoked, it would have been a no. So I think my parents – they met him before, and my brothers had met him – they asked him lots of questions. So it was all based around what everybody had asked him – if he fitted the bill ...

We all [the cousins] went to each other's weddings. It was kind of – all of us got married at the same time. It was amazing. But it wasn't planned like that though, if we didn't find anyone then we'd just come back. It would have been all right. But because everybody else was doing it, [I thought] – 'Oh, I'll get married too!'

Betrothals and even marriages, anticipated or not, often take place when families are visiting Pakistan from Britain to attend family gatherings, the most common being weddings. As Jamilah's comments suggest, there may be something about the excitement of attending a relative's marriage that inspires others to follow suit, particularly given the opportunities such occasions present for networking and identifying matches. In addition, on a rare trip from Britain, families will be expected to visit as many of their relatives' homes as possible, providing a perfect opportunity to inspect potential spouses. These multipurpose visits make greater financial sense than a separate trip to Pakistan specifically to view matches. Iram's wedding, it will be remembered, took place just after both *choti* Eid ('little' Eid, Eid ul-Fitr) and the anniversary of her father's death, allowing the family to mark these occasions with relatives in Pakistan. This logic is also common in Pakistan, with many marriages taking place around the two Eid celebrations, when families are already gathered together. Although weddings do take place across most of the year, this has the effect of producing a kind of marriage season: from after the fasting of *Ramazan* when marriages are not prohibited but fasting makes hospitality difficult, until just after *bara* Eid ('big' Eid, Eid ul-Adha) when the mourning month of *Muharram* begins. This is apparently particularly the case when, as during my time in Pakistan, the period coincides with the more comfortable cool winter months.

Transnational *rishte* introduce a further element into the dynamics of power between the families involved. The implications of this are most visible when British Pakistani women like Jamilah are taken to Pakistan to select a husband. Pakistani girls and their parents often view themselves as fairly powerless, waiting for a suitable 'boy' to come along and hoping that they are chosen. Several young women in Bristol, however, recounted stories similar to Jamilah's of being presented with a number of young men to visit in order to see if any are suitable, dramatically reversing the traditional pattern of viewing visits by prospective grooms. The opportunity to move to Britain, the USA or elsewhere in 'the West' that such marriages present is often extremely desirable to Pakistani residents, and can lead to competition for these *rishte*. In addition, the brief visits that families from Bristol are able to make to Pakistan for the purpose of identifying a match mean that parents of young women cannot sit around waiting to see what *rishte* come, but must be more pro-active than has generally been the custom in Pakistan.

As might be imagined, deciding on a future spouse after very few chaperoned meetings, or even without having met the proposed partner at all, can be difficult. Three interlinked factors – parents, religion and attraction – emerged in conversations with young British Pakistanis as influencing the acceptance of a match. Parents may be a source of both advice and obligation. They are often viewed, or at least view themselves, as able to make better choices because of their greater experience, combined with a concern for their child's best interest. Equally, the young person may feel their parents' wishes should be followed because of the duty to reciprocate the care they have given. One man, for example, eventually gave in to pressure from his mother to marry his brother's wife's sister because his mother was getting old. Another made what he called an 'emotional decision' to accept the match that his mother had favoured while she was dying:

> ... afterwards I thought, 'What am I doing? I hardly know this girl. I don't know what I'm doing, but this is what my mum wanted'. And I think the overriding feeling was this is what my mum wanted. She sacrificed so much for me, I just thought, and my whole family actually, I just thought this is the only way I can repay them. That's not really a religious decision at all. Maybe it's a bit of a thing about our culture – to sacrifice things for our family and to repay them for any debts that you think you owe. And that's why I made the decision at the time.
>
> (Saif)

Although Saif denies that his decision was based on religion, a passage from later in the interview suggests that in retrospect he does see some element of *qismat* or fate in the marriage.

> It's really strange. I've had barriers in front of me for the last eight years that I've been studying and it's like I'm finally getting over these barriers ... These things are finishing one by one. The only thing left now in my life is to get a job, a decent job. Which is my plan at the moment. Once I've got that I've got everything I need really, and a new wife as well. She's brought me a lot of luck since we got married, a hell of a lot of luck. And it's funny – my mum said something along the same line before she

passed away: 'she's a lucky girl' ... My sister said the same thing as well, just talking: 'she's going to bring you a lot of luck.' And it seems to be true. She's bringing a lot of luck at the moment.

After initially saying that this is the kind of thing mothers say to encourage a reluctant son to accept a *rishta*, his sister explained how the idea of a bride bringing luck was connected to *qismat*. People often notice, she said, that when a new wife comes into a family, good things start to happen, as they have done for Saif. Sometimes comments may be made to the opposite effect – that bad things have been happening since the new wife arrived – but more often girls are associated with positive 'luck'. Girls are born with their own *qismat*. A daughter may be destined to fly the nest, but the *qismat* she brings means that she is not a burden to her family. In Bushra's experience, this is borne out in her observation that families with many daughters tend to be rich. When she marries, a girl takes this *qismat* to her new family. Boys also have *qismat*, but they can study and work to improve their life, where a girl is (conceptually) more dependent on her fate. Such comments provide an alternative, or perhaps simply a resistance, to the more widely reported Pakistani view of daughters as burdensome (e.g. Winkvist and Akhtar 2000).

Qismat may be employed to place the responsibility for bad marriages with fate rather than the parents who arranged it. Marriage is a *qismat ki bat*, a thing of fate, so when I asked one mother visiting from Pakistan why she had married her daughter in Britain, she replied simply '*uski qismat yahan hai*' (her fate is here). This is alternatively phrased as someone's *khana-pina yahan likha hua hai*. This literally means their eating and drinking is 'written' here.[6] Religion can be a further source of authority to which young people turn for help with making these important decisions. In particular, a prayer called the *istikhara* may be used to divine the right path to follow. A final factor influencing many of those I talked to was attraction. In this excerpt, Talib, a religious young man from Bristol, gives an explanation of his choice of bride in which religion, parental advice and attraction melt into each other:

> I actually kept praying to God, thanking God and saying, 'If I did marry, will everything be alright?' There is a thing in Islam called *istikhara* ... You actually pray to Allah asking him, 'Well, is this thing that I'm going to do now – is it good for me? If it's good for me then please give it to me now. If it's not good for me then put it away from me'. And I actually made that kind of prayer, there is a special prayer that you have to learn, and I just kept making that prayer ... What happens is you actually see it in your dreams, or you see that the situation is turning good – in other words, you see that people want you to get married to that person, and you can see that situation at the time is good for you.
>
> There were available [other *rishte*] but I did keep on making prayer to God and I didn't see anything within that. And always throughout my whole life, twenty-four years, I've noticed that whatever my parents have

said comes true. Wherever they say, because they've got experience, and because they've lived life. Whatever they say, they always look for the child's goodness, they always want to see that the child, what's best for the child ... Actually my heart was very inclined towards her at that time anyway. I think Allah ... put love in my heart. And I didn't have any problems, to tell you the truth, and Allah ... made it easy for me ... I could see the situation at the time being easy for me.[7]

The next section will explore attraction in transnational arranged marriages a little further.

Doing your own *rishta*: transnational 'love marriage'

Pakistanis both in Britain and Pakistan differentiate between 'love' and 'arranged' marriages, with arranged marriages being the more respectable norm. As Mody (2002b) writes of north India, personal love affairs are seen as disruptive to social relationships and the social order. A Quranic injunction specifies that a woman should not contract a union herself, but be given in marriage by a male guardian (Yamani 1998: 154).[8] In Pakistan, this is sometimes expanded so that Donnan (1994: 307) reports informants saying that a father 'can make the marriage where he wishes'. The social expectation that the process will be controlled by the parents is reflected in the use of the terms 'boy' and 'girl' (in Urdu: *larka* and *larki*) of the potential spouses even when they are well into adulthood, implying their childlike passivity and obedience to their parents in the arrangement.[9]

In practice, the generally opposed categories of 'love' and 'arranged' marriages appear as a continuum, with varying degrees of parental/wider family involvement. At one end of this continuum are the increasingly rare cases in which a couple do not meet until their wedding day, while at the other are the similarly infrequent cases where couples meet and marry in secret. (I am treating forced marriages [*zabardasti ki shadi*, *marzi ke bagair*], arranged marriages without consent, as a separate phenomenon for the purposes of this discussion, and will not discuss them here.) Transnational marriages without meeting used to be more common before the advent of affordable air travel, with reports of weddings being conducted over the telephone, and spouses meeting on the tarmac of British airports. The other end of the continuum, elopements, occur both in Pakistan and among British Pakistanis, but are, for obvious reasons, less possible transnationally. In practice, therefore, even those marriages that are classed by the participants as 'love' marriages usually involve some degree of outside 'arrangement'.

Fischer notes that love marriages are most likely to occur between cousins (Fischer 1991: 102), who are likely to have more opportunity to meet and form attractions than unrelated young people of the opposite sex. A younger brother of Yasmin (whose narrative will appear in Chapter 6), for example, had developed an attraction to a cousin during visits to Pakistan for other family weddings, and asked her parents if he might be allowed to take her out to dinner; they agreed, and the couple's marriage was arranged soon after. Raisa's family had decided that she should marry her paternal cousin, but on visiting Pakistan, she found him 'village-y' and unattractive; she showed me a picture of a thin, dark, moustached man. Whilst staying with her family, however, a maternal cousin was delegated to show her around, and even to take her to meet her intended spouse. This cousin was handsome, fair, fashionably dressed and articulate, and the pair ended up talking to each other into the early hours of the morning. On her return to Britain, Raisa told her mother how much she liked this cousin and, at the cost of rifts within the family, her mother broke off the previous agreement and arranged for her to marry the man with whom she had fallen in love. Fatima, another woman from Bristol, rejected two marriages within the family in Pakistan (in one case only telling her father she didn't want to go through with it just before the planned wedding). On another visit, whilst her mother's brother's family were attempting to bring her round to marrying a son of their household, she found herself falling for another cousin who sometimes visited the house. Her father, feeling bad about the unwanted – and narrowly avoided – earlier wedding, supported her, and the marriage was quickly arranged.

As across South Asia, there is a fascination with romance among the young in Pakistan (Fischer 1991: 102). When Amina's British cousin declared to his parents at the end of a visit to Pakistan that he wanted to marry her, the wedding (including venues, clothes, guests and photographers) was organised in two days. To her surprise, Amina then quickly obtained a 'fast track' visa, and within a very short period of time was leaving Pakistan to join her husband in Bristol. Amina described this whole whirlwind period in her life as 'filmy' – in other words, like something from a romantic Indian film.

The contracting of an 'arranged' marriage can equally be remembered as a time of love and romance, approached 'along with some trepidation, [with] a degree of eager anticipation and romantic expectation' (Mines and Lamb 2002: 8). This is often evident in my informants' descriptions of their weddings. Nabila was born in Pakistan and at the time of our interview had been married to her mother's sister's son Farooq in Bristol for four years. Her mother, mother's sister and maternal grandmother were all keen on the match when Nabila came from Pakistan to visit her relatives in Bristol eight years before, but she was nervous of marrying into an unfamiliar environment, particularly as she had seen the difficulties caused in the household by a family member with mental health problems. It was only when Farooq himself proposed and promised to be faithful to her while he completed his university degree that she was swayed. Her mother was worried about her marrying into the uncertain moral climate of the West, but 'he said to my mother that he loved me and he will die in front of my house, and this and that'. Nabila's eyes shone as she showed me the gold pendant he gave her to mark their engagement and which she has worn constantly ever since. She came on a fiancée visa to Britain and, to avoid antagonising his mentally ill relative, their marriage was a simple affair at home with only two witnesses, but her husband did his best to make the occasion special for her, asking her to dress in her bridal clothes for him once they were alone, and taking her on a two-week honeymoon.

During my research, romance was more often present in the narratives of women than men, and Farooq himself explained his personal proposal as his 'Islamic duty' rather than the romantic act Nabila perceived. Of course, this may be an alternative discourse considered more suitable for a man to present to me, a woman and a non-Muslim, and a romantic impulse is visible in other young men's actions. Bushra's son, for example, got together with the brother of his fiancée in Pakistan, who is marrying his sister (i.e. a brother-sister pair 'exchange'), and the two young men took their future wives out to dinner to present them with rings that they had bought in secret.

The *rishta* as connection

> Because my grandmother, she want to marry [me] with my cousin because my mother and my aunt, they just both sisters [i.e. no other siblings] ... If I married here then they will stay together [*ikhatte rehnge*].
> (Nabila, partial translation from Urdu)

So far the term *rishta* has been translated as 'proposal' or 'match', but in a more general sense it also means 'connection' or 'relationship'. Relatives are called *rishte-dar* (the *-dar* suffix indicates possession), but a *rishta* does not need to be a relationship of kinship, so that my host in Pakistan explained to another guest at a wedding that our *rishta* to the couple was that we were neighbours of the girl's family. These senses of *rishta* are equally important in understanding what people are looking for in a proposal or match: in the connection or relationship of marriage.

Most obviously, and as has been often repeated, South Asian arranged marriages are not simply relationships between individuals, but between families. Connections made through marriage create relationships beyond the couple, and new networks of *rishte-dar*. Some university girls I spoke to in Pakistan told me about marriages in their family between, for example, the children of two men who were friends, and who thought of each other as 'like family' before the marriage (see also Shaw 2000a: 145). In such cases a *rishta* transforms kin-like bonds into kinship, which may then be reinforced by further marriages in the same or subsequent generations. However, given that so many Pakistani marriages are between cousins or other kin – and indeed in many cases the ability to trace a kinship connection is desirable for the *rishta* to be considered a good one – what is the significance of viewing what is sought in a match as a 'connection' when a relationship often already exists?

One response to this question is that not all relatives are the same. A *rishta* may transform someone who is merely a member of the wider *baraderi* kin group, but with whom a precise relationship might not be traceable, into a *rishta-dar*. A person's 'closest' relatives are often those to whom she is related several times as the result of marriage: for example, two women may be both matrilateral and patrilateral first cousins, and sisters-in-law. One result will be that these women will probably meet more frequently at functions held by relatives such as marriages, death anniversaries or Eid gatherings, and through more casual visiting, as many of their close relatives will be in common. Visiting, particularly on significant occasions, is one mechanism for producing and indicating closeness. My host in Pakistan, for example, compares army classmates to family in how close they are, and how much they can rely on each other, giving the example that after his mother died many of those with whom he trained came for *afsos* (condolence) and to lend their support. Such considerations may be taken into account when considering *rishte*, so Gafoora in Islamabad remembered that when she was helping to think of matches for a younger brother, she was in favour of a marriage with a relative living in Lahore so that the two sections of the family would meet more frequently as in-laws visited each other.

As the importance of visiting suggests, kin relationships are not permanent and given, but will weaken without efforts to sustain them. A Punjabi proverb reflects the ephemerality of kinship without continued intermarriage: 'when the fence is old, it is your duty to put new wood into it' (in Werbner 1990: 96); Shaw (2000a: 155) reports the alternative construction: 'a new brick strengthens the wall.' Without marriages as both new relationships between families, and as occasions on which dispersed relatives may gather in Pakistan, the significance of transnational kinship relations may fade. Hence Parveen, who married a relative in Pakistan, told me:

> ... when we were younger, my mum used to always cry – 'Oh, my family is behind [in Pakistan]', and everything like that. We'd say 'Mum, why are you crying?' – you know – 'We're here', and all that. But your family back home, you know, until you don't go [sic – she means 'until you go'] – because that was the first time ... we didn't know our cousins and our aunties and that [in Pakistan] ... until you don't go back, you don't know how special they are ...

Transnational *rishte*

The importance of *rishta* as connection or relationship is thrown into relief in transnational marriages, which are frequently between close kin. For many British Pakistanis, marriage represents an opportunity to strengthen their connections with Pakistan and with relatives who live there. This is partly a matter of identity: Talib chose a bride from Pakistan to 'keep myself with my origins' and Bushra wanted to keep this 'link' with Pakistan so that her children's Pakistani cultural identity would not be too 'diluted' by residence in Britain. This concern is shared with another South Asian group – a Sikh woman in

Bristol told me that an announcement had been made in the local *gurudwara* (Sikh place of worship) to the effect that all those who were willing should be married to partners from India in order to preserve their language and culture (cf. Mand 2003). Her *baraderi* across the country, she said proudly, has taken 200 young men and women to India for marriage. For most of the Pakistanis I met in Bristol, however, the connections sought are to people and places. Without one parent from Pakistan, one British husband told me, there would be no reason to visit; the family would take holidays to Disneyland or Dubai instead of maintaining connections with their ancestral homeland. Talib's father Ghalib explained his reasons for marrying his son to a relative in Pakistan:

> I wanted to keep a link with Pakistan. If I have found all my three kids *rishta*s here, my link to Pakistan would have been broken ... As long as my parents are alive, I will keep going back ... I can go, see my mum, see my dad, my brothers are there, my sisters are there, but as soon as my parents gone, my link will start getting weaker and slowly, slowly it will break. I don't want to break that link to my homeland, to my family, to my country, so that is a main reason which I actually went to Pakistan [to look for a bride]. So that link can only be continued if at least one of my family members is married there. So my son is married there – my link has gone positive again. If I stopped it, my son will continue it ... And then maybe I will retire myself back home. I personally do want it. If I'm going to retire I would like to retire in Pakistan. As you might have seen – you went to Pakistan – [the] elder you are [the] more respect you get. People look at you and ask your experiences. So I don't want to go in an old people's home here and die. That is the reason.

Since he and his wife have fulfilled their desire and obligation to maintain this connection through the marriage of their son, at the time of the interview they were searching in Britain for a husband for their daughter, as he considered that the risks of importing men were too high (see Chapters 5 to 7). In the end, however, this daughter was also married in Pakistan.

Much writing on British Pakistani arranged marriages focuses on the parental motivations of maintaining contact with the land and family they left behind when they themselves migrated (e.g. Ballard 1987), but the young British Pakistanis getting married may themselves, like Talib, also value this connection. When Azra was considering her options, she reflected that if she married in Britain she, and indeed her children, might never again have the pleasure of visiting Pakistan. Marriages are thus used both within Pakistan and in the diaspora to maintain connections, *rishte*, in the face of distance. This power of a marriage *rishta* to renew close kinship between people in different places is clearly illustrated in one case I encountered in Bristol where a marriage was arranged between a woman from Britain and a man resident in America in order to maintain the linkages between relatives living in two different villages in Pakistan. She explained why so many of her relatives had pressed for the match:

> Well basically because there wasn't anybody else and also to start a new link ... They were from a different, sort of, village ... [And our marriage would] bring them closer as well – link up with them. 'Cos I don't think there was anybody else in our family who'd get married there ... We're from near Mirpur and my husband is from Jhelum.

Donnan's study of Pakistani marriage choices documented strong preferences for both geographical and social proximity in choice of spouses, linking distance in terms of geography and kinship. A study of transnational marriage is of course unlikely to uncover strong preferences for local marriage partners, but connections between geography and kinship emerge strongly from my data. As already noted, visiting, encouraged by geographical proximity or kinship ties, produces 'closeness'. As in English, the same term, *qarib*, is used to indicate spatial nearness and immediacy of kin relationship (*qarib rishte-dar*).

The distance people seek to diminish by these marriage connections is not just physical, but also emotional. Just as Gafoora sought to use a marriage to bridge the distance between Lahore and Islamabad, her sister Farida, who migrated to Bristol for marriage in the 1970s, was eager to arrange a match between her daughter Uzma, and Nadir, the son of her other sister (Tayiba) in Lahore. Gafoora's daughter told me that all her *mamu* (maternal uncles) were keen on the match: at the moment their sister visits Pakistan to see her father, although she comes less frequently than when their mother was alive, but given that the bond between siblings is less strong than between parents and children, she will have less reason to visit after his death. Another woman in Bristol compared parents to the roots of the family tree, which becomes weak and can fall apart after their death: 'When the father dies, it shakes, and when the mother dies, everything falls down.' As the next generation are growing up in different countries, they see each other less frequently, so are less emotionally close, and may not keep in contact.

Distance has affected relationships in the older generation. Farida herself told Gafoora during the latter's stay in the UK of her own difficulties since her migration. When Gafoora asked why she had not said anything earlier, Farida replied that there was no point: 'You were so far away.' However, Farida now seems to be trying to include her own children in the closeness born of association between young cousins, sending Uzma and her younger brother Javed to Pakistan to spend Eid with the extended family. According to Gafoora, this visit was primarily in order for Nadir and his parents to see more of Uzma, to increase the likelihood of the *rishta* being secured.

In addition to visiting, Pakistanis create and maintain ties between both friends and relatives through gift giving (Shaw 1988; Werbner 1990). Uzma and Javed took with them whole suitcases full of gifts, mostly jeans and fleeces, for their relatives. Later, Gafoora told me that Farida had won Tayiba over by her generosity in giving without expectation of return. There were also, however, hints that this strategy had simultaneously been divisive: Gafoora, while insisting that she didn't mind, told me several times that Farida always sends far more gifts for Tayiba's family than for her own.

The attempts of Uzma and her mother to secure the match that may strengthen ties with their family in Pakistan appears inadvertently to have reinforced distance with other sections of her kin group. Gafoora's daughter Salma is the only female first cousin of a similar age to Uzma apart from Nadir's own sister, and she and her mother feel that Uzma and Farida have treated her as a threat. Gafoora has told her sister directly that she is not interested in a match with Nadir or his brother for Salma, but tension between the two young women persists. While I was in Pakistan, Salma said that Uzma had emailed her to report on the engagement of a cousin in Bristol, who had at one stage been considered a possible match for both girls, telling Salma that she had 'lost'. Nonetheless, when some time later I asked Salma which 'side' ('boy's' or 'girl's') she would be on at Uzma and Nadir's wedding, as both were first cousins, she replied that although usually you join the party of the person to whom you are closest, she would probably be on the girl's side (*larki ki taraf*) as Uzma has no real sisters and so will need female friends to play their roles in the proceedings. Part of these duties, she pointed out with a grin, is to demand and receive money from the groom's side.

Part of the appeal for many British Pakistanis of visiting Pakistan is undoubtedly shopping. Not only does the money they may have worked very hard to save go a lot further in Pakistan, but particular goods such as *shalwar qamis* and jewellery are available in the latest styles, and in greater choice than in Britain. Lavish consumption may impress some Pakistani relatives, and perhaps give a misleading impression of the standard of living these families enjoy at home. As with the generous gifts presented above, the intention may even be to impress in order to attract *rishte*, or simply prestige, but such displays also have the potential to be divisive. Thus while Nadir and his brothers in Lahore look out for bargains for Gafoora's family, when Uzma talked gleefully about how much money she had to spend on clothes, the cousins decided to take her to the most expensive shops to hasten the end of her spending spree.

The delicate relationship between closeness and division may be intrinsic to the search for a 'good *rishta*'. While matches between close kin generally attract most approval from the kin group, a *rishta* can be an opportunity for making new connections – to influence, wealth, or opportunity – and non-kin marriages have been seen as sometimes risky attempts to maximise such benefits (Ahmad 1978b: 175–76; Donnan 1988: 173–97; Jeffery and Jeffery 1996: 98–99). Within Britain or Pakistan, however, the opportunities for marrying 'up' are limited by the fact that families generally look for *rishte* from similar socio-economic backgrounds. In addition, it has been noted that *baraderis* tend to fracture along class and residential lines into smaller in-marrying groups (e.g. Shaw 2000a: 144). Thus in the Lahori district studied by Fischer

(1991), marriages are usually an expression of status, rather than the vehicle for improving it.

A transnational kin marriage seems to present those living in Pakistan with a particularly attractive blend of a connection to new opportunities in other countries, prestige, and real or imagined wealth, together with social approval for marrying 'in'. From the perspective of British Pakistanis, there may also be gains to be made in terms of prestige in the quality of *rishta* they can attract as British citizens. Several young people I met in Bristol married 'up' in terms of education or social class by bringing spouses from Pakistan: the beautician daughter of a market trader married to a doctor; an unemployed man with no qualifications married to a cousin who gave up medical studies to come to Bristol; or a telesales manager whose beautiful wife came from a wealthy family living in the best area of Lahore. Even for these better-off Pakistanis a connection to the UK or another developed country can be valuable. Professionals such as engineers and doctors are often keen to gain training or experience abroad, although they may not intend to move overseas permanently, but to return to Pakistan after some years with their earning power increased.[10] Nevertheless, from the Pakistani perspective, opportunities abroad are not necessarily the primary motivation for such marriages. During Nadir's engagement to Uzma, he independently obtained a visa to study in London, and hoped to return to live in Pakistan, so it did not seem that this was the principal motivation for his family in agreeing to the marriage. More important was the pressure from Farida and her brothers in Pakistan for connection to be maintained with this British section of the family. This interpretation is supported by the fact that his father, who is not related to his wife's family (i.e. she married 'out'), was much less keen on the marriage. The father did not get on with many of his wife's relatives, and without the multiple ties that unite close *rishte-dar*, he saw the prospect more as losing the son who was to look after him in his old age, rather than, as for his wife's side, cementing, mending and ensuring close relationships despite distance.

Distance, however, also disguises the failures and disappointments of migrants. A man whose financial position in Britain is fairly insecure may still be able to send money back to Pakistan, or it may be easy for a woman to hide marital problems from family in Pakistan to spare them distress or shame. When Gafoora and her family visited Britain, for example, they were surprised at how small their relatives' houses were. She recounted several examples of relations who, although they may have built smart properties in Pakistan, lead less salubrious lives in Britain: working while claiming benefits, sub-letting council houses, or other activities that she had not known about from their visits to Pakistan. These deceptions, however, may be at the price of the often prized emotional closeness with those in Pakistan – as when Farida could not confide in a distant sister, and so reinforced their distance by her lack of communication, a distance that she had more recently been attempting to bridge with visiting, gifting and, most importantly (and, she must hope, permanently), with the marriage of her daughter to her sister's son.

Rishta: connecting strategy and emotion

Rishte are connections between people. Two main strands seem to be intertwined in *rishta* as a proposed connection of marriage. It may be the consequence of, or intended to maintain, emotional connections and kinship bonds with relatives or close friends, and a good *rishta* can be one that brings wealth, prestige or political connections.[11] Focusing on this indigenous term for affinal connections may prove useful in uniting some of the evidence on Pakistani marriages in the literature, by undermining the distinction between preference and practice. Hastings Donnan (1988), as mentioned earlier, divides the factors involved in marriage choice into socio-cultural preferences and 'personal expectations'. This distinction, however, begins to appear a little artificial when it is understood that *both* strategic advantages *and* the value of marrying where connections already exist are part and parcel of the concept of the good *rishta*. In other words, maximising personal advantage is an intrinsic part of the socio-cultural expectations of choosing a marriage partner.

Donnan starts his volume with a review of the debate on marriage preference, and attempts to reconcile a preference for patrilateral parallel cousin marriage, or at least marriage within the patrilineage, with a far more varied practice – many people marry matrilateral relatives – by explanations in terms of strategic behaviour, such as maximising the useful contacts gained though a match. This contrasts with Veena Das's (1973) explanation of matrilateral parallel cousin marriage as the result of dominant mothers insisting on matches with their beloved sisters' children rather than their husbands' relatives. If, as I understand it, strategic matters, kinship obligations and emotional connections are all part of what is understood by *rishta*, then these disparities of interpretation are no longer in need of explanation, but are in fact consistent and cognate phenomena.[12] Transnational marriages emphasise these different facets of the concept of *rishta* by exaggerating both the dangers of losing connections, even between close kin, and the difference in opportunities, wealth or status that may be (hoped to be) achieved by connections through marriage. Other than through this chance of migration, it would be unusual for a person to change their situation so dramatically on marriage, given that marriages rarely take place across great class divides.

It is worth noting that most of my discussions and observations about connectedness and distance have been with women. The differences in discourse on emotion between men and women may help to explain the differences between my focus on emotion, and Donnan's emphasis on strategy and patrilineage, derived more from conversations with men. One young woman I met in Pakistan had a sister living in England, married to the son of a friend of her father, but her father rejected a proposal for her to marry this man's other son. This might be viewed, following Donnan, as socio-economic

84   Zarurat rishta: *making connections*

strategy: having established a connection to the UK, the marriage of the next daughter could be used to fulfil family expectations, or establish other relationships. The girl's explanation, however, was that having sent one beloved daughter so far away, her parents did not want a second to be married overseas. Of course, it could be suggested that this narrative provides a culturally acceptable gloss over 'real' motivations, but given the obvious importance of this demonstration of her parents' affection to this young woman, to dismiss discourses of emotion as mere appeals to convention, or disguises for more important matters, would be to weaken our understanding of the experience and meaning of marriage. It is on such experiential matters that future behaviour is based. To give a final example, another girl's father has withstood *baraderi* pressure for a match for his eldest daughter, the first woman in the family to go on to further education, in order for her to pursue her studies and even continue them overseas. She sees his strength on her behalf as proof of his admirable character and love for her, and she takes very seriously her reciprocal responsibility to him, and to the other women in the family who may wish to follow her, to set an example of irreproachable behaviour and high achievement.[13] The concept of *rishta* thus provides a bridge between the strategic and emotional considerations involved in arranging marriages. The next chapter will demonstrate how these issues emerge again as explanatory factors in the popularity of close kin marriage.

Notes

1 See Jeffery *et al.* 2004 on Islamic views of education for women.
2 Cf. Jeffery 1976b on rhetoric of spouse selection among Muslims in Delhi.
3 The Prophet Mohammed is traditionally held to have taught that marriage should be between equals (Ahmad 1978a: 14).
4 See: www.therevival.co.uk/forum/general/352 (accessed 12/01/2012).
5 Also thought improper here is the idea of proposing a *rishta* simply on the basis of looks, although as the mother of an unmarried girl, Gafoora may be particularly sensitive about this.
6 Cf. something being 'written [by Allah] on the forehead' as a metaphor for fate in Bangladesh (Gardner 1995: 176).
7 His father, however, sees his parental role as more instrumental: 'So one of those girls, I said to him, "Look, I think this is right for you". He was bit fifty-fifty – "Shall I? Shan't I?" Unfortunately he haven't got the ability to make decision. That's another reason why parents involve themselves in the wedding because in young age every shining things look like gold, but it might not be. But if experienced person is with them, he can check it and see it – is it really gold or is it rolled gold? He wasn't sure, so I said to him, "OK, take your time, think about it and then tell me" ... We came home, we talked to her [sic – his] mother on the phone, to his sister, and then we came here and he said, "Well, if you want it – OK". I said, "It's not us – it's your decision, because we don't want to be accused for that all our lives: 'I done it because of you.' So you better make a decision". Unfortunately he's not very decisive. So with a little talk to him he said, "Yeah, fine. I'll get married. That's the girl".'
8 The Prophet Mohammed is reported to have said that marriages should be arranged by 'proper guardians' (Ahmad 1978a: 14), but 'nobody has got the right to give [a woman]

away in marriage without her wish and consent. And if she marries a Muslim by her free choice, nobody can stop her doing so'. Nonetheless, it is 'not proper for a woman to marry anybody she pleases against the wish of the responsible people of her family' (Maududi 1939: 149–51).
9 In addition, Mody (2002a: 225) notes that 'unmarried people are still considered to be dependants on their families and as such, do not qualify for the more exalted "*admi*" (man) or "*aurath*" (woman)'.
10 This path is not always straightforward – an issue which will be addressed in Chapter 7.
11 In somewhat archaic usage, the word 'connection' also carries this range of connotations in English. In the work of Jane Austen, for example, kinship and marriage 'connexions' are valued for the material and social advantages they confer. In her novels, as in Pakistan, such connexions are seen as fragile and prone to dissolution through offence or neglect. Like *rishte*, Austen's marriage connexions also have emotional content: while a disagreeable person may be suffered for the sake of the advantages the connexion brings, the ideal in marriage is to combine wealth and status with personal fulfilment: 'A most suitable connexion everybody must consider it, but I think it might be a very happy one' (Austen 1994 [1881]: 157–58).
12 Further evidence for the importance of emotional relationships in influencing *rishte* is provided by Fischer's (1991) observation of the very large proportion of kin marriages that are between the children of same-sex siblings, a relationship considered particularly close.
13 A potential spouse's character may be judged by the behaviour of close relatives of the same sex, as character traits are thought to run in families and along gender lines (Fischer and Lyon 2000).

4 Close kin marriage
Reducing and reproducing risk

One of the most striking features of transnational Pakistani marriage is the high rate of unions between close kin.[1] A good *rishta* (as proposal), as has been seen, is often one where a *rishta* (as relationship) of kinship already exists. This overlaying of a new marriage relationship on pre-existing ties is a mechanism to reinvigorate the bonds of kinship, seen as particularly vulnerable in the context of migration when physical separation can lead to emotional distance even in relations between siblings. This chapter will take a look at close kin marriages from a different perspective, demonstrating that they are also favoured because they are perceived by participants as reducing the risks involved in what has already been seen to be the delicate process of finding and securing a good *rishta*. This perception of reducing danger stands in marked contrast to the dominant bio-medical and popular view of such marriages as intrinsically risky in genetic terms. However, while I have suggested that the introduction of migration heightens the strategic and emotional facets of the concept of *rishta*, transnational marriages are shown in this chapter to highlight new risks.

Risk, society and migration

The problem of risk has been seen as a distinctive feature of late modernity (Beck 1992; Giddens 1991). For Giddens, risk is essentially a feature of society 'taking leave of the past, of traditional ways of doing things, and which is opening itself up to a problematic future'. The calculation of risk opens up the possibility of insurance, and a 'colonisation' of the future towards which society is now oriented (Giddens 1991: 109–12). Much of this literature, with its focus on the state, science, corporations or the environment (Krimsley and Golding 1992; Sagan 1993; Rose 2000), has little to say about the small-scale negotiations of risks such as those involved in marital arrangements. More pertinent to this topic is work influenced by the anthropologist Mary Douglas's collaboration with Aaron Wildavsky in *Risk and Culture* (1983), and later sole-authored *Risk and Blame* (1992), which situates risks in their social and moral environment. Perhaps the most useful aspect of Douglas's work is the fundamental point that people do not treat risk as a matter of calculable probabilities. Rather, risk is a social matter. Risks are taken after consultation with kin and friends, and moral obligations, values and relationships are taken into account in decisions about risk taking. Hence, in Pat Caplan's edited volume *Risk Revisited* (2000), contributors draw attention to the cultural and the social settings in which risks are evaluated and negotiated. The influence of social and cultural factors is increasingly recognised in risk research (Taylor-Gooby and Zinn 2006), whilst affective elements of risk perception have also attracted academic interest (Slovic *et al.* 2004).

A smaller literature exists on risk in relation to migration. Economic debates have focused on whether migration should be seen in terms of risk taking (Jaeger *et al.* 2010) or risk reduction (Stark and Levhari 1982). Whilst the former argument can be grasped intuitively, examples of the latter include the spreading of household risk by retaining some members in an agricultural setting whilst others migrate to urban labour markets. From a less economistic perspective, risk reduction and risk taking may be less easily separable, as in Gardner's suggestion that the insecurities of the life of Bangladeshi villagers pre-disposed them to risk overseas migration in the hope of economic transformation (Gardner 1995: 262–63). The risks of migration must, furthermore, be understood in a gendered context: whilst undertaking risky migration may serve as a masculine rite of passage for some, women migrants may risk moral opprobrium, or narrate their mobility as self-sacrifice rather than individual agency (Carling n.d.; cf. Gardner 2002b).

The physical risks of some contemporary irregular migration are particularly stark (e.g. Carling and Hernández Carretero 2008). Largely unsuccessful US attempts to discourage unauthorised immigration from Mexico by increasing the hazards involved form the backdrop for Sheridan's (2009) exploration of Mexican migrants' risk management mechanisms, chief among which are transnational family networks providing information and assistance. This posits a model of authorities imposing risk, to which migrants can only respond (Sheridan 2009). The transnational marriages that form the topic of this book, however, in which the risks are (generally) more emotional than physical, are unions between (would-be) migrants and citizen/resident spouses, and so have a more complex relationship to immigration rules which often claim to protect the latter whilst regulating or excluding the former. Here Adams's (1995) suggestion of parallel 'formal' (e.g. governmental) and 'informal' risk management strategies may be useful. Participants' informal strategies for reducing the risks involved in marriage are the focus of this and the following chapters, but informal strategies take formal provisions into account (Adams 1995), and attempts to manage marital risk are set against the background of immigration policies and legal definitions of marriage and divorce. Both assessments of risk are dynamic, part of what Douglas and Wildavsky (1983: 6) call the 'dialogue on how best to organise social relations ... For to organise means to organise some things *in* and other things *out*'. From this perspective, the political debates following ministerial advice to British Asians to seek partners from within Britain in light of the dangers of 'bogus' transnational marriages, the focus on forced and 'sham' marriages in subsequent immigration policy debates, and the responses in British Pakistanis' marital practices, can be seen as a process of negotiation of acceptable risk. This dialogue echoes Adams's (1995: 4) observation that the formal sector tends to try to reduce risk, while the informal seeks to balance risks and benefits. Each system responds to the other. Emotion, genetic risks and the consequences of risk reduction strategies for relations with kin, all form part of this dialogue. The practices described here should thus be viewed as capturing a certain point in this dynamic process, as capable of further change and development, rather than as a fixed aspect of a reified Pakistani culture.

An extended interview excerpt in which Shareen from Bristol talks about her decision to marry a cousin from Pakistan forms the central section of this chapter. Her narrative recalls themes from the preceding chapter, whilst providing a commentary on risk and trust leading into the main body of the discussion. First, however, it is necessary to outline debates surrounding Pakistani marriage preferences. The chapter as a whole moves towards clarifying the position of affinity in this largely endogamous in terms of kinship, but geographically expansive situation.

Endogamy, cousin marriage and genetic risk

The *zat* or *qaum*, commonly translated as caste, is a conceptually endogamous unit. The use of the term 'castes' of South Asian Muslims has been disputed (Ahmad 1978a), and some Pakistanis deny the existence of caste in Pakistani society (Shaw 1988: 86). During my fieldwork, I heard the term caste used frequently, although sometimes with the qualification that the system is different from that in India.[2] Matches between higher and *kammi* (artisan) *qaums* are considered particularly inappropriate (Shaw 1988: 91). However, '[i]n most cases the question of caste status in marriage does not arise explicitly because of the traditional Pakistani Muslim preference for marriage with first cousins'. This, in turn, is related to a desire to maintain the 'purity of the blood' (Shaw 1988: 98). In contrast to ethnographic data on conceptions of procreation from elsewhere in the subcontinent (Inden and Nicholas 1977: 52–53), blood is thought to be transmitted from the father (Jeffery 1979: 10; Werbner 1990: 283), so purity of the blood can be understood to mean patrilineal endogamy. In practice this has been reported to mean a Pakistani preference for marriage with the father's brother's daughter (Alavi 1972; Donnan 1988: 114–51), or another first cousin within the *baraderi*, a term commonly translated as 'patrilineage' (Alavi 1972; Shaw 1988: 102). My informants in both Bristol and Pakistan, by contrast, did not express a preference for patrilateral marriages, and Shaw's (2001) survey in Oxford found no statistical preference for father's brother's daughter marriage, and only a slightly higher rate of marriages to patrilateral than matrilateral relatives. Father's brother's daughter preference is common in other Middle Eastern Islamic societies, and the existence of groups described as patrilineages encourages observers to think in terms of matri- and patrilineages, but given repeated close kin marriage many members of the *baraderi* are related on both their mother's and father's sides. As Veena Das points out, if a pair of brothers marry a pair of sisters, their children will be both patrilateral and matrilateral first cousins (Das 1973: 38). In other cases, the 'closest' link between husband and wife will be stressed,[3] so the majority of marriages I have encountered may be classified by those involved as *man ki taraf* (mother's side) or *bap ki taraf* (father's side). Nevertheless, it should be remembered that although the term is translated as 'patrilineage', *baraderi* members are not only related through the male line.[4]

Baraderi is a concept with a 'sliding semantic structure' (Alavi 1972). As seen in the previous chapter, marriage tends to take place within a smaller sub-group, reflecting the distinction between what Alavi calls the *baraderi* 'of participation' and the *baraderi* 'of recognition' (Alavi 1972), or Wakil (1991) terms the 'effective' *baraderi* and the *baraderi* 'at large'. At one end of the scale, people may talk about their *baraderi* as this former fairly close-knit group of relatives. The next level is that of those they recognise as related, although a precise relationship may not be able to be traced. Another level up, all members of the same *qaum* from the same village might be considered *baraderi* members. Finally, the concepts of *baraderi* and *zat* may collapse into one another, so that when I asked for a definition of *baraderi*, some people responded by saying that it is *zat*. This ambiguity can be useful in negotiating who may be married, as will be seen in Chapter 6.

The Born in Bradford survey of children born in the city reports that 63% of Pakistani mothers surveyed were married to cousins.[5] In a survey of Pakistanis in Oxford, 59% of marriages were with first cousins, and 87% were within the *baraderi/zat*. These figures are substantially higher than those reported either for Pakistan, or indeed for the parental generation in Britain.[6] Moreover, 71% of the marriages surveyed were to spouses from Pakistan, and 90% of the first cousin marriages were transnational in this way (Shaw 2001: 323–27). These data seem to suggest a marked increase over time in the numbers of consanguineous and, in particular, first cousin marriages amongst British Pakistanis (see Shaw 2000b), but this increase was only in transnational marriages: less than half of the marriages to spouses in the UK were to relatives.

Coupled with high rates of close kin marriage, elevated levels of infant mortality and disability amongst the Pakistani populations in Britain have generated considerable research, reaching differing conclusions about the genetic implications of consanguineous marriages (Shaw 2001), although the consensus now seems to be that the offspring of such couples suffer from raised levels of genetic illnesses and disabilities (Shaw 2000b, 2009). Whilst those with whom I discussed genetic risks were aware of the issue, they seldom saw it as a reason to avoid marrying within the family. They may appeal to fate, or assert that children are gifts from God – although Shaw's sensitive work on genetic testing among British Pakistanis demonstrates that religious essentialism would be an inadequate understanding of the issue

(Shaw 2000b, 2009). Many are able to appeal to reasons why this danger would not affect them: there are no disabilities in their family, or their own parents married 'out' and so the probability is reduced. Others narrate stories of the 'Uncle Norman' variety, such as an example of a family who married out and bore disabled children, while others had healthy offspring, despite repeated cousin marriage across generations.[7] Responses to these risks – testing, termination, and indeed whether genetic causes for disabilities are accepted – must also be 'negotiated with respect to the authority of senior and other relatives, and the authority of religious leaders' (Shaw 2005: 28).

Genetic factors were a major concern for two families I met, but did not prove a complete deterrent in either case. One educated middle-class woman in Pakistan declared that she had decided not to marry her children within the family because she attributed her own multiple miscarriages to consanguineous marriage. On other occasions, however, she told me that she had at one point had her eye on a certain cousin as a match for her daughter, and she would not prevent her son from marrying his first cousin if he wished. Another woman who shared her congenital disability with two siblings married a distant relative, but the family intended to have genetic testing carried out on the husband before the couple decided to have children. Some families who have experienced ill health attributed to genetic causes may take information on genetic risks into account when making marriage choices (Shaw 2009). However, finding a spouse for someone with a disability can prove difficult, and it may be that a suggested *rishta* within the *baraderi* resulting from obligations between kin is the only option available. The opportunity to migrate may make marriage to a disabled relative in Britain a more acceptable proposition for Pakistani nationals.

The lure of consanguineous matches is evidently strong. 'As your children grow up,' said one mother in Bristol, 'it just becomes harder to imagine going outside when there are perfectly good *rishte* within your own family.' This chapter will explore the attraction of kin marriage, and attempt to explain its particular appeal to the diasporic communities in Britain.

Obligations and assets

Noting that marriages that go against the preferences for *quam* and *baraderi* endogamy do occur in Pakistan, Hastings Donnan (1988) argues for a shift from an account of marriage practices that gives explanatory priority to marriage rules and preferences, such as 'close kin marriage', to a focus on the purposive strategies involved in marriage choices. Anthropologists, he argues, have sought explanations only for these exceptions, implying that the remainder are 'explained' by the marriage prescription or preference. This situation has arisen, he suggests, because anthropologists treat marriage as belonging to the sphere of kinship,

> ... and have concentrated on marriage rules expressed in terms of kinship. Even though we know that marriage choice can involve political and

economic considerations, we have not worked out a mode of analysis which incorporates them on an equal footing.
(Donnan 1988: 209)

The model Donnan proposes for interpreting marital decisions (introduced in the previous chapter) includes factors in two categories: a set of cultural preferences, and considerations defined by individual goals. Kinship preferences fall into the former category, and may conversely form the basis for claims or expectations to marry a child to a certain person. While requests from close kin may be hard to ignore, decisions are made by weighing the social implications of neglecting these expectations against other priorities (Donnan 1988: 119–51). These other factors, the personal goals involved in a marriage choice, include strengthening kin ties, making new connections, or having a wealthy or beautiful spouse. The considerations relevant to each arrangement vary. A father with many daughters and thus a high financial burden, for example, chose to marry the first few to *baraderi* members to strengthen kin ties and establish the family in the village where this section of the *baraderi* live. With his family size diminished and economic situation improved, however, he was in a stronger position to resist pressure to marry another child within the *baraderi*, and risked arranging marriages to non-kin, thereby forging new networks (Donnan 1988: 173–97). Even marriages identical in terms of genealogy, writes Bourdieu (1977: 48), may have 'different, even opposite, meanings and functions', according to the relationships and strategies involved at the time.

A strategic perspective on marriage arrangements has been pervasive in the study of British Pakistani marriages, although the factors involved in decisions differ from those proposed by Donnan in Pakistan, as they must incorporate the incentives introduced by migration. Varying predictions of British Pakistani marriage patterns have been due to the different weighting given to the factors employed in the calculations. In Shaw's (2001) schema, socio-economic interests in Britain are balanced against obligations to kin and opportunities for financial connections in Pakistan. In earlier writing, she had predicted that local socio-economic interests would outweigh those in Pakistan, so that 'families may tend to select a spouse from among kin in Britain rather than in Pakistan, on the basis of economic interests, equality of status and the compatibility of spouses', and might for the same reasons increasingly marry non-relatives in Britain (Shaw 1988: 107). As it became evident that the trend has been towards increasing transnational marriage, largely with close kin, she revised her assessment by introducing two additional explanatory factors. The first is that under current immigration restrictions, marriage is the primary means to continue labour migration to the UK. However, the fact that equal numbers of (less economically active) women come to Britain for marriage suggests that this is not the main motivation. Instead, she stresses obligation to family in Pakistan as the chief factor in British Pakistanis' choice of a spouse from Pakistan for their children (Shaw 2001). Fulfilling these obligations, she notes elsewhere, has the additional benefit of enhancing reputation. Close kin marriage is thus publically 'expressive' of the solidarity of the kin group (Shaw 2000a: 154).[8]

In 1987, Roger Ballard wrote that Pakistani parents in Britain:

> ... usually find themselves under intense pressure to accept offers of marriage on behalf of their siblings' children back in Pakistan. And they also know that if they refuse, they are likely to be charged with having become so anglicised that they have forgotten their most fundamental duties towards their kin. These pressures are extremely hard to resist. So as more and more migrants' children reach marriageable age, the frequency of marriage with partners back in Pakistan is rising rapidly.
>
> (Ballard 1987: 27)

A major part of the obligation to kin is economic. One of the stock answers an ethnographer receives in Pakistan when enquiring about the reasons for close kin marriages is that they are arranged in order to keep the family assets together. As sons inherit land and property, and daughters receive their dowry, intermarriage between siblings' children prevents the fragmentation of resources. Pakistani university students told me stories to illustrate how women may suffer as a result: girls married to unsuitable men (younger/much older/disabled/ugly) simply because they are cousins; or Pathans or 'tribal lords' who marry their daughters to the Quran Sharif under the guise of a religious act, to prevent them marrying out for lack of a match within the family. Some of my Bristol case studies could be interpreted in this light. Nabila's marriage to her mother's sister's son in Bristol, for example, was described in the last chapter as arranged in order to strengthen the relationship between two sisters. However, Nabila's grandmother also desired the match to strengthen her descendants' claim to a row of shops in Pakistan. The old woman's British-resident daughter's husband had given power of attorney over the shops to his step-brothers, who then refused to relinquish it, so marrying a granddaughter into this son-in-law's family might re-establish a right to the property. A similar story of seeking access to lost assets through marriage is told by Junaid in Chapter 7. Forms of cultural capital, particularly education, may equally be guarded within the family. On hearing of my project, one British father's first words to me on the subject were, 'If a boy – it used to be a boy in those days – has a degree or something, [then] the family should benefit'. This father's statement, however, suggests an additional perspective on the role assets play in marriage. Rather than an obligation to keep assets within the kin group, marriage can be an opportunity to share benefits. So one woman told me that her friend wanted to marry her daughter to her sister's son, despite the daughter's doubts, in order to give her sister in Pakistan a large dowry. While men living in Britain commonly remit money to their family in Pakistan, a woman's family (as outlined in Chapter 1) is generally not expected to receive anything from her after marriage, so the wedding of a child presented an opportunity to share the comparative wealth of life in Bristol with a sibling.

However, as the argument over family property above indicates, discussion of sharing, obligations and mutually owned assets should not give the impression of the extended family or *baraderi* as a homogenous or necessarily harmonious unity.

> The [marriage] choices that are made have a far-reaching impact upon the parents, their siblings, their siblings' children, and a range of other relatives, affecting the futures and socio-economic positions of a much wider range of kin than just parents and children. For this reason, decisions about marriage are a matter of corporate, not individual, concern. At the same time, the interests of those with a stake in the outcome of a marriage negotiation are often quite conflicting and competing.
>
> (Shaw 2001: 325)

Differing interests within the *baraderi* do not just concern socio-economic matters, but extend to considerations of power within the kin group. A Bristol taxi driver elaborated on this theme, describing a system called *hath* (hand) or *bawan* (arms) (cf. Kurin 1984: 211), in which spouses are chosen on the basis of 'points' in a network of male power. He himself was married out of the circle of cousins, to his brother's wife's sister, and so if he needed support within the family, the only 'hands' he had to help him were his own brothers. Those who married cousins, on the other hand, can count on support from all the cousins, with whom consanguineal bonds have been strengthened by affinity. In addition, if a man's wife has many brothers, they gain more 'points'.[9] 'It's all about power', he said, relating a story from their village in Pakistan where a 'Beauty' was married to a 'Beast' from Bristol:

> Everybody wanted to marry her, but they were all two points, four points. The Beast was twenty points, because he was her first cousin. That gives the most power, family-wise. Not just with the brothers and sisters, but all the cousins. Power means if anything happens in the family they will back you, be with you.

Although only a few older women among my other contacts in Bristol recognised the term *bawan*, and those who did said that it had fallen out of use, many old and young recognised the advantages of marrying into a large family within your close kin group.

Bawan, how many hands or arms you have behind you, only gives power within the extended family. Nonetheless, networks of male relatives do operate to defend family interests if threatened from outside. During earlier research in Bristol, a young man in charge of the family shop boasted to me that if there was any trouble, he could make one phone call and summon immediate back-up from relatives in businesses around Bristol, and such a network did appear to be put into action after an attack on a member of another prominent shop-keeping family. Brothers may feel they have to defend family honour by challenging men or boys who may be involved with their sisters (e.g. Shaw 2000a: 169), and in a few cases, 'blood feuds' between families in Pakistan have led to murders in Britain. I will return to issues of masculinity, honour and rifts within kin groups in the final chapters of this book.

The advantage of a large family in terms of support is only one side of the coin. Just as involvement in the 'community' is both valued and resented, there may be negative aspects to marrying into a large family. Hence, one mother who had recently arranged her daughter's marriage said she was glad that the fiancé's family was small because her daughter would face less competition from sisters-in-law.[10] Significantly, this also hints at something that does not feature in models of marriage choice as strategies for maximising assets, social capital or social power: the wish to protect yourself, or those you care about, from hurt – in other words, to manage risk.

The other side of the benefits of marrying 'in', are the dangers of marrying 'out'. I have heard Sumera from Bristol, who married a non-relative from Pakistan, described as 'alone' because her male support networks were weak: her father had died and her brother was disabled. When her husband mistreated her and married again in Pakistan without her permission, I was told that he was able to do this only because of her lack of support. The plight of a woman 'alone' is considered so great that in this case other members of the community stepped in as surrogate kin: work-mates ostracised the husband, and one even offered to have him arrested or injured the next time he went to Pakistan.

The issue of risk in transnational marriage re-occurred time and time again during my fieldwork. Lutz and White (1986: 421) suggest that frequently appearing emotions may illustrate 'points of tension' in social structure:

> The fact that emotions are, in many societies, a critical link in cultural interpretations of action implies that emotion concepts are likely to be actively used in the negotiations of social reality ... Attention to emotional rhetoric and discourse, then, should be a fruitful focus for ethnographic investigations of social life as an active and creative process.
> (Lutz and White 1986: 420)

The risks involved in transnational marriage present one such 'point of tension'. As such, the issue may be used to illuminate the wider field of marriage and kinship negotiated over distance.

Shareen's cousin marriage: already I know him

At this point, I would like to introduce Shareen, a 27-year-old Bristolian woman who married her mother's brother's son in Pakistan when she was 19. Whilst much of the literature above focuses on parental motivations for marriage, Shareen provides information on her own involvement in the process. The couple now have children of their own, so she is able to talk not only of her own decisions on which *rishta* to accept, but also of her thoughts on her own children's future marriages. In her narrative themes recur from the last chapter, such as the desire to keep connections with Pakistan, but are interwoven with new threads concerning trust, risk and kinship as she describes how her family tried to ascertain which of the young men would make a suitable match. Her options included kin and non-kin, and British and Pakistani candidates. She speaks rapidly in a soft Bristolian accent.

> When we went to their houses, my mum would say to me ... [whispering] 'This is the one that we were thinking of giving you to'. So anyway, my eyes were sort of sealed at them. And then I'd look, I wouldn't just focus on him, 'cos at the end of the day – OK, I'm going to marry him – but it's the family, the people, everything, that you need to look at. So obviously I had my sister with me for an opinion, my brother, and my mother there – other people doing their observations as well as my own. But we never ever had an opportunity to be alone. Because it wasn't allowed for us to be on our own unless something official was sort-of said [i.e. the match was agreed]. So we were never on our own, it was always with the family. So there's certain things you can say to one another, rather than getting more to know each other.
>
> We had our meetings with a few of the families ... they were family – my dad's side of the family, and my mum's side of the family, and there were one or two of my dad's friends. So we went to all of their houses because my mum and dad said, 'Well, we'll go and see them all' ... They called us for a meal and everything, and we sort of sit together and have a chat ... And he was actually the third family that I'd seen. Because he was obviously my relative anyway, I already knew his parents and the sisters and everything – it was just straight in there, have a chat. It was a lot more easier. Anyway, it wasn't the fact that that was why I thought I want to marry him. I don't know – I liked his dad, my uncle, my *mamu*. I really liked him from the beginning. When we were little he used to talk to me, and he used to always send me things, and I used to always really like him. I thought, 'It'll be really nice if I have a nice father-in-law'. Because he was already so sweet and nice with me from before, you know, I'll always have that nice with him [i.e. things will always be good between them], already I know him.
>
> So I said to my mum, I want to go to their house again ... and this time it was OK because it was me, my sister, and his sister. And we had our little group, and just talking. But Oh! – it was a bit shy; bit shy to say your words and everything! But we got there in the end. Sort of spoke about each other, and what do you do and everything. And I said to my husband that actually, yeah I quite like him and everything, even though we'd just had two times to visit each other. But I said I could understand, and I could see from what I could see that I'd be quite happy with him. Said you know, 'His family's nice, his house is nice and everything, his

sisters are nice'. And I said, 'You know I think I'll feel more comfortable there than going to somebody that I'm not even sure with, and family that I've never heard about … I don't think I really want that'.

I did have other people ask me proposals from over here, but I said to my mum, I said, 'You know, boys' understanding is a lot more different to what they are over there … I've seen the boys here, but I also want to go and see families there'. And I said 'You know, if I'm happy with somebody there then I'll go for it. If not, then I've got all these people who've asked for my hand here anyway' … Their understanding of, their life is a lot more different, they're more laid back. Thing is here is like, I don't know, I've just seen lots of people and their marriages here and I think you know you don't probably have that more respect that you probably do with a husband over from Pakistan. I think you understand the culture, whereas if you get married here you never go back to your own country, you never ever show your kids that … the only way to have that bond is for you to get married to somebody like from over there. And I said, 'I quite like that actually'. But I said to my mum, 'You know, we'll go and have a look'. 'Cos my brothers were married you see and they're from that same sort of: married-over-there-and-come-here … So I did have *rishte* [in the UK], but my mum said [to them] we're going to go hopefully [to] Pakistan and if we do find somebody for her, get married, if not then we'll think about yours when we get back.

… We had loads of proposals from my dad's family as well as friends and everything, so obviously if [non-relatives] weren't in mind my dad could have said no to them – just said we're not interested in friends and whatever, but they never [did]. They said if it's a good family, good people then I don't see why … [but] I think it's quite a bonus, because if you marry in the family, you know, they know you. You've got that strong bond before you even start from like day one getting to know the people. And then you've got the family support as well. And instead of a person coming from all that distance to here, and not having a family here apart from his wife, and building that – it's hard for them … but I feel that it's more comfortable for a girl or a boy to come into a family which they don't, OK, *know*, but they're related to in a sense. Just makes it a lot more easier and everything. And I felt that I wanted it like that anyway.

… I've got my dad's cousin-sisters here [i.e. first cousins], and I've got my mum's cousin-brothers and their kids and that here, but I didn't really want to marry them. They're more like dosser sort of boys. I just thought, I don't think I could see them being married and settled! I said they're already into their life here and you can't really develop or change them in any way. If a person's come from there, they're obviously going to change because the lifestyle's different. And I thought, well – it will give them a time to do something better for their life. I may as well give somebody an opportunity from there than somebody that's already here, d'you know?

Two [of my sisters], the two after me, they went to get married. And I've given them the same advice. I said, 'Go and have a look ... Spend a bit of time with them, as well as with the family'. And I didn't say there are things that you should look out for – I said, 'Don't just focus straight on the boy'. OK, you do that automatically, but I do say the family is equally important. 'OK, look at the style of life they've got, the way they do things. That's how you're going to be able to fit yourself in that picture. If you can't see yourself fitting in there, then', I said, 'you need to think really seriously' ... I said, 'Don't just do it thinking that you want to go ahead and do it, and your parents aren't really happy for you. I said don't make that decision, because you can't lose your family over your husband to be' ...

I went over [to see her future husband], I had my brother with me, so my brother was asking lots of questions. And they went out together with my husband there, and my brother said, 'It's really good, he's not a waster and he doesn't even smoke!' And he goes, my brother was saying to him, 'Come on, let's have a fag!' or something, just like boys do, just sort of testing. He said, 'No, I don't smoke, and my dad's never taught me to smoke, and I'm not going to smoke'. [So the brother said] 'Oh, I'd better put my fag away then' – but my brother don't smoke, it's was just, you know, a test that you do. And my brother said they went to a café to have a drink and everything and my brother said to him, 'Let's go and sit over there. There's some girls over there, let's go and tease them!' – just to see what the person's nature's like. And my husband said, 'No – we shouldn't really do that because we've got sisters of our own, and somebody could do that to our sisters'. And my brother said, 'He's a good lad, he's a decent guy – you'd better go for it!' ... I said [to my sisters], 'Get to know his sisters and they'll be able to tell you a bit more about him'. Because I said, 'You're not going to go to him directly and ask him, so you've got his family there as well, so why not use them' ... If you're happy, mum and dad happy, they're happy – then I said, 'Go for it – you've got nothing to worry about! It's only a matter of time that you have to wait to get them [to Britain], that's the only hardest bit!'

Well it's difficult [to say where her children will be married], because all my family lives here, you see. All my brothers and sisters live here. And my husband's only got two sisters, and they're not even married yet, so they haven't got children that match with my children. And my brothers, they've got kids. I'm not saying, 'Yeah – they'll marry there' [to her brother's children]. Somebody good can just come from Pakistan, because my husband's brought up there and he's really in contact with his friends and everything there. Some of them are married and everything and I went to see them when I went to Pakistan. You never know, if it's a good friend and it's a good family, persons like each other and everything, you never know. I would never say, '*Yes*, they will marry from Pakistan'. I would never say, 'They'll marry from here'. 'Cos at the end of the day, we have to look where they're going to be happy.

Because our time was different – how we were brought up. And we're a lot more independent with things, so our children will grow up like that. But at the end of the day, I will tell them of families over there because again, I don't want them to stop having that relationship that we did. So I will encourage them and take them to Pakistan, but I would never force them or I'd never say to them that this is what we've chosen for you because it didn't happen to me and I don't see why it should happen to them.

I say to my sisters, 'It's a shame my husband hasn't got a brother', 'cos I would have asked my sisters to marry my husband's brothers. Then they could have been my sister-in-laws!

Reducing risk: knowledge and nature

'At the end of the day,' said Shareen, 'we have to look where they're going to be happy.' Arranging a marriage is an emotionally risky business, and the marriage of a daughter is considered particularly difficult. The literature on South Asia stresses the financial burden of marrying a daughter, providing a dowry which she will take to another household: 'Feeding a daughter is like watering a tree in another man's garden' (Brown, cited in Bradby 2000).[11] However, for the Pakistani mothers I talked to in Bristol, it was the danger of causing their daughter unhappiness by an unwise choice that was of most concern.

A wife, at least conceptually, is in the vulnerable position of moving to her in-laws' home. In Bristol, Humera told me that 'everything depends on the husband, what he's like'. Stories circulate among women in Bristol about husbands who have serious drug or alcohol problems, are violent, have left their wives for other women (most often non-Pakistanis), or contracted second marriages. However, even if her husband is good to the bride, her sisters- and mother-in-law may not be. This fear is evinced by the stereotypes of cruel mothers-in-law that abound throughout the subcontinent, and in the traditional attempt to divine whether the mother-in-law will love the bride by the strength of colour given by her bridal *mehndi* patterns.

Humera complained that women are always blamed for any trouble in a marriage. If the marriage does end in divorce, suspicion that the woman may have caused the problem may contribute to the difficulty for the woman to remarry (cf. Jeffery 2001).[12] By 2008, it seemed to me that divorce and remarriage were becoming more acceptable in Bristol, particularly among younger people, but they remained more problematic for women than men. Even if a second match can be found, their motivations for accepting a wife who has already been married might be suspect. Lifestage also makes a difference: if a divorced woman has children, for example, the second husband might not treat them well, or even insist that they be sent to live with their father's family. Hafza in Bristol, who endured years of verbal and physical abuse before leaving her husband, said she had seen one man – '*bas!*' (enough/stop). Nighat, a Mirpuri woman whose husband left her and her daughters for his Indian girlfriend, attempted to commit suicide rather than face the prospect of life as a divorced woman. It is no wonder, then, that parents of girls are described as *majbur* (helpless; oppressed; in need) in the matter of arranging marriage, with the knowledge that if it goes wrong, their daughter is likely to come off worse. For this reason, as many people have told me, 'if a good *rishta* comes [for a girl], you take it'.

Ghalib married into Britain in 1976. He explains the risk he would be taking if he found *rishte* for his children outside the family:

> I'm a really very open-minded person ... but I must admit my weakness. I'm still stuck in that family resistance [i.e. tied to the idea of marriage within the kin group] ... I don't know why, but it's just in my mind. I think if I stick in my family it will be better than if I go out. And that's only a fear. And that fear is I don't know what they will be ...

The most common reason given for marrying close kin is that they are known and so whether they would make a good match, and whether the in-laws will treat a daughter well, can be more effectively judged. As Shareen said of her mother's brother as a prospective father-in-law, 'already I know him', whilst another woman in Bristol described her migration as 'a bit like going from my house across the road to my auntie's house to live but just further away'. 'Because it's family,' she said, 'there wasn't really that much of an adjustment for me to make. I already knew the family.' Her husband's brother's wife, meanwhile, who did not have this close 'blood' link, reported that she received harsher treatment from her in-laws than did her sister-in-law (the cousin-wife). In Pakistani fiction, matches with non-kin are often disastrous. In one cautionary tale reported by Das (1973: 36), an outspoken educated wife dragged her husband to England, where his life was so miserable that he contracted tuberculosis. The need for knowledge of the spouse's nature is particularly important in transnational marriages, with the fear that Pakistani spouses may just be 'marrying a passport', or that British Pakistanis' values may have been contaminated by growing up in the decadent West, leading to unacceptable behaviour such as alcohol use or premarital liaisons.[13] Marrying within the family provides a range of trusted referees in the form of mutual kin, who can advise on the character of the proposed spouse and their family. In other words, risk is managed through trust based on the bonds of kinship.[14]

The 'nature' of close kin is also thought more likely to be similar (cf. Carsten 1997; Fischer and Lyon 2000). Fischer and Lyon suggest that Pakistani understandings of similarity between kin help account for the statistical preference they found in Lahore for marriage between the children of same-sex siblings. Brothers, they write, 'are more like each other than they are like their sisters, and *vice versa*'. Similarity travels down the generations, so the children of same-sex siblings are likely to be most alike from the pool of available first cousins (Fischer and Lyon 2000: 305). A couple who are similar in this way are more likely to 'understand' each other. Along with wealth, the female university students I met in Pakistan rated this 'understanding' – the mutual compatibility of their personalities – very highly in what they hoped for in a husband. Although girls are told from a young age of the need to 'adjust'[15] and compromise in marriage, parents hope that similarities will ensure the couple's compatibility, and therefore their children's future happiness. At the British High Commission, an official told me that many British Pakistani women who report being forced to marry a Pakistani relative say that they later came to love or be contented with their husband, as parents want their children to be happy, and so tend not to choose someone completely unsuitable. One woman who was married at 16, while stressing the trauma of the experience of being suddenly married to a man she had never met before, told me: 'I was lucky, I was forced to marry a really nice bloke.'[16]

Mines, writing of Tamil Muslims in south India, goes so far as to suggest that endogamy is based not on notions of substance, but on the desire to arrange matches between 'spouses who share the same economic backgrounds and the same cultural and, especially, religious traditions' (Mines 1978: 164). One woman I was told about in Pakistan rejected all proposals from outside the family for her son because she could not stand the idea of visits by people she did not know, but who were relatives of the bride. Couples who are relatives are more likely to be able to 'mix up' easily with each other and each other's families, as their lifestyles will be closer. Gafoora's daughter Salma had mixed with her male cousins, so she and her mother could judge their suitability for marriage with each other on this basis, but as the family had decided not to choose a match within the *baraderi*, these known quantities were not to be pursued, Gafoora's plans for her daughter again involved looking for similarities: for example, she did not want a family much richer than theirs because their lifestyles and values would be too different, and she felt that Salma would not adjust well.[17] In the end, Salma's marriage was arranged with the brother of one of her classmates, a relationship that allowed for the development of knowledge of the other family, and avoided the typical 'viewing' experience.

Continua and processes of relatedness

Similarity and compatibility is not simply due to sharing substance, being 'of one blood', and attributed to all members of the *baraderi*. Ties of kinship may be created, as Carsten (1997) has demonstrated in work on the 'process of inship' in Malaysia, documenting how marriage and everyday acts such as feeding and exchange incorporate newcomers and create and maintain bonds of relatedness. In her work on Pakistanis in Manchester, Werbner (1990) discusses a 'process of ethnicity', in which the flow of gifts and marriage partners between Britain and Pakistan underpins 'ethnic renewal'. Undermining the separation between spheres of ethnicity, kinship and friendship, she suggests a continuum of relatedness, created through and indexed by a 'hierarchy of exchange', and postulates a single scale of increasing 'value, exclusivity and trust' linking the categories of neighbours, workmates, business associates, close friends, kinsmen and close kinsmen (Werbner 1990: 221) in a 'friendship-cum-kinship network' (Werbner 1990: 128; cf. Baumann 1995). Hence, one migrant wife in Bristol described how her mother had felt unable to refuse a transnational request for her daughter's hand from a longstanding family friend, and who her daughter called *mamu* (mother's brother): 'it's the first time my brother has asked me for anything in all the years we've known them and I don't want to say no.' Just as friendships are made through exchange and unmade through quarrelling or refusing gifts, kinship relations can be made or unmade through marriage or residential proximity, which sustain or neglect connections (Donnan 1988). As demonstrated in the preceding chapter, geographical distance mediates 'closeness' between kin in purely genealogical terms, so that a first cousin residing in the same city in Britain will often be considered 'closer' than another living in Pakistan.

The linear image of a continuum should not, however, be allowed to obscure differences in the nature of these relationships. In a study of relatedness among Hindus in north India, Lambert (2000a) suggests a continuity in the conceptualisation of consanguineal and 'optative' relations created by substance and sustenance (which correlate with affection), but a contrast with relationships of kinship alone with affines. Such a division is, however, unlikely among Pakistanis. For exogamous Hindus, the non-sharing of substance is a pre-requisite for marriage, whereas in Pakistani marriages between close kin, the non-separation of kin and affines is reflected by the fact that only husband and wife alter their use of kinship terminology towards each other after marriage (Das 1973: 42). Bonds of kinship are ideologically divided from friendship by notions of shared substance (Das 1973: 175), and marriage choices are influenced by hierarchies of caste and class where friendships are based on relations of equality.[18]

In Shaw's (2001) Oxford survey, informants categorised marriages as either with kin or 'outside', but Werbner (1990) notes distinctions within the category of kin: the *ghar* (literally house, meaning extended family), close kinsmen, and kinsmen. Kinship, to make a rather weak pun, is evidently relative. In discussing matches, my informants make clear distinctions between close kin (usually first or second cousins), and more distant relatives (e.g. *dur se* – far). Where a relationship was distant and complicated, or the exact connection between husband and wife unclear, they might be described as 'just *baraderi*'. The closer the relative, the more secure the knowledge about the potential spouse, and so the safer the marriage is considered to be. In theory, then, a match with a close friend's child might be considered preferable in terms of security to one with a distant relative. It will be remembered that Shareen has her eye on the children of Pakistani friends of her husband, with whom he maintains close contact, as possible matches for her children.

In practice, multiple factors can deter matches with non-kin. One of the reasons for a preference for kinship-based similarity, above, was that the spouse should be able to fit in socially with their in-laws, and there are limits to the extent of difference that families will tolerate. Some elders insist on marriage within the family. In Bristol, one man's father threatened to cut him off financially and did not speak to him for months until he abandoned his plans to marry the woman of his choice and accepted a match with a relative, while a middle-aged woman said her father was 'very strict': if you married outside of the *baraderi* you were 'ex-communicated' for seven generations. Some will accept marriages out of *zat* but may, as Punjabis, object to a Mirpuri spouse, or vice versa. Such considerations may be mixed with ideas of class or rural/urban difference, so one migrant wife in Bristol from an urban Arian family commented of her family's marriage preferences: 'we would be happy to do it [marry] in Jat [a different caste] – but like people from Mirpur, that's so far we can't be mixed with them ... because they're in a different part of the country and their standard of living is different. There is a difference in how people are brought up in cities and villages.' For others, the boundary is the ethnic group: a father who has accepted that his children will marry out of the *baraderi* told his daughter she could not marry an Indian Muslim because the wider family would not accept it. 'Some people are brave,' he said, 'but I won't allow my children.'

Baumann (1996) has documented the commonalities that transcend ethnicity in friendships and interactions in Southall, and most young Bristol Pakistanis have friends from different ethnic groups, but marriage is often another matter. Although many younger people appeal to the laws of Islam to argue that the limit should be religion, many families would object to a marriage with a non-Pakistani.[19] In addition to the ease with which the spouse could mix within the family, and a concern with cultural reproduction, the issue of trust based on similarity is a further important factor. There is a general sense, writes Werbner (1990: 71), that 'relations between Pakistanis are underpinned by a set of shared cultural premises', such that *kameti* rotating credit schemes, for example, can operate on trust. This ethnic bond of cultural morality should extend to marriage: when Sumera's husband married again, she complained that although she knew Pakistani men used white women to gain visas, she hadn't expected him to do it to 'one of his own'.

Rayner (1992) suggests that people deal with risk not as the standard calculation of 'probability x consequences', but are concerned with 'fairness', rooted in considerations of 'trust', 'liability' and 'consent'.[20] Kin links provide the basis for all three: trust based on moral obligations and similarity between kin, group sanctions to hold a transgressing spouse to account, and kinship provides networks along which marriages can be negotiated. Harriss (2003) suggests that formulations of trust are based on characteristics, process/experience, or institutions such as societal norms, and that character assessments can be specific or generic. Close kin marriages, I suggest, are felt by many of my

Close kin marriage: reducing risk 103

informants to hold out the possibility of solid and multiple routes to trust. Specific knowledge of the character of a close relative is cemented by trust in the general commonalities felt to exist between kin and co-ethnics. The success of other relatives' close kin marriages may further increase confidence in this type of match, whilst the values of kin solidarity and mutual obligation provide a further basis for trust.

One angle on the betrayals perceived by British Pakistanis such as Sumera is to question whether her husband in fact felt that his wife was 'one of his own'. Ethnicity, it has often been noted, is contextual (e.g. Nazroo 1997: 8–9). In Chapter 2 I described situations in which young British Pakistanis perceive and present their identities as separate from those of Pakistani nationals. The security of close kin marriage, on the other hand, relies heavily on commonalities and a shared identity.[21] Moreover, ethnicity has a dual nature: the identity a group claims for itself, and that attributed to them by others (Guibernau and Rex 1997). It seems that the assessments of transnational ethnic unity, or even kin-based solidarity, relied upon by some of my informants in Britain for the purpose of arranging marriages, are not shared by all Pakistani immigrant spouses. The converse may be true of cases in which Pakistani spouses are mistreated or abandoned by British relatives with whom they have contracted marriages. The transnational 'trust networks' providing social insurance and social control described by Tilly (2007) as crucial to many forms of migration, here appear as more perspectival constructs. They are, moreover, potentially riven by competing interests which may undermine the basis for relationships of trust – the 'human dynamics of transnationalism' (Carling 2008) discussed further in subsequent chapters.

In Muslim and Hindu marriages in north India, knowledge and trust are crucial, not only in assessing matters that may affect the future happiness of a son or daughter, but also in predicting dowry and other demands. Ahmad suggests that the security of endogamy is a feature of low-status marriages among Muslims in India, whereas the socially mobile are more likely to take the risk of exogamy with its possibility of new and fruitful alliances, and increased status (Ahmad 1978b: 175–76). Jeffery and Jeffery, however, report hearing that even urban Hindus were adopting close kin marriage for just the reasons of trust and risk outlined above (Jeffery and Jeffery 1996: 98–99). Transnational marriages introduce an additional distance, and therefore additional risk. Even between close kin, for example, the distance between the two countries may increase the chances of concealing love affairs, or rumours of love affairs, which could damage reputation and marriage prospects, particularly for a young woman (Shaw 1988: 175). In this sense, migration has introduced additional risk by undermining the trust based on knowledge of one's kin. Nonetheless, this section has suggested that the concern to reduce risk plays an important role in Bristol Pakistanis' frequent choices of relatives as spouses for their children. Assumptions of similarity and greater knowledge, together with cultural deterrents for marrying 'out', mean that they are likely to prefer matches with close kin. Moreover, transnationalism and close kin marriage may be mutually reinforcing. The hazards involved in transnational marriage, and the perceived danger that British-raised children have developed unacceptable behaviour, intensify the need for security, leading many to cling to what is perceived to be the safety provided by close kin marriage.

Thus far, the discussion has focused on similarity between spouses, but affinity 'is always a precarious balance between too much and too little closeness' (Carsten 1997: 191).[22] Again, geographical, emotional and genealogical proximity combine in creating what is thought of as 'too close', just as they create distance that is held to entail risk. Among Muslims in north India, for example, Jeffery and Jeffery write of the need to balance the physical distance between a girl's natal and marital homes carefully. The parental bond must be adequately broken to avoid interference in the daughter's married life, but if a marriage is arranged too far away, then kin are physically missing and emotionally missed (Jeffery and Jeffery 1996: 216–17). A mother in Bristol, for example, said that she would prefer to find a *rishta* for her daughter outside Bristol. Whilst she would love to keep her daughter close, if she lived nearby the danger of becoming involved in the couple's marital problems and making the situation worse for her child would be too great. The other side of such concerns was illustrated with regard to transnational marriage in Chapter 3, when the father of a student in Rawalpindi decided he could not bear to send both his daughters overseas in marriage.

Marriage migration is thus a double-edged sword. It may strengthen relationships between kin in disparate locations, but simultaneously reproduces distance between the migrant and the kin they leave behind; it creates 'orphans'. In addition to the loss of companionship or emotional support, there are practical implications of 'missing' kin, as women with no mother-in-law to assist with children may be burdened with an unusually heavy workload.[23] Other families compensate for the loss of resident kin, so that Asma may not have her Pakistani husband's relatives around to help care for her two young children, but she spends a great deal of time at her mother's home, where sisters, brothers and her mother all help with childcare. Chapter 7 will consider the implications of such situations for immigrant husbands.

Place of residence and the environment in which the young person has grown up are also thought to influence their character. Here, too, there may be such a thing as too much similarity, as I have heard of marriages between two British-raised people described as unlikely to succeed because they will both be too strong-willed. The implication is that in marriage it is necessary for at least one party to compromise. Pakistani girls may be taught from a young age that they will have to 'adjust' to their husband's family's ways of life, but some view young women raised in Britain as less likely to heed this traditional advice. Residence in Britain thus seems in this respect to erode gendered difference, damaging the complementarity between husband and wife, and leading to potential conflict.

Some Pakistanis in Bristol are wary of matches with other British Pakistanis for fear that they will have been contaminated by what they perceive to be the amoral climate of the West. This issue comes to the fore in the context of the cultural and religious reproduction implied by marriage and childbearing. A spouse from Pakistan may be thought to be more religious, or more traditional, bringing another element of difference that will benefit the marriage and prevent the loss of such traits in the next generation through two similarly 'modern' or religiously lax British-raised parents. When Gafoora visited Britain, she heard the term 'practising Muslim' for the first time, and finds the phrase ridiculous. Nevertheless, the idea that a *rishta* in Pakistan may be a connection to more Islamic behaviour is pertinent to British Muslims. When Gafoora asked one of her relatives why she was looking for a *rishta* in Pakistan, the woman replied with a list of marriages between British-born Pakistanis that had failed, suggesting that one hope is that a Pakistani will bring with them a more committed approach to marriage as a result of growing up in a Muslim country.

One young man in Bristol, Wasim, told me at length about the failings of the local Pakistani community: children affected by the behaviour of other pupils at rough inner-city schools, the proliferation of mobile phones leading to illicit communication between the sexes, and fathers who neglect their children's moral development in order to devote their lives to working long hours in shops or taxis. He said that when he was ready to marry, he decided to abandon his desire for a beautiful wife, in order to have 'someone who won't be going out all the time and who'll always be there for me'. Aware of his own lack of religious practice and knowledge, he hoped that a wife from Pakistan would be able to teach their children about Islam. Talib similarly explained why he preferred to marry a woman from Pakistan:

> I really didn't actually want to marry somebody from this country – not really, no. I really wanted to marry with somebody from back home, to keep myself with my origins, you know. I didn't actually really want someone who was, you know – bossy and pushy ... That's how people are here, and that's how the Muslim girls especially, the environment that they're brought up in nowadays, I don't think I could have adjusted with one of them – any of them. That's why I really wanted someone from Pakistan. I wanted someone who would be quiet, loving, caring, understanding. You know – someone to be with you in joy. And someone in the family ... And that's what Allah Tallah wanted, that's what God wanted, and he set me up with a nice person.

For many British Pakistani men there is a conceptual opposition between the archetypal British Pakistani girl who wants to go out all the time, may be loud and argumentative, 'does fashion' and might have indulged in immoral activities, and a quiet, cooperative, sheltered, religious Pakistani girl who will make a good mother. The latter is described as 'simple'. Wasim, whose desire for a simple bride is mentioned above, also hinted at the perceived benefits in terms of domestic power relationships (cf. Lievens 1999) that a 'simple' wife might bring when he asked her only to address him in Urdu so that she would use the respectful '*aap*', similar to the French 'vous', a distinction unavailable in English.

When looking for a *rishta*, outward symbols of religious commitment can be employed to make judgements in the context of limited interaction before making a decision. For women, the *hijab* is the most powerful such symbol, and some young men specifically look for wives who wear it. Concerned over the morals of British-raised Pakistanis, Omar, from Karachi, was reassured when he saw that the young woman from Bristol who had been suggested for him wore a headscarf.

> My opinion after college – it's my wish to get married a girl who is wearing *hijab*. So [wife] wears *hijab* yeah … So that's why I was ready to marry her – 'Oh yeah she's wearing *hijab*' … The thing is actually, as I told you earlier on, I really like it because [in] Islam – to be a wife, you've got to be, nobody can see her like in the dress … she wear in front of me. Obviously my wife I know better than *anybody* else. After marriage, even her parents they don't know … obviously what I know about her … because obviously there is no secrets between husband and wife. So that's why I wanted to get married to a girl who wears *hijab*, because it's part of Islam as well.

Azra, a religious young woman from Bristol, was specifically searching for someone who shared her commitment to Islam. She was looking for 'A kind person, and a beard! [giggles] Because it's religious you see, it's *sunnat*, which means Muslim men have to have a beard'.

A match between two religiously committed people tends to be considered ideal, but one such spouse in a marriage is often seen as preferable to the dangerous similarity of a husband and wife, and later mother and father, who both neglect religious knowledge and practice.

In terms of kinship, there are obviously clear rules as to who is 'too close' to marry. Whilst the children of parents' siblings may be married, one's own siblings may not. This may seem a facile point, but has interesting linguistic ramifications as people create and narrate levels of closeness and distance between those who are potential spouses and those who are not. The term *bhai* (brother), it has been noted, is used by Punjabis to address cousins and indeed acquaintances of similar age, but seldom as a term of address for actual brothers (Das 1976: 216–18). Baumann (1995) reports the widespread use of the classification 'cousin' among young people in Southall, and suggests that Sikh parents encourage relations of cousinship for their children in order to discourage love relationships. Muslims, he observed, used the term less, because of its directly opposite connotations of marriageability. In Bristol, I heard the term cousin used frequently, but often in combination with statements like 'he's my brother', or in the compound nouns 'cousin-brother' or 'cousin-sister'. I would suggest that the ambiguity of these terms – *bhai*, brother/sister, cousin – in terms of what they imply of marriageability is employed by young people to negotiate the category of potential spouses.

Many young British Pakistanis, influenced by the dominant discourse of disapproval of cousin marriage in Britain (see Shaw 2001), consider their local cousins 'too close' to marry. Nineteen-year-old Leyla reflected:

> It just wouldn't seem possible to get married to someone in England who's your cousin, because we've got quite open relationships with each other, cousins, and brothers and sisters. It's all like one big family, we just regard it as a family, rather than, you know. And then when it's mentioned – there's a possibility of you getting married – it's a very strange way of understanding. But there it's very common.

Asma, it might be remembered from the previous chapter, attributed the fact that she knew her British cousin 'too well' to marry him, to the well-trodden linkages between residential proximity, association and emotional closeness: 'I've lived with him, went to nursery with him, school with him. He's like your brother and you're like, "Yuck, I don't want to marry you!"' These young people might otherwise be considered by their elders to be potential matches on the basis of close kinship links and knowledge derived from residential proximity. By saying that these cousins are like brothers, or indeed calling them *bhai*, or cousin-brother, these young women are indicating to their families that they are in fact too close to marry. This sentiment may even be extended to unrelated men living locally, so that one young woman explained that she would not like to marry a boy from Bristol as she would 'know too much about him'. A certain distance, then, is necessary to make space for affinity within bonds of kinship and locality.

Young British Pakistanis often do not have these uncomfortable feelings of excessive closeness about cousins in Pakistan whom they may only have seen occasionally. Some young people to whom I have spoken retained a slight uneasiness about the situation, as, for example, they might have to justify their marriage with a cousin to non-Pakistani friends. Saif, Leyla's mother's brother, worried about both the closeness and the generational difference in his arranged marriage:

> I wasn't sure whether it was legal or not, but they convinced me. I was a bit wary. I mean cousin's quite close in itself, but cousin's daughter – I think it's even worse. It sounds even worse when you explain it to people. If they understand the generation gap and the number of years between us – nine years between us – I guess you can get away with it. But it's still a bit scary. 'Cos it's my two brothers – their two wives, [are] Aisha's eldest sisters. Sorry – I even get confused by that. My elder brothers … their wives are the sisters of Aisha's mother … Yeah, Aisha's aunties.

Nevertheless, many British Pakistanis agree to marriages to cousins in Pakistan rather than Britain. Transnationality thereby doubly influences their negotiations of the position of affinity in kin relations. Exposure to British ideas on close kin marriage may lead them to attempt to place the boundaries of the marriageable further away in genealogical terms among their cousins in Britain. On the other hand, the possibility of transnational marriage introduces potential spouses who are equally close in terms of kinship, but distant enough in other ways to be acceptable partners, whilst fulfilling the criteria of connection needed to be confident of social approval and the reduction of risk involved in such arrangements. Leyla's mother Bushra is happy with the decision for her daughter to marry in Pakistan.

> Both my sisters [in Britain] have got sons, but my daughter has always said that she felt they were like her brothers. And she always made it a bit clear that she'd seen them more and more often – they were more like cousins and brothers rather than to see them in that sort of light. And I wasn't sure about it anyway because she'd been brought up with them and they'd seen each other quite a lot. Whereas because they were in Pakistan, we didn't see him that often. It just seems more of a – kids find it easier. It does happen here, kids marry cousins here as well, but with my kids that's how it was.

Reproducing risk: dangers of the 'double *rishta*'

A final reason often given for viewing kin marriages as less risky comes into effect when marriages do run into difficulties, or where one partner is behaving badly. Unions within the family are thought to have more chance of enduring because the family will get involved to resolve the problem. I have heard accounts of couples on the verge of divorce whose differences were solved by the interventions of parents, but I also encountered many examples where this safeguard did not appear to operate. One of the common complaints from women is that their husband's family take his side in disputes, making the conflict worse.

Although one intention of a kin marriage may be to strengthen family ties, if conflict does occur between husband and wife, and particularly if they divorce, the effect can be to cause rifts within the family as other relatives take sides (cf. Carsten 1997). The root of this problem is what some called the 'double *rishta*', meaning a relationship of both blood and affinity, which leads to the fragmentation of allegiances within the family. The breakdown of a transnational marriage can be particularly serious. If the imported spouse has not yet been granted permanent residence rights, they may be deported, but women who have secured their immigration status may still face the choice of returning as a divorcée to be a cause of shame and financial burden to their families, or remaining in Britain with limited support networks. The implications of the rifts among kin groups that can result from divorce will be examined in detail in Chapters 6 and 7.

However, if marriage choices can cause family conflict, the same can be said of refusals, as parents may be insulted by the rejection of their child. One man from Britain proposed a childhood engagement between his daughter and the son of a relative in Pakistan, but the boy's father declined as he disapproved of marital decisions being made for the very young, resulting in bad feeling for years. Nabila had several proposals from relatives in Pakistan, who were jealous when she married in Bristol, and tried to sabotage her visa application by withholding documents sent by the British High Commission. Later, when she did not get pregnant for over a year, rumours were spread that her husband never touched her. Her grandmother began to worry over the state of the marriage and phoned frequently to ask the boy's father whether she was expecting yet. Another woman, who came to Bristol as a fiancée 20 years earlier, told me she did not really want to come to the UK, but her sister's husband's brothers were all fighting over her hand. She did not want to cause a long-term rift by marrying one and rejecting the others, and so accepted a proposal from abroad.

The dangers of the 'double *rishta*' may also undermine one of the sources of security in arranging marriages: the use of kin as referees and informants. A group of sisters I know in Bristol were scandalised by the engagement of one of their British cousins, a notorious womaniser by their account, to a cousin in Pakistan. They had heard that he was even chatting up a girl on the plane to Pakistan, and everyone in the family in Bristol was aware that he had a girlfriend. 'Didn't anyone tell the Pakistani girl's family?' I asked. They replied that relatives would be too afraid of being accused of causing trouble or being jealous, and of being blamed for the failure of the *rishta*, to have said anything about the situation.

One response to the hazards of marriage arrangements is to take someone from a family, or 'house' that has already been proven – where one marriage has been seen to be successful. Jamilah, who married a cousin from Pakistan, told me about a *rishta* her husband's brother had received from a relative:

> ... [the proposal] was a very recent thing – after [her husband] came to England ... Can you understand how that changes people's view now? Because there's already someone here, they can see that someone's already in a house where he's financially stable, so [they think], 'If I was to marry my daughter in that house it would be very easy for me'. Whereas to bring somebody from a different family is much more difficult. So I think there would be less chance of somebody else going [i.e. another transnational marriage being arranged with the husband's family] if he wasn't here to begin with.

Shareen, it will be remembered, wished that her husband had brothers so that her sisters could marry them. Not only would this provide husbands from a tried and tested source, but would negate some of the difficulties of the double *rishta*, as her sisters-in-law (her sisters) would be allies rather than potential

110 *Close kin marriage: reducing risk*

rivals. However, for a parent, putting all your marriage eggs in one basket does negate the possibility of compensating for rejecting a *rishta* from one side with the marriage of a subsequent child to someone from that family. Bushra told me about the proposals for her children from her husband's family, which occurred while she was visiting Pakistan.

> She [husband's sister] said, 'What it is, I wanted to bring your daughter into my family, but I wanted to also give my daughter to your family' ... That was new to me because I thought it was just Leyla, and I thought, 'OK'. And then straight away without even consulting my husband – it was his sister [who was suggesting the match] – but without even consulting him, we were sort of stood talking in the kitchen, and I said, 'What else could be better!' Because, the thing is, the children match up very well – the way they've been brought up, and we're quite similar. They're lovely kids and it just seemed like it would be OK, and I said 'yeah, that would be great!' And she was like over the moon, suddenly 'yes' had been said – because I think she was always afraid. The other thing is I've got sisters and they've got sons and daughters as well, and I think she thought that by taking both my children, you know, my sisters might not feel good about that. Because you know when you're in our families, when you've got your husband's side and then your side, there's a lot of problems sometimes where your sister wants your daughter's hand in marriage and your husband's sister as well – your sister-in-law. And there's always problems and your husband might side with their sisters, say they want your daughter to be married on that side ...

This kind of marriage represents in effect an exchange of opposite-sex siblings. This type of marriage is known as *watta-satta* (Eglar 1960; Wakil 1991), meaning giving and taking.[24] This arrangement may reduce the costs of marriage as dowry expectations will be low (Eglar 1960; Wakil 1991). It is also intended to provide security, but for many women I know in Bristol, *watta-satta* epitomises the dangers of the double *rishta*. Some told me that it was a village custom and that only a few families kept up the tradition, although Bushra is from an educated urban background. Most people I spoke to about the practice agreed that it is dangerous, running the risk of direct revenge being taken out on your daughter should your son's marriage run into difficulty. So when one man in London refused for a decade to apply for a visa for the wife he had not wanted to marry, her brothers in Pakistan retaliated by preventing their brother from co-habiting with his wife, the British man's sister. Another woman in Bristol praised a male relative as 'really good' for staying with his wife, despite the fact that her brother had divorced his sister. So, for many, *watta-satta* represents the point where the balance shifts in the risks and benefits of close kin marriage; where an attempt to reduce dangers by marrying close kin ends up producing other equally serious risks. Rifts within the family are a hazard of all unsuccessful consanguineous marriages, but in *watta-satta* each side has the potential to inflict a direct blow to the other's family honour, and cause suffering to a daughter of the other's house.

The marriage of same-sex sibling pairs is considered ideal, however, leading not only to harmony with spouses' siblings' spouses, but to a situation in the following generation where there is no conflict between matrilateral and patrilateral first cousin unions (Das 1973) – a double reduction, it would seem, of the double *rishta*'s potential for conflict. The *watta-satta* exchange marriage, on the other hand, represents a complication rather than simplification of corporate interests within the kin group, as affinity and consanguinity become entangled in a dangerously unstable web where delicate connections may be torn apart by these opposing forces.

Conclusion

This chapter has argued that whilst the move from a concern with marriage prescription and preference towards an understanding of the strategic, pragmatic and symbolic considerations involved represents a step forwards, it neglects a powerful motivating force in most Pakistani marriages that comes to the fore when considering transnational unions. I have suggested that interpretations of marriage choices among Pakistanis and the Pakistani diaspora must incorporate an understanding of the role of risk in these deliberations, and that concern to protect against the dangers intrinsic to marriage should be given a more prominent position in analyses. Discourses concerning the daughter's best interests have been described as 'rationalisations', 'best regarded as symbols of the values of "real" or "fictive" kinship solidarity' (Shaw 2000a: 158). Such marriages undoubtedly have a symbolic function as public representations of the trust between kin. However, just as the last chapter argued for the incorporation of both strategy and emotion in models of spousal selection, this chapter demonstrates the value of making space for issues of risk alongside pragmatic considerations in interpreting the popularity of close kin marriage.

Barbalet (1998) suggests that fear can lead to social change through efforts aimed at containment of the danger. Close kin transnational marriage is here presented as one such attempt to contain the hazards involved in marriage. Risk theorists have stressed the dialogic, processual nature of risk selection and management (Adams 1995; Douglas and Wildavsky 1983; Douglas 1992). Nevertheless, Adams (1995) points to what he calls the 'cultural filters' through which information on risks and benefits are understood, and which produce a cultural bias towards certain responses. Here I have outlined aspects of Pakistani conceptions of relatedness, and perceptions of the dangers and benefits of selecting spouses from Britain or Pakistan, or from within or outside the kin group. Although the mechanical metaphor of cultural filters inserted into a flow chart of rational decision making may not be appropriate, this chapter has demonstrated multiple reasons for the thus-far enduring appeal of close kin transnational marriages as a response to the various risks involved in choosing a spouse.

The interactions between transnational marriage and the selection of close kin as spouses are multiple. British Pakistanis may find Pakistani spouses preferable to locals either because of doubts over the character of British-raised young people, or because they perceive local cousins as too close to marry. In transnational marriage, on the other hand, the dangers involved encourage families to seek the security of close kin marriage. Such over-layering of affinity and consanguinity can promote good relationships by removing conflicts of interest, but some types of double *rishta* are seen as particularly prone to the danger that difficulties within one marriage will then spread to the wider kin group. Further, as will be seen later, in Yasmin's story, the incentive of migration can undermine the assumed solidarity between kin. The following chapter suggests alternative mechanisms that may be employed to reduce the risks involved in transnational marriages, whilst Chapter 6 explores the consequences when these measures fail.

Notes

1 For a review of the history of cousin marriage in Western countries, see Shaw 2009.
2 Other possible translations for *qaum* are: tribe, nation, sect, people, and religious or ethnic group (Donnan 1988: 47).
3 Compare Good on Hindu India: 'All marriages are terminologically correct in retrospect because the relationships they create supersede those existing beforehand' (in Barnard and Good 1984).
4 See Boddy 2003 for an interesting discussion of the suppression of matrilateral linkages to create the impression of patrilineages in Sudan.
5 www.borninbradford.nhs.uk/pdf/results_from_the_baseline_questionnaire.pdf (accessed 18/09/2012).
6 Cf. reports of higher rates of consanguineous marriage amongst Turkish and Moroccan migrants to Belgium than in the countries of origin (Reniers, in Lievens 1999).
7 In the literature on social medicine, Uncle Norman is the folk model of the man who flouts health advice and lives to a ripe old age (Davison *et al.* 1989).
8 Our interpretations have since converged, see Shaw and Charsley 2006; see Chapter 6 for an outline of the importance of such solidarity for *izzat* (honour).
9 Jeffery and Jeffery (1996: 208) report a north Indian wife's description of her husband without brothers as 'alone', and so vulnerable to mistreatment and exploitation.
10 Patricia Jeffery reports north Indian informants pointing out that large families can also create heavy burdens in terms of cooking for in-marrying brides (personal communication).
11 Note the contrasting discourse on daughters bringing luck in the preceding chapter. Although Muslims and Hindus in north India state preferences for sons, Jeffery's (2001) survey found gender ratios less weighted to the masculine amongst Muslims. This may suggest that ambivalence surrounding the desirability of daughters is translated into practice. Equally, however, it may reflect Islamic views on abortion and the God-given nature of children (cf. Shaw 2000b).
12 There is no prohibition on women remarrying after divorce or the death of their husbands, but the acceptability of the practice seems to decline with age. Sumera,

who was still in her twenties when her marriage broke down, was encouraged by family and friends to consider marrying again. On the other hand, I have heard an older widowed woman who wished to remarry ridiculed by other women, and Shanaz's declaration that she wouldn't want to remarry after the death of her husband was met with approval.
13 The dangers are discussed at greater length in the remaining chapters of this book.
14 Cf. Caplan (2000) on willingness to eat British beef during the BSE crisis, where trust was also based on 'knowledge'. Knowledge in this case came not from kinship but from locality – knowing the locals who raised and sold the meat.
15 The students in Pakistan and Pakistanis in Bristol both use the English word 'adjust', even when speaking in Urdu: 'adjust *karna*' (to adjust, *karna* being the verb to do).
16 I should stress that reporting these comments should not be taken as in any way condoning forced marriage.
17 Note that this family was comfortably-off.
18 Werbner (1990: 81–120) suggests that the independent ideologies of hierarchy and Islamic equality are mediated by the *baraderi*, conceptualised not only as a 'brotherhood', but also as the local marriage unit.
19 See Chapter 6 for an example of one woman's creative solution to this situation.
20 A triptych he frivolously contracts to 'TLC'.
21 In Mary Douglas's terms, on the assumption of strong 'group'.
22 See also the discussion of mock fighting in Pakistani weddings in Chapter 1.
23 My thanks to Roseanna Pollen for stimulating comments on this matter. It might also be noted, however, that women may also appreciate escaping the control of a mother-in-law, but see Jeffery *et al.* (1989: 49–52) for the costs and benefits of living with the mother-in-law or *alag* (separately) in terms of the level of and responsibility for household chores, and freedom to visit natal kin.
24 The spelling used by these authors differs from that employed here. Alavi (1972) reports the practice to be called simply *watta*. The term comes from *satta-batta*, meaning 'interchange, exchange, barter; a mercantile transaction' (Platts 2000 [1884]: 641). 'W' and 'b' sounds often change between Urdu and Punjabi. (My Punjabi informants in Bristol use a mixture of these two languages. They say that Sindhis speak *saf* (clean or pure) Urdu.)

5 Married but not married
The divisibility of weddings and the protection of women

This chapter will detail ways in which legal pluralism, migration and individual circumstance lead to the stretching out of the marriage process through both the addition of British legal requirements, and the possibility of separating the Pakistani wedding into its constituent parts. In particular, two ceremonies will be highlighted: the *nikah* and the *rukhsati*. In Pakistan, in common with some other Muslim societies, the religious marriage ceremony (the *nikah*) may be held some time before the rest of the wedding, and I will describe some reasons why this occurs. In the transnational marriages that have been the subject of my research, however, delaying the *rukhsati* (when the bride leaves her natal home to go to her in-laws' house) also appears to be common practice. Taking up the theme of risk from the preceding chapter, I will argue that the primary motivation for this delay is to protect brides from the risks involved in transnational marriage. The chapter concludes with a discussion of these dangers, and of the inadequacies in Pakistani practice of Quranic provisions for the protection of women in marriage through the payment of *mahr*.

Legal pluralism and the multiplication of marriage rituals

Pakistani weddings tend to be lengthy and complicated affairs consisting of a variety of events normally spread over several days. These most commonly include three main festivities: the pre-wedding *mehndi* celebrations, the *barat* (fêting of the groom's party), and the *walima*. The signing of the *nikah-nama*, the Islamic marriage contract, takes place on or before the *barat*. When the *nikah* is carried out in Pakistan, it is recognised as a legal marriage by the British immigration system, but when carried out in Britain the *nikah* alone does not fulfil British marriage requirements. Not only are officiants and venues often not registered for marriages, but Islamic marriage declarations can be made by the couple in separate rooms, while in English law the bride and bridegroom must both be present to recite set vows (Yilmaz 2002: 348). Hence, if a couple marry in England, they will usually have a civil ceremony so that their marriage is legally registered in the UK. Since the early 1990s, changes in legislation have allowed more mosques and community centres to become registered as venues for weddings, and some mosque officials have been empowered to wed couples on behalf of the registry (Yilmaz 2002: 348), but many couples still employ the services of a separate registrar.

Yilmaz (2002: 343) draws attention to this legal pluralism in England, where in particular, marriage, divorce and polygamy are dealt with very differently by Muslim and English law. 'Muslim law,' he writes, 'is still superior and dominant over English law in the Muslim mind and in the eyes of the Muslim community; and many Muslim individuals follow Muslim law by employing several strategies in England.' Where 'classic' legal pluralism refers to a colonial and post-colonial context in which foreign law was superimposed on pre-existing indigenous practices, this is an example of 'new' legal pluralism, which 'pertains to the existence of plural normative orders within modern, western societies in particular' (Fuller 1994). Three phases of ethnic minority legal pluralism in Britain have been suggested: in the first, marriages and divorces were not registered due to lack of knowledge of civil procedures; then both customary and civil marriages and divorces took place; after which an informal hybrid 'Angrezi Sharia' (English Islamic law) developed, featuring both new versions of religious law, and the incorporation of some aspects of religious marriage into British law, for example by treating the *mahr* payment as a personal contract (Menski 1988).

Transnationalism produces another type of legal pluralism, as marriages become involved in the legal institutions of two countries. Crucially, the requirements of the dual national legal contexts, and of immigration, may be negotiated by various multiplications or separations of the rites of marrying. Other significant differences exist between the marriage laws of Britain and Pakistan. Polygamy, for example, is permitted in Pakistan.[1] Second marriages require court permission, taking the views of the existing wife into account, although marriages occurring without this permission are still considered legally valid (Yamani 1998: 156), providing a loop-hole that allows men to remarry without their first wife's consent or even knowledge. During my fieldwork I encountered several examples of polygyny in the older generations, where it seems to have been not uncommon practice for an immigrant man to have one wife in Britain – sometimes a white woman – and another in Pakistan.[2] Since the closing of a legal loophole (Yilmaz 2002: 349), immigration regulations permit only one wife to be resident in Britain. Even before this, wives in Pakistan were often never brought to Britain, or at least not while the first marriage was 'subsisting', in the Home Office's terms, and these cases still occur. Bilqis, a young woman I met in Pakistan, had only just been granted her visa to come to Britain after 10 years of marriage as her husband did not apply for her to join him until his first marriage, to a white woman, ended in divorce. On the other hand, Manzoor, who is in her sixties, told me how her husband did manage to bring a second wife to Britain, where she lived until the polygamy was discovered by the authorities and she was returned to Pakistan. Even within Britain, however, the duality of Muslim and English law can be manipulated to allow a man to have more than one wife resident in the UK: I have been told of rare instances in which a man has married one woman by *nikah* only in Britain, and another either in a British civil marriage, or in a Pakistan ceremony later recognised by UK immigration (cf. Shaw 1988: 57).

The concept of legal pluralism has been criticised on the grounds that 'the coexistence of multiple plural legal or normative orders is a universal fact of the modern world [so] the concept points to nothing distinctive; it merely reminds us that from the legal perspective (as from any other) isolated, homogenous societies do not actually exist'. Furthermore, it risks blinkering the researcher by its focus on law, 'reproducing law-centred misconstructions' (Fuller 1994: 10). In the British Pakistani context, such a perspective tends to privilege these religious and legal marriages over the 'common-law' unions that some Pakistanis form, particularly with non-Pakistani and non-Muslim partners. Nevertheless, such privileging is common amongst British Pakistanis themselves – relationships not solemnised by *nikah* may not be recognised by the community in Bristol and are generally subject to disapproval. Hence it was only towards the very end of my fieldwork that I learnt that the son of a woman I had been meeting regularly was cohabiting with a white partner (and may even have been married), as the matter was never mentioned.

Plural, transnational and dynamic legal situations provide the context for significant variation in marriage practices. Over the course of my fieldwork, the UK immigration regulations relating to marriage underwent several changes. Most notable among these was the extension of the probationary period before spouses are granted permanent residency rights from one to two years in 2003, the raising of minimum ages for spouses from 16 to 18 (in 2003–04) and then 21 (in 2008), and the introduction in 2005 of the 'Certificates of Approval' Scheme requiring temporary migrants to apply to the Home Office for permission before marrying in Britain – under which permission would not be granted to irregular migrants or those with less than six months left on their visa.[3] Prior to this, the use of civil marriages to 'buy time' in immigration terms was more straightforward. Rasham, for example, now in her thirties with teenaged children, married her husband while he was in Britain as a visitor. They had two weddings – a quick registry office marriage before his visa expired, allowing him to stay in the country, and the 'proper' Pakistani wedding a few months later.

The stories of two weddings in one family expand upon the factors that can lead to the multiplication of marriage ceremonies. Riaz and Uzma are brother and sister. During my first fieldwork, Uzma's Pakistani fiancé Nadir came to Bristol on a one-year student visa, and lived next door to Uzma in another house owned by the family. The plan at that stage was to hold the civil marriage while he was in the country, although the couple would not cohabit until after a wedding in Pakistan the following year. They had been advised that this would be the simplest and quickest route to secure his immigration status in Britain. When I told them that the Home Office had recently proposed closing this option, they considered doing without the expense of two weddings, and concentrating on the celebration in Pakistan.

Nadir living next door meant that the couple could not be accused of cohabiting before the marriage, whilst Uzma's family could provide him with meals and any assistance he required. Early on in the year, Uzma's grandfather visited from Pakistan, and his daughter, Uzma's mother, decided this would be the perfect time to hold the official engagement party – partly inspired by the excitement of attending another family wedding. During another visit by her father (at short notice due to the serious illness of a relative in Britain), the family considered staging the *nikah* while he was there to enjoy it: on these visits the grandfather had been remarking that he was old and unlikely to live much longer. These plans were shelved, however, when a friend of the family died and festivities seemed inappropriate. They decided to stick to the earlier plans of having a joint *nikah* and civil ceremony, with a large function for their relatives in England. The couple's marriage would finally be completed, they hoped, with a full three-day affair in Pakistan to celebrate in style with Nadir's family and other relatives there. In the event, however, the ill health of a close member of the family meant that they could not travel to Pakistan when they had planned, so the *rukhsati* was held in another function at a hotel in Bristol six months after the civil and religious wedding. A few months later, when Uzma and Nadir were travelling to Pakistan to attend Nadir's sister's wedding, they planned to hold a party to celebrate the union with relatives in Pakistan, although the wedding was theoretically complete as the *walima* had taken place in Bristol.

When Uzma's brother Riaz became engaged to Sarah in Pakistan in 2006, they wanted to avoid a long separation after the wedding whilst they waited for his wife's visa, but in this case there was a different permutation of the marriage ceremonies. After the engagement, the couple applied for a fiancé visa which would allow Sarah to enter Britain for a period of six months during which the marriage could take place, but the family returned to Pakistan to hold the 'full' wedding with both sides of the family in attendance. Although legally and socially married, Sarah thus entered the UK as a fiancée. The family then had to hold a registry office wedding in the UK to fulfil the immigration requirements, before applying for a spousal visa.[4] The occasion was not an elaborate affair, partly because the ill health of a member of the family made it impractical, but as Sarah also explained:

> We didn't do any party – we just went there to that place [the registry office], all Riaz's relatives, close relatives. Because we already had lots of functions in Pakistan ... we just had to do that because my visa was running out, we had to do that quickly ... I just wear that white gold little set, not the proper gold set, just a little set, with the light earrings and all that, I didn't wear any gold bangles ... I was properly ready with the proper make-up, hairstyle and everything. But it was not the way I was in Pakistan with the proper, you know, jewellery – it was light jewellery. *Lehnga* [outfit] was – it was quite heavy [i.e. elaborately beaded], but still it was not the one in Pak ...

These siblings' stories demonstrate the many interacting factors – cultural, geographical, legal, political, financial and emotional – that can result in the multiplication of the ceremonies of marrying. The transnational family means that visits can be such rare occasions that important life events that cause a gathering of kin may be scheduled to coincide with them. The ability to hold the religious marriage as a separate function increases such possibilities. Legal pluralism creates another opportunity for division because a separate civil ceremony can be held, and immigration policies may provide incentive for such 'paper' marriages (which are, however, by no means 'sham'). A wedding in Pakistan presents opportunities to celebrate in much greater style than would be possible in Bristol. In addition, given the difficulties of obtaining visas, marrying in Pakistan is the only realistic way of enabling the family of the Pakistani spouse to be physically present. It is also a chance for parents who migrated to Bristol several decades ago to mark this important life event – the marriage of their child – with the siblings and other relatives they left behind. Where the main events of the marriage are held in Pakistan, a later function may allow friends and family in Britain a chance to celebrate the union.

The divisible wedding

The addition of the British civil ceremony represents a multiplication of the rites of marrying, whilst holding a separate *nikah* is a division of the conventional Pakistani wedding celebration. Over the course of my fieldwork, it became apparent that the normal way in which Pakistani marriages were described, as consisting of the *mehndi*, *barat* and *walima* – which may be reflected in the titles of three different cards within a wedding invitation – did not really reflect the most important elements of marrying. Some rituals that occur during these days came to appear more essential than others, and some were occasionally dispensed with altogether.

Religious reasons why people may not have a *mehndi* were mentioned in Chapter 1. Several informants stressed that the *walima* meal held by the groom's family to celebrate the arrival of the new bride is a religiously prescribed element of a marriage, while other festivities are merely Pakistani customs. Nevertheless, I have come across occasional cases where no *walima* was held. In one wedding in Bristol, for example, the *nikah* took place at an elaborate *mehndi* celebration, the *barat* and *rukhsati* were held the following weekend, but plans for a small *walima* were put on indefinite hold when a relative became ill. The *barat* day is in any case generally the most extravagant, in keeping with the general pattern across South Asia for the woman's side to spend more on the wedding. Nabila, however, was sent off from Pakistan as a fiancée, and had a simple *nikah* ceremony at her husband's home in Bristol, so missing out on the *barat* – conventionally thought of as the wedding day – altogether. Photographs from the family celebration in Pakistan, however, show the conventional *rukhsati* leave-taking scene being enacted, with Nabila being guided (although not, as would be normal, to her husband's waiting transportation) by relatives holding a copy of the Quran over her head.

It seems that the two elements of the wedding that always occur are the *nikah* and the *rukhsati*. It is of course hardly surprising that the *nikah* is indispensable, as without this the marriage would not be recognised as legitimate by members of the religious community. *Rukhsati*, meanwhile, refers to the final ritual of the wedding day when the bride is sent off to her new home, accompanied by lamentation and weeping by her female relatives. It is also understood, however, to have the more general meaning of leaving the parental home to cohabit with the husband, and implies the consummation of the marriage. As such it is an equally inevitable element of being wed: where the *nikah* is the contract that establishes the union as legitimate, *rukhsati* is the practical act of marriage that transforms the virgin bride into a wife.[5] This double meaning of the term *rukhsati* was reflected in occasional confusion in talking about the issue, such as when I asked Jamilah and her husband Omar whether they had had their *rukhsati* in Pakistan. Jamilah first said that they had not, but then her husband disagreed:

OMAR: The thing is it *was rukhsati*; they did *rukhsati*.
JAMILAH: But they didn't send [me] home with you.
KC: So you did the crying and everything?
JAMILAH: No, no, no, we didn't.
OMAR: Yeah you did – when you were making the movie and everything.
JAMILAH: This is what happened. We went home together and we had dinner – because we didn't have dinner in the hall because it's difficult to eat at them [presumably because of the ban on serving food at weddings mentioned in Chapter 1]. And then he went to his house [and] I went to mine. So it was like a *rukhsati* but not a *complete* … We went home together, but we did not actually, if you know what I mean. And then I went home. He stayed for about a week … not even a week – couple of days … We arranged for him to stay at a family member's house.

In this case it seems that the dual meanings of *rukhsati* have been reified by temporal separation: the ceremony of leave taking and joining the husband was performed, but the consummation of the marriage took place at a later date. Although the sequence of the marriage ceremonies is somewhat different, this can be compared to Nabila's case in which the *rukhsati* conventions were enacted when she left her parents in Pakistan, but the consummation of the marriage did not happen until after her *nikah* in Bristol.

Saying that there was no *walima* is sometimes the same as saying there was no *rukhsati*, as the *walima* is not held until the *rukhsati* has taken place and the bride has gone to her husband's home. Other people talk about their marriage in Pakistan as not having been a 'full wedding'. The *nikah* and *rukhsati* can thus be separated and held on different occasions, sometimes with many months or years intervening. The reasons for doing so are diverse, as we shall see, but for the purposes of this chapter, I will separate this phenomenon into two categories: the 'separate *nikah*' and the 'delayed *rukhsati*'. In the former case, a smaller function is held for the *nikah* some time before the marriage celebration proper. In the latter, the normal wedding is held, with the arrival of the *barat* and the signing of the *nikah*, but the 'complete' *rukhsati*, in Jamilah's terms, does not take place. The bride may, like Jamilah, initially depart with the groom, or the conventional *rukhsati* scene may be staged for the cameras, but the bride will not accompany the groom to his home to spend the night with him and consummate the marriage. Of course, the two types may theoretically be combined in one marriage: a *nikah* could take place, followed some time later by the wedding celebration, but the consummation of the marriage could be delayed until after the Pakistani spouse has been granted a visa and arrived in Britain. I have not, however, come across any such cases.

The separate *nikah*

The *nikah* and *rukhsati* often take place on the same day, or at least within a few days of each other. This is not, however, essential: the *nikah* may take place several months or years before the couple start to cohabit. This practice exists in Pakistan as well as amongst Pakistanis in Britain. Gafoora in Pakistan told me that the *nikah* was really a 'strong engagement': the couple weren't really married yet, but it would be unusual for the match to be dissolved once the *nikah-nama* had been signed. Many Muslims, however, would be unhappy with the term 'engagement', as it undermines the importance of the *nikah* as the religious marriage.

When I asked one woman from Mirpur why her *nikah* to her Bristolian husband had been held years before she came to Britain, she simply answered that this was their culture. Other women in Bristol, though, told me of a variety of motivations for holding the *nikah* separately. If the families were not well known to each other, this time might allow them to get to know each other better and make sure that the *rishta* was indeed suitable. Parents might want to finalise the *rishta* before the couple were ready to marry: they might still be studying, the groom might wish to establish his career, or the families might need time to save for the wedding. In addition, one woman told me, families might push for an early *nikah* if they feared that the groom might change his mind later on. Other reasons for a separate *nikah* might not concern the couple themselves, such as when Uzma's mother wanted to hold the *nikah* for the benefit of her father. This is not a new practice in the family. The *nikah* of her sister in Pakistan, 20 years or more ago, had been two years before the wedding. An uncle had apparently been visiting Pakistan from Britain and the *nikah* had been held at that time in order to gather the family for a celebration during his stay.

As a religious marriage, the *nikah* has a legitimating effect. As such, an early *nikah* can permit behaviour that might otherwise provoke disapproval, or be considered dangerously 'modern'. If a couple are already religiously wed, for example, they may sit side by side at a joint *mehndi* celebration. When Sonam, from Pakistan, was about to embark on studies abroad at the same university as a male cousin, her *nikah* to her British intended husband was carried out so that she could travel with this theoretically marriageable young man without causing worry or gossip. In Bristol, one couple took advantage of the freedom provided by this state of being religiously but not practically married by going out unchaperoned on shopping trips to buy jewellery during the year in which they were '*nikah*-ed' but not living together, overcoming the traditional prohibition on contact between engaged couples. There was another reason that this couple had their wedding so long after their *nikah*, however, and here we return to the issue of legal pluralism raised above: they could not have their civil marriage, or publicly celebrate their union, until the groom's divorce from his non-Pakistani first wife had been finalised, so they chose to solemnise their relationship initially through the religious marriage contract.

A separate *nikah* may therefore be held for a number of reasons: to secure the *rishta*, as an excuse for a party that gathers kin together, to circumvent the British legal or immigration systems, to legitimate behaviour, or to buy time. Finally, for Shareen, whose *nikah* was held very quickly after the match was decided, it was largely a matter of practicality, as she needed to return to Bristol quickly. She could also, however, see other benefits:

> ... we didn't do the *rukhsati* then because I was short of time because I was working and I had to go back. And I wanted to spend time with him after marriage [rather] than me just staying with him [for a] couple of days after marriage and then going back to England ... So that was all fine. And in that time I said [to husband]: 'You can do your training and everything, and then by the time I come up [i.e. back to Pakistan], you can save a bit more money and then we could do the wedding like that.'[6]

The delayed *rukhsati*

While the separate *nikah* seems to be an accepted practice in Pakistan, during my fieldwork I came across several cases of transnational marriages in which the *rukhsati* was delayed, so that the marriage would remain unconsummated until the Pakistani spouse arrived in Britain. I did not hear of this situation in Pakistan when international migration was not involved. Moreover, among those I interviewed, this arrangement was more common where a British bride was marrying a Pakistani groom, than vice versa.

Where motivations for holding the *nikah* separately show wide variation, those for delaying *rukhsati* were remarkably consistent, centring round a desire to protect against future difficulties and distress. The stories of three sisters, Asma, Nasreen and Rubina, help to cast light on why delaying the *rukhsati* may be attractive to the families of British Pakistani women. Nasreen and Rubina did not have their *rukhsati*s when they were married in Pakistan.

RUBINA: Basically my parents – they've seen it a lot that people go to Pakistan, they have the wedding – full, full wedding – they have a wedding night together and everything, the bride gets pregnant and the husband doesn't get a visa. So she's here and she's a single parent and everything. So my parents wanted to avoid all of that.

NASREEN: The *rukhsati* means, obviously, spending the night together. Everybody was worried – like we don't really want babies and things involved if we're trying to get you over [i.e. during the visa application process]. And we knew it was going to be complicated for me because … I wasn't working. And um, I think that was it really. That was the only main reason … Me and my mum and dad all sort of thought that it was a better thing to do. I don't know really. I guess if you become heavily physically involved with someone, it's not necessarily the right thing to do I suppose – to not see them for months and months in that same situation. Maybe it's not mentally healthy or something.

As I suggested in the Introduction, the period during which many of those I worked with married transnationally may well come to be seen as one in which the UK was unusually receptive to spousal immigration. Acceptance rates for spousal visa applications rose considerably after the abolition of the Primary Purpose Rule, and were relatively high at the time of my fieldwork, before new restrictions were imposed. Nevertheless, I did encounter cases of 'immigration widows' whose husbands' visa applications were refused, but who had conceived children on visits to Pakistan. The risk of rejection may help to explain why *rukhsati* was more often delayed for British women. Not only is the risk run by women higher than that for men – as the plight of an effectively single mother is unenviable – but there was considered to be greater risk of husbands than wives being refused visas. Entry clearance officers I talked to in Islamabad reflected the observations made by others of a greater burden of proof on male applicants than female (c.f. Wray 2006b). They understood that it was normal for women to move on marriage and to be economically inactive, whereas men were considered more likely to be motivated by the economic incentives of migration and so were treated with greater suspicion. Moreover, as Nasreen suggests, prolonged separation might be difficult after embarking on a physical relationship. Pakistanis believe sexuality to be a powerful force: a common justification for purdah practices is that an unrelated man and woman left alone together would be unable to resist each other. Whilst this temptation towards illicit sex is seen as wicked – one woman in Pakistan told me that the devil runs through all our veins – regular sex within marriage is considered healthy, and the separation of husband and wife thought difficult for both. Veena Das, writing on Punjabi conceptions of kinship in north India, much of which is equally applicable in the Pakistani

Punjab, notes that 'shared sexuality is considered to create strong natural bonds which are extremely difficult to resist' (Das 1976: 205). Parveen, in her mid-thirties when I interviewed her in 2008, illustrates the attachments that can form in even a brief union. She says she 'just went along with' her family's plans for her marriage in Pakistan when she was 16. Her youth caused suspicion that she had been forced into marriage, delaying the granting of her husband's visa. Her sister, meanwhile, who had married on the same day, had been reunited with her husband. 'And then my mum said, "do you want to go back to him?" Because if I see that couple [her sister and her husband, together] and then I'm in tears. And my mum said, "you can go back and stay with him until he comes back". And then that's what I did – I went and stayed for a year and half until he got his visa.'

Jamilah was encountered earlier in the chapter talking with her husband Omar about her delayed *rukhsati*. She added another matter in which her father sought to protect her:

> We had a *nikah* – that guarantees that you're married. We had that straight away ... No engagement. Straight away we had the *nikah* – two, three weeks after we first saw each other. I saw him one day, [and] on that weekend I went back to Lahore – because that's where my parents are originally from – and we held the *nikah* in Lahore, because the girl's side of the family is who actually arranges that. And the *barat* came from Karachi to Lahore and then they went back. I didn't see him afterwards and all that. [No *rukhsati*] ... because my father had doubts in his mind that what if he never got to England, the visa was rejected, and then [she said in giggly whispers] he still wanted me to be 'pure'. I'm the only daughter you see, so my dad's very protective of me.

If a husband's application to enter Britain is rejected, not only will the fact that the marriage is unconsummated protect against the dangers of children born without a resident father, and emotional attachments generated and then severed, but the young woman will have remained a virgin. As such, not only should it theoretically be simpler for her to obtain a divorce, but it may be easier for her to remarry. Jamilah's father is thus reducing that which the family stands to lose in the risks of transnational marriage and negotiating the immigration system. Of course, parents in Pakistan may have similar concerns for their daughters who are marrying British men. As already noted, however, it is considered easier to bring wives from Pakistan than husbands. Moreover, it may be that the British side, with its promise of a better life, holds greater sway in the negotiations over such matters. So while Pakistani families may wish to delay the consummation of a daughter's marriage to a man from Britain, they may not be in a strong position to press for this to happen. In one case, however, the uncle who was acting as go-between in the marriage discussions apparently told the British groom that he would be taking his new bride home, whilst assuring the bride that she would only have her *nikah* and be able to continue with her studies – a duplicity that was discovered only after the ceremony. In the end the Pakistani bride did get her way. When Talib from Bristol married Zahida from Pakistan, his mother clearly recognised that the consummation of the marriage might cause her new daughter-in-law problems, but avoided shouldering responsibility by employing the common discourse of fate:

> Well people do – they don't consummate the marriage because they have other plans ... but we said, 'They're married and why shouldn't they? It's now their destiny how quickly she gets here ... It's their right and why should we get in the way'.

Amina, a young woman from Lahore whom I met in Bristol, had a 'full' wedding, but her *rukhsati* did not have a great impact on her as she returned to live with her parents while she applied for a visa. The sexual bond between husband and wife may be strong, but the ties it creates are, at least initially, weaker than those between children and their parents. Amina's real *rukhsati*, she told me, was when she had to leave her parents at the airport in Pakistan.

Fears for British Pakistani women

Even if a husband's visa application is successful, there are other fears for British Pakistani women marrying men from Pakistan, and for Nasreen and Rubina it seems that delaying the *rukhsati* was also intended to protect against these additional dangers. The sisters' marriages were held in age order on three consecutive days, with the eldest, Asma, married first, and Rubina the youngest last. Asma's husband came to Britain first. The two other young men were granted visas on appeal, after a second visit by Nasreen and her father to Pakistan left her feeling confident about the match. The family brought Nasreen's husband over next, with the intention that Rubina's husband would follow after a few months. In the event, Nasreen's marriage failed. Worried by this experience and the fact that the two sisters' husbands are friends, the family decided not to bring Rubina's husband to Britain at all and sought a divorce.

My assertion that the main reason for separating the *nikah* and *rukhsati* – not having a 'full' wedding as they put it – was to reduce the various risks to Nasreen and Rubina, is backed up by the contrast with their sister Asma's wedding. Although the family took care that all three functions were identical in all other respects, Asma's *rukhsati* took place on the day of her marriage. This difference can be explained by the divergent degrees of danger perceived in these matches. Nasreen and Rubina married in the family, but to relatives who are not considered very close as the families did not mix much at the time. Nasreen's husband was her second cousin, while Rubina is unclear as to her direct relationship to the man she married, although one of his brothers is married to Nasreen's husband's sister. She put it this way:

I felt to one degree that I was still in the family, because my mum knew them while we were kids and they were kids, but she didn't know them that well, so to that degree maybe it was out of the family …

Asma's match, on the other hand 'is really close' (Rubina). Her husband is her mother's sister's son. While Asma's husband had professional qualifications, the other two men were relatively uneducated and from poor families. As will be clear from previous discussions of risk, then, Asma's close kin marriage to an educated boy whose family was well known was considered far less risky than those to two lesser-known quantities with clear potential incentives for economic migration. The family could thus feel much more confident in allowing Asma's marriage to be completed by cohabitation.

The regulatory practices of the Primary Purpose Rule, and the subsequent focus on a couple's 'intention to live together' and more recently on 'sham marriage' have been the subject of criticism (Charsley and Benson 2012; Wray 2006c), but many British Pakistani women marrying men from Pakistan shared the concern that their marriages should not be contracted simply for the opportunity for economic migration.[7] However, as I argued in Chapter 3, connections to wealth and opportunity are an accepted and intrinsic part of the search for a *rishta*. Accordingly, young British women may be realistic about the economic aspect to their marriages. In the last chapter, for example, when Shareen was deciding whether to marry in Britain or Pakistan, she thought: 'I may as well give somebody an opportunity from there [rather] than somebody that's already here – d'you know?' Nevertheless, the potential or perceived gains from such marriages are such that they may undermine confidence in the Pakistani husband's commitment to the marital relationship. Most serious is what the immigration regulations term the intention to 'live permanently with the other as his or her spouse' – in this case, the husband's intention to stay with his wife once he has gained the right to remain in Britain. A few husbands in Bristol have deserted their wives, either having gained 'permanent right to remain' after the probationary period, or (and in my impression, more commonly) having waited until they 'get their British passport' (i.e. are granted British citizenship). In some cases, such as that of Sumera, once the husband's position in Britain is secure, he has secretly contracted a second marriage in Pakistan. It is difficult to judge whether this was the husband's original intention, however, or a decision made later as a result of dissatisfaction with his first marriage.[8]

The literature on Muslim marriage notes that polygyny can be a source of severe anxiety for women (Usmain 1991: 35; cf. Abu-Lughod 1988: 228–29; Jeffery 1976a: 10). Manzoor, the woman in her sixties mentioned at the beginning of this chapter, was clearly still upset several decades on as she told me how her husband had married as she was giving birth, and neglected her for his second wife, taking money from her wages to send to the other woman in Pakistan. The instances with which I am familiar where men imported as husbands for British Pakistani women then marry again have indeed caused great upset to the first wife (and no doubt also to the second if she was not aware of the situation). In Pakistan, when a man marries a second wife without court permission, the first wife is allowed to petition for divorce (Yamani 1998). For women involved in these transnational polygamous marriages, however, this decision can be further complicated by the fact that if she does divorce her husband under British law, he is then free to bring his second wife to Britain. Iqbal told me that his first wife, who demanded he issue a *talaq* (religious divorce) when she discovered he had married again in Pakistan, then attempted to delay the civil divorce in order to 'give me a hard time' by preventing him from bringing his second wife to Britain. Many women in Bristol advised Sumera against a divorce for this reason, but she went ahead with it to allow herself to remarry, although she viewed the prospect of her husband bringing his new wife to live in the same city as deeply unfair.

The possibility of being deserted, perhaps with young children to support, while your husband of only a few years gains the right to remain in Britain and even import another wife, understandably worries many of the British Pakistani women to whom I have spoken. These concerns are intensified when news of such an event spreads through the Bristol grapevine. When it emerged that Nasreen's husband intended to leave his wife once he had gained settlement rights, her (at that time) happily married sister caused great upset to her own husband by asking if he was going to leave her too. One of the young women's friends from school caused arguments with her own new Pakistani husband over similar concerns. A further fear is that the husband will not be sufficiently oriented towards his new commitments in Britain, neglecting duties to his wife and children in favour of his relatives in Pakistan. The aspect that women most commonly mentioned was the issue of remittances. Many, if not most, women accept that their husbands will fulfil their filial duties by sending money to support their parents, but I have heard of some cases in which British families feel they have been forced to live with severe financial constraints in order to finance luxuries in Pakistan. As will be seen later, wives' families' attempts to influence a husband's remitting become a bone of contention in some relationships.

Some men are considered more of a risk than others, and other tactics may be employed to reduce these dangers. Zaynab, for example, has suffered two failed marriages. One husband's visa application was rejected, while the other left her immediately after gaining his British citizenship and is now married again. Zaynab says she has been offered other *rishte*, but has rejected them. She would not marry someone in Britain on a visitor visa who might only be looking for a way to stay in the country, and was hoping for an older man who, she felt, would be less likely to leave her for another (younger) woman. Poor men are thought more likely to be driven by economic gain, so several women have told me that the fact that their husbands were from financially stable backgrounds was a factor in agreeing to the marriage. Azra, who feels strongly that their finances are too limited for her husband to remit money to his family, told me why she rejected another proposal:

> His mother came in to see my mother. It's funny, because she said she wants her son to get married to me, and she wants her son to send money to them when he's over. And I thought, 'I really don't like that'. She just came out with this ... and I thought, 'I don't want to get married to him'. I know my husband – they're quite wealthy and they're doing OK, touch wood, so I know he won't be ... I had some sort of indication, but at the end of the day you don't know how a person may behave – only God knows. But they're all wealthy. They're OK – they're doing fine. He doesn't seem *lalchi* [greedy].

This sentiment was repeated by Jamilah:

> ... when we were looking in Pakistan, we did look for financially stable people. Because there's always a problem when people are coming to England – it's more boys than girls – to try and support families at home. If they're not stable already then we have a hard life to support two families you see.

Nasreen and Rubina's family, who did take boys from poorer backgrounds as husbands for their daughters, apparently tried to reduce the financial incentive for the marriage by refusing to offer a dowry.[9] With hindsight, after Nasreen's husband had proven very much motivated by money, one relative criticised the decision not to give a dowry, telling me that it only increased his family's financial hardship and therefore made them more desperate.

I have been told that another of Nasreen's relatives in Bristol brought a man from Pakistan to Britain as a daughter's fiancé on a trial basis. The marriage did not take place in the end, as the family had developed doubts over his character during his stay. In two other cases, I met people in Bristol whose future spouses had come over on visits, allowing the families concerned to see how they acted in this environment. This option is not, however, open to all. Those without financial securities in Pakistan may find it harder to obtain a visa, and it is commonly thought that visitor visas are less frequently given to the young and unmarried for fear that they will try to evade the normal spousal immigration routes by marrying during their stay.

Later in our conversation, Jamilah summed up the uncertainties faced by several young women I spoke to in Bristol, expressing a range of concerns, anxiety and frustrations:

> Your permanent stay shouldn't be given in one year, it's too quickly [this interview took place before the extension of the probationary period]. You've got to remember these people don't know each other. First it's hard enough putting people in a house together that already knew each other but we've got two steps in one if you know what I mean, so I think it should be five-year period at least ... We've had this really bad experience in the family ... and it wasn't fair at all. I think it all comes down to how

easy it is. I know we pester [the authorities] to say we want to bring our husbands over, I know it's our fault as well partly, but you should have checks on it again and that the permanent stay be delayed. Maybe not delay them coming over, but [make sure] that they are suitable. Half the people you've got coming here ... have got nothing to do with us [i.e. their wives] any more. They've all left – maybe gone back to Pakistan and married someone they really wanted to. It's all using – lots of it is. I mean I couldn't say it doesn't happen in the family because it happens everywhere now, it's very common to be used ... but this is fraud. You're using someone to come to England, pretend to get married, pretend to have children with them, pretend to love them and then – not even five years some of them – after two, three years turn around, go back to Pakistan and get married again and leave those people to live on government benefit. You could have done that in the first place, why do we have to have them living here and paying our taxes towards them? ... I don't think it's fair ... They think it's going to make their homes more financially stable back home. They don't give anything about people here and they say, 'Oh, you live in a trampy lifestyle and I'll keep sending money back home'. Rich them up, make them go upper class or whatever it is they want to do. And their needs are not even essential any more, they're like, 'I want a mobile phone, or a stereo system, so you can't have your dinner tonight'. So it's not very fair ... That's not us though [she and her husband], but it happens ... They seem like the best people when you first meet them, very kind – you wouldn't think they could ever do a thing like that. Then they do. Very cold blooded.

Mahr: Islam's protection of women in marriage

Islam does make provisions to protect women against casual divorce and hardship after the end of a marriage. In the *nikah-nama*, a sum of money to be paid by the groom to his new bride must be specified. This payment, the *mahr*, should be made before consummation of the marriage, but may be deferred or 'forgiven' by the bride.[10] At the latest, however, it should be paid to the woman if her husband divorces her, and as such has been viewed both as a deterrent to divorce and a kind of alimony to support the divorced woman.[11]

Wakil notes that the institution of *mahr* is flexible: 'the amount of *mahr* varies, the mode of payment varies, the subjective motives and meanings vary, and so on' (Wakil 1991: 55). Studies show that the amount and implications of *mahr* differ greatly both cross-culturally and within societies, and change over time, so that while a token sum of one Jordanian dollar has recently been gaining popularity in Palestine (Moor 1991), in Sumatra, some *mahr* payments were so large that they could not be paid in the lifetime of the groom (Tugby 1959). In pre-1950s Palestine, prompt payment of the *mahr* gave women direct access to productive property (Moor 1991), whilst Tugby (1959) reports that in Sumatra, the deferment of *mahr* payment was more advantageous for the wife, incorporating her securely into her husband's lineage through debt. It did not, however, provide an effective deterrent against divorce, as a man might separate from his wife without pronouncing the final *talaq* to complete the divorce, leaving her to renounce the *mahr* if she wished to remarry.

In Pakistan, Donnan (1988: 109) reports that *mahr* is usually deferred, although another work suggests this may be a recent development (Wakil 1991). Studies demonstrate that higher sums correlate with, and indeed confer, higher status (Donnan 1988: 150; see also Wakil 1991: 55–56). Wakil suggests that families of low economic standing may engage in exchange marriages such as those discussed in the previous chapter, in which costs, including *mahr*, are low.[12] Small *mahr* payments are not only, however, driven by economic constraints. In Britain, Shaw reports that small symbolic amounts are traditional, and seen by older women as symbols of trust in close kin marriage (Shaw 2000a: 243). In addition, prestige may be gained by an agreement on the 'Prophet's *mahr*' of 32 rupees, also known as *rasuli mahr*, which 'may indicate faith in the stability of the marriage and a concern with religious tradition rather than with material benefit, since this is the amount said to have been pledged on the Prophet's daughter Fatima' (Donnan 1988: 150). Several of my informants reported this amount (or one approximating to it), which is in effect a token *mahr* given the current value of the Pakistani rupee, and which they more commonly called *shar'i mahr*, i.e. the amount prescribed by Islamic law.[13] In addition, a woman in Bristol told me that large sums were not required in kin marriage, as this type of union is expected to provide its own security. Moreover, to demand a large *mahr* is to risk appearing *lalchi* (greedy). In any case, a 'good wife' is often expected to excuse the payment of *mahr* (Shaw 2000a: 243). In this context, to attempt to manage risk by asking for a large *mahr* could produce other dangers by calling into question the presumption of trust between kin.[14]

Islamic feminists argue that the reduction or omission of *mahr* runs counter to the provisions for women's rights in Islam, and criticise the custom of husbands asking their wives to forgive the *mahr* on their wedding night, perhaps with the incentive of a gift of a ring. It is worth noting, however, that even the tiny *shar'i mahr* may be forgiven, in which case a gold ring may make this a very good bargain. Sarah reported that her *burri* gifts were registered as constituting her *mahr*.

> In Islam it has to be whatever you can afford easily. So whatever the gold they give me, they just put that in *haqq mahr*, say we are giving everything to Aisha that all belongs to her now. The gold was more than five *lakh* [*lakh* = 10,000, so 50,000 rupees] but they just put five *lakh* ... So we have paid the *haqq mahr* to her now ... Because it says in Islam that the husband cannot touch the wife until and unless he has paid the ... *haqq mahr*. Until and unless the girl don't forgive him, say that I don't want that. But mum

and dad [i.e. her mother and father-in-law] said that we have already paid, there is no condition of like Sarah is letting it off ...

For several of those I spoke to in Bristol, *mahr* seemed so unimportant that they could not remember the amount that had been specified, or whether it had been paid. In some cases there was confusion about what was *mahr* and what were other marriage prestations. The *munh-dikhai* custom, in which the husband gives his new wife a present to persuade her to let him see her face, sometimes seems to be confused with the issue of payment or forgiveness of *mahr*, which should be done before the husband first touches his wife (i.e. consummates the marriage), unless a deferral was specified in the marriage contract. This confusion seems to be most common among young men. Thus when I asked Tahir from Lahore about his *mahr*, he answered:

> *Mahr* – yes, well the first night ... let me remember what I did with it a little bit ... I had to buy a present for the first night, so what happened [was] that I didn't really have the time – or I didn't know what I was going to do the first night. People told me at the last moment, 'Oh you have to give a present, you have to give the *mahr*' ... My mother told one of my aunts to bring over a present and they gave me it as a surprise and said, 'You give it to your wife' ... It was a watch ... [Then on reflection he says:] No – it hasn't anything to do with the *mahr*, but I paid around 5,000 rupees – but I didn't know it was *mahr* at that time until later on. My father asked me in the morning, 'Well, did you pay your *mahr*?' I said 'Oh right, did I have to pay that as well?' So next day or a few days after I asked her to just forgive it if she wanted to. Otherwise I could have paid it to her. It's not that much ...

His wife's memories are similarly vague, and differ from those of her husband. When I asked about her *mahr*, she said:

> *Mahr*, yeah ... I can't remember how much it was. But there was a lot of money given. 'Cos he gave me a watch on the wedding night, as a present from him. And I think it was 10 thousand rupees – *salami* I think it's called, and he gave me that. And the *haqq mahr*, it was a wee little bit – 35 rupees I think it was. He hasn't given it to me, but I said just give me it whenever, he probably already used it on me! 'Cos it's only a little bit of money, but he said whenever you want it just tell me, so I said, 'Oh when we go next time I'll just take it then'.

In this statement, *mahr* is again viewed as a matter of little importance. Saif, from Bristol, seems to have been even less aware of the practice. He told me what he and his wife had done with the *salami* money gifts from their wedding:

> Well we spent it. She keeps ten thousand rupees. I don't know if you know that – ten thousand rupees she keeps for, um, [tries to think of the

word] *haqq mut*? [I suggest *haqq mahr*] *haqq mahr*. So she kept that. That was on the wedding night itself. That was something completely – I wasn't sure if she was pulling a fast one on me! But I just accepted it anyway. She said, 'Right – this is ten thousand rupees for me, this is my *haqq mahr*.' And I said, 'All right then ... What's *haqq mahr*?'

For many Pakistani women, therefore, *mahr* does not seem to provide any kind of marital or financial security. This may be because the amount involved is very low, particularly with the value placed on the *shar'i mahr*, which has by now become a token payment, but even a large *mahr* may not be paid if the wife 'forgives' it.[15] Moreover, even if *mahr* were operating effectively in Pakistan, it is unlikely that it could afford any real protection to British Pakistani women engaged in transnational marriages to men from Pakistan. Even the most generous rupee *mahr* would provide neither an effective deterrent to divorce once the husband is earning in Britain, nor any kind of adequate financial support to the divorced wife. Given the heightened risks that British women and their parents run in arranging transnational marriages, it is hardly surprising that other methods of protection have been sought.

In the preceding chapter, I suggested that close kin marriage is often one attempt at reducing these risks. This chapter has detailed ways in which the divisibility of Pakistani weddings can be employed to protect brides further.

Conclusion

In Pakistani weddings that do not involve international migration, the *nikah* may be held some time before the rest of the marriage. In the transnational context, however, the possibilities and motivations for the multiplication of marriage rituals are increased. British, Pakistani and Muslim laws relating to marriage combine to create a kind of double legal pluralism in which the co-existence of civil and religious law in Britain is complicated by the involvement of the Pakistani legal system. The meaning of marriage rites then depends on context: a *nikah* held in Pakistan is treated as legally valid by British law, whilst the same procedure carried out in the UK is not. The mechanisms of divorce are also complicated by the situation, and women in Britain who were married in Pakistan may find it difficult to obtain a religious divorce from the Pakistani authorities (Shah-Kazemi 2001). In Bristol, I heard of a case in which a British Pakistani woman divorced her Pakistani husband under British law, but he denied that the divorce was valid as the religious marriage had not been declared at an end. Nasreen and Rubina spent many months negotiating the complex system of divorcing their Pakistani husbands from a distance and against the young men's wishes.[16]

I have outlined ways in which pluralistic situations can be used to the advantage of those involved, including circumventing the British prohibition on polygamy. In other cases, it is simply the need to fulfil the requirements of both religious and British civil law that leads to the multiplication of wedding ceremonies, as when a registry marriage allows a spouse's immigration status to be secured. In addition, however, migration leads to further motivations for additional ceremonies as families hope to celebrate with relatives in both countries. In the end, it will be remembered, the process of Uzma's wedding was extended to include multiple functions in Britain and a party in Pakistan in response to the family's need to allow her fiancé to remain in Britain, the practical demands of health and travel, and a desire to celebrate the union with kin in both countries, or on the occasion of valued visits from Pakistani relatives.

An additional picking apart of the elements of marriage is the practice of delaying the consummation of the marriage until after a Pakistani groom has been accepted for immigration to Britain. I have argued that the 'delayed *rukhsati*' is designed to protect British brides from dangers that are specific to transnational marriages, which I have outlined above. It is used in combination with other methods such as the selection of a husband from a financially secure background, and in response to the assessment of risk involved in the marriage, a calculation that includes the perceived security of close kin marriage. Finally, I described a religious institution for the protection of women in marriage, *mahr*, and documented its widespread lack of financial impact on those with whom I have worked. The dominant model of reduction of risk through marriage to close relatives is again seen to interact with other methods of protection. In this case, the effectiveness of *mahr* is undermined in two ways. Participants are encouraged to think that a token payment will suffice, as a financial guarantee is not necessary in arrangements between trusted relations, and the giving of a small *mahr* is promoted as a demonstration of that trust. A picture has thus developed over the course of these chapters of multiple and interacting modes of risk reduction in transnational marriage, which have led to distinctive patterns of spousal selection in terms of high rates of transnational close kin marriage, to new forms of marriage ceremonies, and has further reduced the practical importance of *mahr* to the point that some young people seem to have very little knowledge of the custom.[17] The narrative interlude at the start of the next chapter takes up the story of Yasmin, whose *rukhsati* was delayed, to provide further illustration of these practices, and introduce an example of what happens when all these safeguards fail.

Notes

1 See Shah 2008 for an account of the regulation of polygamy in UK immigration law.
2 A Pakistani man having a wife in each country featured in the 1999 British film *East is East,* and was a central theme of the 2010 sequel *West is West.*
3 A scheme later judged discriminatory and eventually dismantled.
4 Riaz's family were not aware, however, that they would need to pay a second costly visa fee to transfer from fiancée to spouse status. A steep increase in the level of immigration fees is a feature of contemporary British attempts to regulate immigration.

5 In the *nikah-nama* the term for a virgin (*kunwari*) also means an unmarried woman. It must be specified whether the bride is a virgin, divorced or widowed.
6 In Bangladesh, Gardner (1995: 167) reports the opposite phenomenon, as the traditional delaying of the couple's cohabitation is relaxed in some circumstances where grooms must quickly return to work abroad.
7 The criteria on which Entry Clearance Officers decide whether a marriage is 'genuine' are somewhat vague, but, as set out in the Introduction, include attempts to ensure that such marriages are not motivated primarily by immigration or financial advantage. Immigration regulations, writes Menski (1999), are peppered with the potential for subjective judgements by individual officials in terms such as 'adequate' and 'satisfied', with rumours of 'hidden quotas' and 'secret instructions'. In 2011, a Ministerial Authorisation was revealed which permitted discrimination against a secret list of nationalities (likely to include Pakistan) in immigration applications: www.free movement.org.uk/2011/05/31/secret-race-discrimination/ (accessed 31/01/2012).
8 This issue is discussed further in Chapter 7. See Charsley and Liversage 2012a for a lengthier discussion of polygamy.
9 As Gardner (1995: 178–80) points out, distinction should be made between the various parts of a dowry. In this case, although the family did not send money or goods to Yasmin's groom and in-laws, they still presented their daughter with substantial quantities of gold jewellery and clothing.
10 My informants in Bristol generally referred to the payment as *haqq mahr*, *haqq* meaning true, just or appropriate.
11 For a discussion of the interpretation of *mahr* by Western courts, see Fournier (2010).
12 This practice has also been noted in Palestine (Moor 1991).
13 In north India, Jeffery's (2001) informants report the amount of the *shar'i mahr* to be 125 silver rupees.
14 This might be compared to the distrust between couples in Tanzania that may be engendered by requests for condom use to reduce the risk of AIDS (Bujra 2000).
15 Jeffery (2001) describes confusion and scepticism surrounding *mahr* in rural north India. Whilst many of her informants either did not know the amount of their *mahr*, or reported a low figure, not one of them had actually received the money.
16 The Islamic Shari'a Council in Britain (www.islamic-sharia.org) has developed a service in response to these issues. Most of the 95% of enquiries it receives that are marriage-related concern women seeking a divorce (*khula*, as opposed to the male *talaq* divorce pronouncement). In these cases the Islamic Shari'a Council will consider issuing a religious divorce certificate, after sending the husband a series of letters and invitations to interview.
17 I wish here to differentiate between the practical importance of *mahr* as protection for women in marriage and divorce, and the religious importance of the practice.

6   Conflicting interests
Rifts, concealment, *izzat* and emotion

Yasmin's marriage

Here Yasmin from Bristol, whose *rukhsati* was delayed and whose marriage later failed, will tell her story in her own words. This narrative provides a bridge between the questions of risk, trust and protection explored in the last two chapters, and the issues of rifts within families, *izzat*, and the position of in-marrying husbands, which will form the remainder of the book.

When Yasmin's older sister's marriage had been arranged, the young women's paternal grandmother suggested to their father that it was time to think about Yasmin's marriage. At the time, Yasmin, born and raised in Bristol, was 19. Her father thought that it would be difficult to find a husband for Yasmin because she suffers from a physical disability, but he asked his wife's brother in Pakistan to make enquiries. The uncle later phoned to recommend a match, a maternal second cousin. Her parents spoke with the boy and his parents, and photographs were sent over.

> I personally was amazed because I always said to my mum that I don't think arranged marriage can work for me because I didn't think anyone would agree to marry me on arrangements – it would have to be a proper love marriage, as it were. He would have to know me because of the disability factor. But I think my dad was quite reluctant, and he sort of thought, 'No, it can work'. And I was quite flattered that there had been a proposal, so I agreed.

The family went to Pakistan two months before the wedding, and she got to know her fiancé.

> Because of living here [my parents have] got a bit more Western ideas. I mean, a lot of people aren't even allowed to talk to their partners-to-be before marriage … I saw him nearly every day, or every other day, or spoke on the telephone and I thought, 'Yeah, this is fine' … He seemed caring and genuine.

The wedding took place, and they applied for his visa. The application was rejected, but later granted on appeal. During the appeal process, Yasmin and her father went back to Pakistan.

> But I was only *nikah*-ed so I didn't live with him. I stayed with my dad when we went there, but he came around and brought me flowers, brought me gifts, constantly phoned me, met me at the airport when I got there. And he was really upset when I had to leave ...
>
> Basically, when he got here, we had booked the halls and arranged for the rest of the wedding ceremonies to take place. I think it was a Friday when he got here and we had the wedding ceremony on Saturday, *rukhsati* was on Saturday, *walima* was on Sunday ... [His father's younger brother] lives in London and he's married, he's got his own kids. The other thing that might be of importance is that one of my mum's sisters is married to another of his dad's brothers ... She was at the airport as well to receive him ... and when he came out she sort of whisked him away and I found out later that was to show him how the telephones work ... And the next day was the *rukhsati*, which is supposed to be the wedding night, which he spent mostly talking about how long it takes to get permanent in the country, how long it takes to get British nationality, which is I think three years now ...
>
> I was on the pill because I didn't want to get pregnant. Most Asian brides, they're pregnant straight away, and because of my disability I wasn't sure if I wanted to have kids or even if I was ready to have kids, 'cos the doctor said they could do genetic tests on my husband to see if he carried the genes of [her condition], in order to know if my kids would have the [disability] as well. So I wanted to wait for that, and I had already spoken to my doctor to send a referral. So I remember the wedding night, he was really, you know: 'Surely it's not important.' He's not interested in this genetic stuff. He was quite under-educated so he didn't understand. I am the worst in my family in Urdu-speaking or Punjabi-speaking. English is my best language. He didn't speak any English, although my parents had been telling him from here: 'Learn English and driving.'
>
> ... My uncle that set up [the match], he's my mum's brother, but his wife is also my husband's mum's sister, right? So the reason why I remember these things really, really well is because I had a lot of feelings of anger towards my uncle and his wife because I think they were doing it as a favour to her sister – get him married so he can come here. Personally, I think a lot are motivated by money – arranged marriages abroad ... He wanted us to have kids as soon as possible, probably because that's what people over there do, and probably because that's what he was told – that you can stay [in the UK] if you have a baby or something. The next day was Sunday, the *walima*, and that night it continued. I got a fever because it was winter and the clothes weren't really warm. It was rainy and we had to stand outside and get our pictures done. I got really, really sick and he

said I was deliberately being ignorant, 'cos I said I wanted to go to sleep 'cos I didn't feel well. And he didn't like it that my parents – they're very protective about … [me] because of the disability thing … and when I was sick they came upstairs to bring me medicines and hot milk and things, and he got really annoyed at that.

When the husband arrived in Britain, he came to live with Yasmin in her family home.

And he sort of looked around the room and saw – we had a lot of cultural differences, which he thought was a reason to argue. Like, he was into Indian movies and Indian music. I'm into R'n'B music and English films. And he said, 'I don't like the kind of clothes you wear', 'cos obviously, for going out here we wear trousers and stuff like that. Although I would say, our sisters, we're a lot more cultural than most of the girls in our family because we do wear a lot of our own *shalwar qamis* and stuff at home as well … I really love shoes – and he was really annoyed: 'There's no need to have so many shoes.' Most of it revolved around money, expenditure, things like that. So he spent most of that night disagreeing and after that, 'cos Monday it was just normal life, it was supposed to settle down into normal life. We'd visit lots of people for dinner, and the family thing where you go round to visit people, and you wear your fancy clothes and people usually give money. And he kept all of that money even though it was supposed to be split between us … And he spent a lot of the time going out, saying, 'I'm going for a walk'. Which I found out later was to make phone calls from public telephones to his uncle in London.

Then it came on to comparing my physical appearance, my attitude … If he slept in later than I did I went down and sat with my family, but he was like, 'Why are you sat with your sisters? It's different now, you're married'. Or he'd get out of bed at two in the afternoon and say, 'Go upstairs and make the bed!' And it would be directly like that, no 'Can you make the bed please?' or, 'I'm up now'. Like an order. Like I'm a servant girl or something.

He started complaining: 'Your sister's a bad mother. Your mother's cooking's not that nice. Your dad's so forcive [forceful] and he doesn't understand and he doesn't listen. Your brothers have got attitude problems. Your mother hasn't taught you much about marriage and being a wife' … I was willing to accept if he said things about me. And a lot of people in my family told me that everybody has problems, and settling in takes a while … But when he came to insulting my family I couldn't stay quiet and it got into major arguments. And he started saying things like, 'I didn't want to marry you anyway, it was all your uncle who set it up'. He wouldn't say it was his auntie because she was his direct blood auntie … 'They said that your dad would send eight thousand rupees to my house every month for looking after you.' And he didn't intend to work basically. Just expecting money to be sent to his house for being married to me ... We did ask, but obviously they denied it. And ever since then it's been really difficult in my household 'cos my dad says, 'He must have said it, it can't have come from nowhere', and my mum says, 'No, he can't have said it', because that's her brother, 'He wouldn't have said anything like that'. Because that uncle had changed, he was different to me after I got married ...

... Everybody got involved. Whenever anything happened I told my dad and he had a word with him, and he said, 'Why do you always tell your dad? It's our marriage, it's got nothing to do with your parents'. [Another of his mum's sisters] came down and said, 'I'll take him to London, maybe he needs a bit of space, and I really sympathise 'cos I've got daughters of my own' ...

My parents were getting a lot of hard time from my dad's brothers who all live here. [Her father's older brother is married to her husband's aunt] ... So that family had a lot of problems with us. [His aunt] came here and tried to talk to me about it. She took him to her house and told him stuff like, 'Try and apologise, try buying her flowers and chocolates and stuff like that' ... I later found out that all the letters and cards he sent me with all that meaningful stuff in them from Pakistan, they were all written by one of his friends because he doesn't know English so he got one of his friends to write them. He told me things like, 'All my friends read your cards and letters' ... I like writing poetry so I wrote all these poems to him on Valentine's Day and stuff, and it was all just a big joke to him.

He came down with his auntie and uncle and they sat down and talked to my dad ... 'Cos that day my dad asked his brothers to come down to help represent our side of the family as well. And they all said, 'No, we don't agree with what you're doing. Once someone is married they should stay married. Your daughter probably isn't putting all the effort in and you haven't taught her what you should have, so we're not going to represent you'. So we had nobody to represent us and he had all his family with him. For the sake of my parents – and my mum and dad were really affected by it – I said that he could stay and I'd give it a go, try and make it work.

... So he was back to normal in front of me and sweet as pie in front of my parents. So that was the problem, my parents thought I was being too hard on him and I was being difficult and things like that. And that's what my brothers and sisters thought. And there was a lot of disagreeing and a lot of arguing and I think that was making me more and more ill. Plus it was *Ramazan* and we were fasting. The other thing is, I don't know if you're aware in Pakistan they sell these 'blueprint' movies about sex and things ... A lot of wives are getting abused by their husbands because of those videos, because of the violent things they've done to their wives. And he confessed to me that he had watched a lot of those.

And he told me threatening things like how his dad beats up his mum and that's how he's got her obeying him and she does everything he says. Which really told me that that was the way it was going to be with us once we moved into our own house. 'Cos a lot of the time he went on about, 'When are we going to move to our own place?' The worst thing was when I told him about council flats he said, 'Well why do they give us a flat? Can't they just give us money that we can do what we want to?'

He saw pictures of my school dance, we had a school dance when I was leaving, when I was sixteen, and he saw photos and he accused me of having boyfriends, illegitimate relationships. And he wouldn't believe me if I told him that I hadn't ... And he was really, really violent. If I didn't do something that he wanted me to he would grab me and pull me around by the wrists. I had bruises on my wrists. And he was sexually being violent as well ... After a couple of nights, I used to stay up. I used to send him to bed and then I'd go up later. And then I used to wake up really early, and basically I spent most nights not sleeping. I was really out of it – not eating, not sleeping. Now when I think back to it it's like a dream, it's really airy everything that went on. It just went by really quickly. But he was really, really violent. I had a lot of bleeding and a lot of pains ... I told my parents about that, which is the point where my dad, my dad was the one who totally flipped out: 'Verbal, I can handle, because she can handle that, but when it comes to physical!' – because it's a known natural scientific fact that men are more strong than women. That was the point where it had gone too far for my dad, he didn't want to even push for it to be sorted out any more.

... One of my aunties, she's a bit younger and a bit more blatant and she just comes out with it about sex and stuff, whereas my mum's not so open about it, and she found out about the kind of experience that I had, from my parents. And his auntie ... said 'Well that's just the way it's supposed to be. My daughter had a hard time with her husband and these things happen, but girls don't have rights, they're supposed to do what their husbands say'. She had a lot against me. She said a lot of things about me to people in public in Pakistan. We have not got on with that family for years and years. Recently [they] went to do Haj ... It is the duty of all other Muslims to forgive the things they have done. And that's the only reason I'm speaking to them now ... otherwise even if we saw each other in public nobody said hello or anything.

I just pushed for it. I said there was no way he was staying here. I didn't want to live with him. People said to me, 'If you let him stay for about a year either it'll get sorted out or you don't have to let him get permanent', 'cos it takes [at that time] about a year to get a permanent visa, 'and then he can go back. At the moment it's not right to send him back' ... I just wanted him out of the house, I didn't care where he was, in Pakistan or in England ... He was stalking me round the house, I was scared to get up in the night, I was scared to go to the toilet, I used to have to take one of my brothers or my dad with me. He just kept pulling me around: 'Why won't you listen?' The worst thing was, there were so many people in the house but no one could stop him.

So my dad booked his ticket and said, 'I think you should go back for now and I'll try and talk to my daughter and sort it out, but it's safer if you're not here at the moment because she doesn't want you around'. My parents weren't happy, they were just sending him because that's what I wanted ... And on that day [his aunt] phoned my husband's uncle in London ... She denied doing it, but it's too obvious because she was the only person who knew and she knew because my dad told his brother ...

Everybody during this time span was telling me about [bad] experiences they had had when they were newly-weds ... [But since then] so many of my cousins have said that, 'It's so good that he's not here anymore. Because if we're still finding it hard – we have to raise the kids by ourselves, we have to do everything for ourselves, we have to do all the outdoor work, the bills, the statements, the washing, the cooking and if [you're disabled] it would never have got done, he would never have changed'. 'Cos my cousins have been married for ten years, eleven years and their husbands have not changed. They don't do nothing.

Yasmin's husband, with the help of his London relative, attempted to evade being sent back. When this failed ...

> he said, 'Why don't you drop me off at my uncle's?' This is what he said: 'I'll work there in his shop and I'll pay you back the money for the ticket that you lost.' So there was nothing to do with the marriage, he was happy to live in London and just work there ... [Dad] brought him back and everybody in the family abused him and he got dumped on the downstairs living room to sleep on the floor, and the phones were unplugged so he couldn't phone anybody. He wasn't allowed out of the house ... His family started phoning from Pakistan as well saying, 'What's the problem? Let me talk to him, we can sort it out' ... In that time I heard [listening at the door] that when our *rishta* had been set ... a year before we were married, his relatives in London had phoned his family in Lahore and told them that, 'What are you doing? That family is the wrong family to get your son married into. You should not be getting him married there. The girl is [disabled], she can't do anything, she's useless, no education, no nothing. She's totally not going to be the right kind of wife for him – you're making a mistake'. And his parents had said, 'It doesn't matter, at least he'll get there. When he's permanent there he doesn't have to stay with her'. So his auntie and uncle had arranged that in a year's time when he got a permanent visa to stay here, because obviously they would need my signatures to do that, so for a year he would have to cut it with me. And then that's it, he was going to leave me and get a new wife ...

This time my dad did not even tell his brothers about the flight ... the only people who knew were the people in this house ... When my dad got to the airport with him he saw another guy that was related to the London relatives, who was also going on the same flight to Pakistan ... He said to him, 'Listen, if you phone and tell anyone that you've seen us here, you're going to have me to deal with' ... The next thing you know my husband's uncle and auntie turn up at the airport ... and said that the boy was being forcibly taken to Pakistan, by which time my dad thought that was it, he was going to get away again because there was nothing my dad could do about it. It was his legal right to stay here for a year. All of a sudden, being crafty as he is ... 'cos my dad had really enticed him with the idea that [he] was going to give money to [Yasmin's husband's] dad to open a proper shop and a new house in Pakistan ... [he thought] 'I'll just tell the police people that I want to go to Pakistan 'cos my mother's ill ... I'm going to come back later' ... It was like a movie!

... [My parents] are there now. They've gone to a wedding in Karachi, but they don't intend to go to Lahore, because that family is lethal. There are people in that family, not directly my husband's family but their relatives, they've got murder charges on them and everything. So my parents don't want to go to Lahore. Even though one of my mum's sisters has passed away a year ago and my mum hasn't still been there to pay her condolences ... We have heard from other people, rumours that they want money otherwise they won't divorce me.

The year that I was married for, because he came in 1999 and I was married in '98, I was really happy ... I never ever would have predicted things to turn around to be that way. It didn't turn around, that's the most scariest thing of all, because they were planned like that before the wedding even happened ... his dad sort of admitted it [to my father], 'Yeah, that was the way it was planned, but he sort of rushed it – he did it all a bit too quickly'. His mum said, 'We're really poor. You did the right thing to get her married to him because religiously you would have done a good thing for someone poor. Can you please take him back with you?' She was phoning my uncle ... to say that, 'Try and get him away from them and sent to London so he can get to stay there'. And that's why I think even more that my uncle, even if he didn't know, his wife definitely knew.

Yasmin's father returned the clothes and other *burri* items.

I didn't want none of their stuff. They gave me clothes which if you wash them the colours were going to run anyway, and they gave make-up which just didn't suit my skin colouring anyway because it was all light fair skin make-up, and all really cheapy stuff you know ... The stuff that my parents gave me I've just kept. There's all the gold jewellery that my parents gave me obviously which I don't wear. I mean I wear some of it, but most of it is stuff you wear when you're married and you're out with your husband and stuff. But the clothes they gave me I wear them to weddings and when we go to parties ... My parents gave him a gold chain and a gold ring which we kept because he was here and we went through his stuff and kept it ... My mum gave his mum gold bangles ... and my parents also gave all of his family loads of clothes and there was all the extended family, because all his sisters are married, so we had to give to all of them. And we know that's stuff we're never going to see again. His family gave me clothes, make-up and some gold jewellery which we didn't return ... because we thought there's so much we've spent on them and we're never going to get it back ... [there was *mahr*] but I don't think it was a large amount, because it's family nobody thought it was going to go wrong. Nobody expects this to happen to them anyway. Especially when it's family – you just think it's family, they won't do that kind of thing.

The preceding account gives an example both of the failure of a family's attempts to manage the risks involved in a marriage, and of some of the dangers that they were trying to avoid. This chapter takes a close examination of Yasmin's narrative, together with other examples from my fieldwork and the literature, to illustrate several sets of potential tensions in Pakistani kinship. One issue that runs through the discussion is tension in the most literal sense of conflicts between family members surrounding marriages. In addition, having discussed concerns for British Pakistani women marrying men from Pakistan in the preceding chapter, the second section will examine difficulties that face some women coming from Pakistan to Britain for marriage. Finally, I will explore the role of honour in the type of conflicts outlined here. Two alternative explications will be proposed: one relying on a distinction between personal and group honour, and the other on a tension between honour and emotion. In the final analysis, however, I will suggest that such conflicts point towards a re-examination of the concept of honour that contextually dissolves these oppositions.

Taking sides: rifts in the family

While close kin marriages are thought to deter divorce, I have noted that there is parallel awareness that difficulties within a marriage between relatives can lead to the splitting of the kin group as individuals take sides, often with those to whom they are closest in either genealogical or emotional terms. The archetype of such risks is the *watta-satta* arrangement in which families 'exchange' daughters, with the danger that if one of the women is mistreated, revenge may be taken on her husband's sister (her brother's wife).

Rifts in the family can be related to marriage in two ways: either pre-dating and helping to channel *rishte*, or forming as a result of the breakdown of the marital relationship. Yasmin's marriage featured both varieties. First, her mother's brother in Pakistan seems to have colluded with his wife's relatives in arranging *rishte* for the two young men in England under false pretences, against the interests of his more distant sister, brother-in-law and British nieces. Then, when her marriage ran into difficulties, other family members became involved in arguments over whether Yasmin should be allowed to divorce and deport her husband. These conflicts led to lasting ill feeling. As this case shows, these disagreements can be very serious, entailing a reported complete halt to interaction. In a few cases a denial of kinship can result, such as when parents disown children (declaring them 'dead', or saying that they have no son/daughter) over severe disagreements (cf. Mody 2002b; Rytter 2012).

It may seem obvious, but matches may be more likely between sections of the *baraderi* (patrilineage/kin group) who have good relationships with each other. It was only gradually, however, that such information emerged in discussion about the choice of marriage partners. Raisa, for example, whose 'love marriage' to a cousin from her mother's side of the family was mentioned in an earlier chapter, let slip that the original 'unattractive' cousin whom she rejected was from her father's side of the family, with whom there is bad feeling. Azra, on the other hand, had originally liked her father's sister's son, but her mother does not get on with her father's side of the family. Over the years she came round to the idea of marrying a maternal cousin and now sees serious flaws in the man towards whom she was originally inclined. I did come across one marriage that took place across such a rift, although the details of the case only serve to reinforce the importance of these divisions. The couple in question were first cousins, but I was told that while one family had become extremely prosperous, the other had not done so well.[1] The two families did not get on and visiting relationships between the women of the two sides had apparently ceased. Nevertheless, the pair fell in love and married. The arrangements were carried out by the bride's family in secret because of the sensitivity of the match, but when the matter came to light it only served to worsen the split because offence was taken at both the secrecy and a decision not to invite some close relatives to the wedding.

As the above account suggests, the process of arranging marriages and choosing *rishte* can be a source of tension. Not only does rejection of proposed matches have the potential to cause offence, but competition for desirable matches can in itself be divisive. Shabaz, the taxi-driver in his thirties who explained the *hath* (hand) system of assessing power within the kin group, described cousins as 'like vultures':

> If I had a daughter and she's 15, 16, 17, if I went back, all the cousins will treat you like royalty, give you anything, treat you so nicely – you'll think they're your best friend. They're trying to come round you [i.e. persuade you to agree to a marriage between your children]. This is if you have daughters or sons. It's blatant – you know what they're doing, but they treat you so nicely you go along with it.

He described how his elder sister's husband's elder brother used to pick him and his siblings up and make a fuss of them when they were young. As soon as Shabaz's sister was of an age to marry, this avuncular character asked for her hand for his brother. However, after this marriage had taken place and his brother's migration to England had been secured, Shabaz said with bitterness: 'he forgot us.' Further examples of attempts by relatives to influence *rishte* in this way can be found elsewhere in this book, as when Uzma's mother besieged one sister with gifts while trying to secure a *rishta* between their children, leaving another sister feeling somewhat neglected. It may also be remembered from the chapter on close kin marriage that Shareen's choice of husband was influenced by her memories of the attentiveness of his father to her as a child.

Shabaz went on to give another example of a relative in Pakistan who was once a close friend. This cousin stopped being friendly towards him, Shabaz said, because he did not want to damage the chances of a *rishta* between his family and another relative with whom Shabaz does not have a good relationship. Of course, this very negative portrayal of marriage negotiations is likely to have been influenced by Shabaz's experience of a number of conflicts within his family. Others may have a less critical view of family members, so one woman in Bristol told me that they were indeed treated 'like royalty' by relatives when they visited Pakistan, but that this was because they had come all the way from England, and not due to any ulterior motives. However, most of those with whom I spoke were keenly aware of the potential for *rishte* to cause division. Many told me tales of rifts if not within their own, then in other families, and Bushra, who has arranged the marriages of both her children to relatives on her husband's side of the family, repeatedly said how lucky she was that all her siblings were fine with this arrangement, as her sisters could easily have been upset that their children were not chosen.

Concealment, hope and fear in marriages of Pakistani women to British men

In discussing the dangers of the 'double *rishta*' connection of both consanguinity and marriage, I noted the potential of mutual kin networks to inhibit referees from mentioning problems with proposed matches for fear of attracting blame. The distances involved in transnational marriage can facilitate the concealment of undesirable characteristics, so that they do not emerge until after the marriage had taken place. It is not only, however, the families of young men eager to migrate to the West who attempt to cover up their flaws. This danger also exists in intra-national arrangements. Jeffery and Jeffery, writing of north India, for example, report a case in which the young woman who arrived as the bride was not the same as the one who had been originally 'viewed' (Jeffery and Jeffery 1996: 98–99). When marriages span continents, the ability of families to visit potential *rishte* is curtailed. This section will examine instances where the families of young women from Pakistan were misled about the character, and in one case the physical health, of husbands based in Britain. Some of these deceptions may be carried out in hope: parents may believe the marriage will redeem their son's defects and be successful, but the failure of this optimism to be realised can leave migrant wives in very difficult situations.

Most Pakistani families are intensely concerned about the fate of daughters after marriage. Their fears can be increased when the daughter is marrying overseas into an environment which, although perceived to offer a 'better life' in material terms, most believe to be morally decadent and corrupt. Not only are American films increasingly available through the proliferation of new media, and Western pornographic sites appeared to be frequently visited by the predominantly male clients of the internet cafés I used in Rawalpindi and Islamabad, but Pakistan is party to the pervasive rhetoric found across the Muslim world in which 'the West' is held to be opposite in every way to decent Islamic values. When Nabila's mother's sister's son in Bristol proposed marriage, she and her mother were very worried about the prospect of her coming to live in this *mahaul* (environment). It's not that they don't trust the 'British-born', she said, but they know they are independent – 'they don't want to stay in'. Not having seen the young man since he was in Pakistan 10 years before, her mother worried that he might have a girlfriend in the 'free environment' she had seen in films. For Saba's mother's sister, these worries were too great, so when an old friend who had migrated to Britain through marriage many years before suggested a match between their children, she refused:

> ... my auntie said, 'I like her and I've kept in touch with her on the phone and so on, but I still can't trust her because ... you know her son is brought up in a different environment and I don't want to give away my daughter so far away. I know her but I can't take the risk'. And so they just said no.[2]

A few women do indeed arrive in Britain to find that their new husbands have partners, or even pre-existing families. One of the women who provided the inspiration for this study was in just such a situation. When I first met Tasneem she invited me to the sparsely furnished terraced home where she lived with her toddler son, while her husband lived with his white partner and their children. She told me that all she did was cry. Several years later she claimed still to have hope that her husband might return to her. He must have liked her when they married, she insisted, pointing to the existence of her son as supporting evidence. My suspicion, however, is that some of these cases are concealed forms of male forced marriage (Samad 2010) in which a young man's behaviour, such as having a girlfriend or using drugs, is worrying his parents. They are taken to marry a Pakistani woman in the hope that this will bring them back to the desired path. Bushra, for example, told me of a family she knows who got their son married in Pakistan in an unsuccessful attempt to put an end to his drug-taking lifestyle. Another man told me that his brother was forced to marry a cousin in Pakistan, but left home as soon as his wife came to the UK, whilst Asiya, who had hoped to marry her secret boyfriend, told me of her heartache when he was pressured into marrying a cousin on a family holiday to Pakistan, his involvement in his father's business meaning refusal would have cost him both family and livelihood. The corrective power of marriage to someone from a less 'corrupt' society is certainly given as a normal justification for forcing young women to marry (cf. Samad and Eade 2002). Mariam, for example, who was forced to marry a cousin, told me that her parents had arranged the marriage because she was 'running wild' as a teenager. The option to resist such compulsion by refusing to consummate the union is probably more readily available to men than to women – Asiya told me her boyfriend swore that he had not touched his cousin-wife (cf. Das 1973: 34; Das 1976: 204) – but it may be that many decide that the easiest path is to go along with the wedding and immigration application, in the knowledge that, unlike most women in forced marriages, they may be able to carry on with their chosen lifestyle after their spouse has come to Britain. The 2009 court case of Naseebah Bibi, jailed for imprisoning three imported Pakistani daughters-in-law and forcing them to work, whilst by no means the norm, provides another example of reluctant grooms: two of the sons reportedly already had white partners, and had little to do with their Pakistani wives.[3]

Other men who turn out to be very different from the image portrayed of them to their Pakistani wife and her family may have been very much in favour of the marriage. Hafza, for example, told me how her cousin from England had visited Pakistan. He had liked her and told his *ghar-wale* (family, lit. house-people) that he wanted to marry her. After arriving in Britain, however, she found that he and his friends drank heavily, moving on to injecting drugs in the house while she sat frightened upstairs. He abused her verbally (*tang karna*) and physically, and said that if she told anyone she would be sent back to her parents in Pakistan. She hoped that things would improve once they had children, but the beatings became worse after her son was born. Unaware of her legal rights, she withdrew several statements to the police for fear that she would be deported and lose her children.

In perhaps the most extreme case of concealment I came across, one family from Pakistan did not find out until the day after their daughter's wedding that the man settled in England whom she had married was physically handicapped, unable to work and requiring constant attention. This marriage was *bahar se* (outside the kin group), however, and it is unlikely that such a visible problem could have been hidden from family members. Indeed, it is sometimes seen as a duty for family to provide spouses for disabled or otherwise unmarriageable children. Sometimes the benefits of migration are explicitly weighed against the problems of the potential spouse. Nabila says that many people have suggested that she should get her brother married to her disabled sister-in-law so that he can come to Britain, but she thinks that this burden would ruin his life. Another woman I met, however, did come to Britain as the wife of a relative with a mental disability. Whilst others I know in Bristol criticised this decision, the new wife professes herself happy, and enjoys the fact that her husband holds her hand affectionately in public despite the obvious disapproval of older South Asian women in the community.[4]

As I noted in Chapter 3, some women with severe marital difficulties said they had not told their parents of their problems, despite their distress and loneliness that is often compounded by lack of language skills and support networks. Women may wish to protect their parents from worry (cf. Jeffery 2001). Hafza did not tell anyone about the abuse she was suffering for fear of being sent back to her parents in Pakistan, which would be experienced as an insult by them. The word Hafza used to describe how this would be perceived was *besti*, a contraction of *be-izzati*, which translates as 'ingloriousness, disesteem, dishonour, disgrace, ignominy' (Platts 2000 [1884]). It is to the role of *izzat* in conflict over marriage that the next section will turn.

Izzat and emotion

Izzat has been translated as prestige (Eglar 1960; Raheja and Gold 1994), status (Fischer 1991), and as opposed to (generally sexual) shame (Jeffery 1979), but is perhaps more commonly translated as honour (Abu-Lughod 1988; Fischer 1991; Lefebvre 1999). All of these inter-linked meanings are present in the term, and which definition is employed may depend on the context under consideration. While 'prestige' has been the most appropriate English term for some writing on the accumulation of *izzat* through gifting (Eglar 1960; Raheja and Gold 1994; Werbner 1990), sexual issues come to the fore when discussing purdah practices (Jeffery 1979). For the purposes of the current discussion, I will employ the term 'honour' as the character which, as will be seen, emerges as primary in the context of marital conflict.

A substantial volume of writing on honour has emanated from the anthropology of the circum-Mediterranean. In this scholarship, however, the concept has been the subject of two inter-linked lines of criticism: that the primacy given to honour in the analysis of these societies has led to a premature conceptualisation of a Mediterranean unity, and that the term conceals significant difference in concepts (Delaney 1987; Gilmore 1987; Herzfeld 1980, 1984, 1987). In Turkey, for example, *seref* refers to honour in a general sense while *namus* relates only to sexuality,[5] and the 'confusion or conflation of these interrelated but separable forms of honor has marred the discussion of this topic' (Delaney 1987: 36). In the context of migration, coverage of 'honour killings' may pathologise minority groups, constructing them as a homogenous and problematic cultural 'other' (Apkinar 2003; Korteweg and Yurdakul 2009). A focus on 'honour' has also been accused of privileging the values of dominant men, masking those of non-dominant groups and ignoring processes of change (Lever 1986). As many of these critics nevertheless agree, some concept of honour may be a near universal, as public opinion arbitrates by evaluating conduct against ideal standards (Peristiany 1965; Pitt-Rivers 1965). The term *izzat*, moreover, is one that is understood and employed by many of those who participated in this research. Rather than avoid the concept of honour, therefore, these next two chapters will attempt an exploration of the multiple connotations of *izzat* in a way which leaves space for alternative constructions by men in non-dominant positions, and which questions the image of unfeeling masculine adherence to codes of honour that underlie so many stereotypes of Muslim men.

Whilst the category of 'honour and shame societies' glosses great variation, ethnographies discussing 'honour' in various circum-Mediterranean societies nonetheless provide elements that can be of use in illuminating the Pakistani concept of *izzat*. Campbell, in work on the Greek Sarakatsani, gives one foundation of the concept as the qualities on which the reputation of the group or individual are dependent (Campbell 1964: 268). This general formulation provides scope for variation of the precise content of these qualities between societies. Moreover, for the Sarakatsani, as for Pakistanis, these desired attributes are gendered: while men are judged by their 'manliness', women achieve honour through demonstrating sexual shame (Campbell 1964: 269). Abu-Lughod (1988) expands on these observations by adding other power dynamics to the gendering of honour so that women and low-status men who share the inability to achieve 'honour' through the dominant model of autonomy may attain it instead by voluntary deference, itself a sign of independence. Similar observations have been made about Muslim women in north India (Jeffery 1979).

The Bedouin value of autonomy is closely related to the ability (of a man) to control assets and other people (Abu-Lughod 1988), and similar ideas of control emerge strongly in the literature on honour in Pakistani society. Land ownership is one powerful method of gaining *izzat* (Eglar 1960), whilst Fischer (1991: 108) writes that *izzat* is also based upon the control over women, most importantly, followed by younger males in the family, and then by that over other men in the extended family. Veena Das, writing on Hindu Punjabis with strong parallels to Pakistani concepts of honour, suggests that honour also implies controlling the ties and emotions that are thought to stem from local concepts of 'the biological facts of procreation and copulation', so that:

> ... honour, which is one of the most valued ideals among the Punjabis, is acquired and enhanced by transcending natural forces rather that succumbing to them. The transcendence, insofar as it violates human nature, is often represented either as a mask which is worn to disguise the pre-social or anti-social currents operating in the biological substratum, or it is represented as a sacrifice which lifts an individual from his 'lower-self' to his 'higher-self'. The negation of honour is expressed in shame or 'loss of face'.
>
> (Das 1976: 198–99)

These categories parallel Islamic conceptions of *nafs*, the animal self, which should be curbed by the opposed category of *'aql*, or reasoned discrimination (Metcalf 1984; cf. Kurin 1988), and echo Campbell's observation of the Sarakatsani that, 'One aspect of honour, then, is a struggle of self-discipline over cowardice and sensuality, flaws of animal nature that continually threaten to limit the natural nobility of man' (Campbell 1964: 269).

Arranged marriages may be viewed, at least in the abstract, as based on 'social' matters and carried out in a cool and controlled fashion. The 'personal' choice of a 'love' match contracted in the heat of passion, on the other hand, can bring dishonour (Mody 2002a: 226). The picture of honour that emerges, therefore, is of a dual system of value in which the powerful gain or lose through the extent of their control over assets and persons, and all – men and women, powerful and powerless – aim to exert control over their 'natural' impulses. To make Das's categories completely clear, 'natural' here refers not to the assertion of a scientific 'truth', but to a cultural understanding of the substances exchanged in procreation and childrearing and the emotional bonds that these, Punjabis believe, inevitably create. In other words, there are two co-existing Punjabi discourses and models for behaviour concerning kinship, one viewed as 'natural' and the other as 'social'. Honour, she suggests, is gained by overcoming these 'natural' impulses and relating to others in accordance with what are seen as the 'social' rules of kinship, depicted here as wearing a mask.

We now return to Yasmin's story and the second role of rifts in the *baraderi* – those stemming from the difficulties and dissolution of marriages. Pakistanis in Britain and Pakistan regard divorce as a serious and shameful matter, particularly for the family of the woman involved. Fischer notes that:

> [t]he marriage of daughters is seen as difficult, for if daughters are badly married this will reflect on the family. Women are the core of the family's *izzat*. They define its range and their behaviour reflects on this. After marriage the family of the husband assumes responsibility for her behaviour. If that responsibility is not taken, this reflects on the family of the girl; they take the blame, although she is not under their direct control, because it was their responsibility to find a respectable family and to provide a woman who would maintain the honour of both families ... If she behaves badly, such as abandoning her husband without cause, or has sexual relations with men other than her husband (*zina*, fornication), then it is the responsibility of her family to remedy the situation, in the latter case sometimes by her death.
>
> (Fischer 1991: 104)

Further, as a social evaluation, the idea of honour connects the individual and the group. For Pakistanis, 'all the members of a *biraderi* have a feeling of collective honor, the protection of which serves as collective security' (Eglar 1960: 79). Conversely, the dishonourable actions of one member of the kin group entail a loss of honour for all, which may deter future *rishte* (Eglar 1960: 78). Disharmony between kin demonstrates a lack of unity or control, and so is bad for the *izzat* of the group. Divorce makes public all of these failures: the choice of an incompatible spouse, lack of control over a daughter and disunity among kin.

Yasmin's wider kin group put pressure on her father to control his daughter and so maintain his and the family's honour. The criticism came in particular from relatives who were 'close' to her husband through links (*rishte*) of kinship and affinity, such as the maternal uncle married to her husband's mother's sister. Yasmin reports that her father was criticised for failing to maintain control when his brothers refused to represent him, saying ' ... we don't agree with what you're doing. Once someone is married they should stay married. Your daughter probably isn't putting all the effort in and you haven't taught her what you should have ... ' In other words, the loss of honour was cumulative. Perceived to have lost control over his daughter, he could no longer command the support of his brothers, with the ultimate result that his son-in-law was in a stronger position in negotiations and Yasmin was made to drop her demands: 'For the sake of my parents – and my mum and dad were really affected by it – I said that he could stay and I'd give it a go – try to make it work.' Finally, however, something happened that made Yasmin's father change his mind. This was the point when Yasmin's parents came to know that their son-in-law was being physically and sexually violent to their daughter. In Yasmin's words, her father 'totally flipped out ... That was the point at which it had gone too far for my dad, he didn't want to even push for it to be sorted out any more'. Despite the efforts and opposition of his relatives, and risking the ultimate loss of honour as a man rejected by his kin, he himself took the young man back to Pakistan.

I would like to propose two interpretations of the turning point in Yasmin's marriage, one based on the concept of honour through control, and the other on the relationship between *izzat* and emotion. Here the importance of recognising differences not just in conceptions of honour, but in their social contexts comes to the fore. Campbell notes that for the Sarakatsani, where the 'elementary family' is the 'only relatively enduring kin group', the fact that honour has two points of reference, the individual and the family, 'rarely leads to any conflict of loyalties since the solidarity of the elementary family is so complete' (Campbell 1964: 268). For Pakistanis, however, the concept of honour has a wider spread, encompassing relatives outside the household, and potentially the whole *baraderi*: a Punjabi proverb both differentiating and linking family and *baraderi* says that 'one does not share bread but one shares the blame' (Eglar 1960: 75). The potential for conflicting aims in terms of honour is thus far greater. From this perspective, it could be argued that Yasmin's father was faced with a conflict between the demands of his own personal honour, undermined by losing control over a junior male member of the household to the extent that he was being violent towards his daughter, and the demands of group honour in preventing divorce. Threats to the personal honour of others involved may also be imagined. Having arranged a marriage to facilitate the migration of his wife's sister's son, for example, Yasmin's mother's brother in Pakistan might well feel that he would lose honour if this project failed and the bridegroom returned ignominiously. From this interpretation, a picture emerges of individuals vying for control over each other and the situation, and with the definition of the interests of the group's honour.

Another viewpoint sees Yasmin's father trapped not only in a conflict between individual and group honour, but between the pulls of *izzat* and emotion. This tension can most clearly be illustrated by a brief examination of the issue of 'honour killings'. When an individual, most often a woman, is felt to have brought shame upon the family, commonly for having committed or being suspected of sexual impropriety or an inappropriate union, there may be calls for her to be killed to protect family honour. Such cases occur both in Pakistan and amongst Pakistanis in Britain.[6] In one widely publicised British case, Rukhsana Naz was killed by her mother and brother for being pregnant by a man other than her husband, who was still in Pakistan (Boggan 1999). In practice, however, notes Abu-Lughod (1988: 286, note 16), such killings are quite rare as 'the ideals of honour and the realities of family closeness ... are in conflict in such cases'. For the Pakistani Baluch, the potentially disruptive *nafs* is valued in certain context, such as when it provides aggressiveness in confrontations. 'A praiseworthy man must be able to juggle these two conflicting elements of human nature', but when '*nafs* and *'aql* collide ... the former is at least as likely to prevail as the latter' (Pastner 1988: 168–72). Equally, when emotional ties and honour are in conflict, the former may win. In other words, the strength of emotional bonds between family members means that fathers, for example, are unlikely to kill their daughters to satisfy the demands of honour. Veena Das phrases this in terms of the distinction in Punjabi thought between the 'natural' bonds of kinship as locally perceived, and the requirements of what is thought of as 'social' morality. The belief in an underlying pre-social force, she suggests, provides an alternative discourse and source of justification for action. Thus while Ahmed told me of the importance of marriage within the *baraderi* and the maintenance of family assets, his daughter says that he has told her affectionately that when she is ready to marry he will make all the available men line up for her, so that she can choose the best. This duality of moral codes also explains the varying moral judgements Das encountered in one case of honour killing:

> Some of my informants felt that the sister had been a victim, but the victimisation was for higher ends. Surely, they argued, the brothers had to sacrifice their own *selves* in killing their beloved sister. Other informants were plainly horrified and repelled. An old man said that he would have preferred to live in shame than have the murder of his own daughter on his hands. This shows that as in the smaller victories and defeats, in the

larger victories and defeats of life also, a person can make choices deriving the legitimacy of his conduct from biological or social kinship.

(Das 1976: 214–15)

Following this line of argument, Yasmin's father's ultimate actions in going against the wishes of the *baraderi* to protect his daughter may be viewed as acting in accord with his emotional ties rather than the duties of honour, or in Punjabi terms, prioritising natural over social kinship, even being true to himself. 'The social symbols *are* masks and the father who preserves his honour by killing his errant daughter may save his face, but he is doomed to irredeemable alienation from his true self' (Das 1976: 222). Thus the brother in the British 'honour killing' mentioned above is said to have wept while he strangled his sister (Boggan 1999). Hafza and other migrant wives' decisions not to tell their parents about their difficulties may be seen as avoiding putting them in this difficult position of choosing between the impulse to rescue their daughter, and the prospect of suffering *besti*, loss of honour.

The choice Yasmin's family faced was stark, but in other cases seeming to present similar dilemmas, solutions may be found that allow the maintenance of close emotional bonds whilst avoiding obvious damage to group honour. In some instances, people decide on a 'love marriage' against their family's wishes. A standard reaction in this type of case is for parents to threaten to disown their children in the hope that this will deter them from going through with the union, or that severing relations will protect family honour if the couple do marry (cf. Rytter 2012). Saif, for example, told me that his elder brother had called off his wedding to the woman of his choice at the last minute after his father had threatened to disown him if he did not agree to his pre-arranged engagement to a relative in Pakistan. In other cases the repudiation is temporary. Once parents have got over their anger and upset, the wayward couple may be recognised by the family once more. Although such instances can damage the honour of the family, particularly in the case of a daughter, the temporary estrangement of the child seems to be recognised as at least a token defence of this honour, but one that allows emotional bonds to be maintained in the long run. So when Shabaz secretly married his girlfriend of six years without his parents' permission, they accepted the situation after a week and allowed him to return home with his new wife.[7] Related examples are found in Perveez Mody's sensitive analysis of the construction of elopements as abductions in New Delhi. In one enigmatic case, she suggests that while it is possible that the young woman in question staged her own violent abduction, the family themselves might have initiated the deceit in order to save themselves from dishonour. Despite the fact that the elopement came publicly to light, after her father initially disowned his runaway daughter, she was eventually taken back by her family. Her family then filed charges against her husband for abduction (Mody 2002b).

One woman in Pakistan told me about a female relative in Britain whom she described as 'very clever'. Several of this woman's children had contracted what were widely assumed by relatives to be 'love marriages', some with non-Pakistani partners. In each case, however, the mother had asserted that she herself had arranged the matches, so that one son-in-law, for example, had been a regular visitor to the house as a friend of the daughter. She told relatives that she had observed that he did not eat pork, and would make a good match for her child, and had arranged the marriage after he converted to Islam. A Pakistani relative, however, cast aspersions on his conversion, suggesting that only his mother-in-law calls him by his Muslim name. I later heard from a different relative that another of this woman's children was to be married, this time to a university classmate. The mother was again saying that she had arranged the marriage, this time after assessing the suitability of all the potential South Asian candidates in her child's graduation photograph. The relative who told me of the *rishta* said that everyone else in the family was fairly sure it was a love match. Although she has obviously not avoided gossip about her children's marriages within the *baraderi*, this woman has managed to negotiate the presentation of these unions to avoid public smears on the family's honour without sacrificing her relationship with her children. She has maintained her honour by asserting that she still has control over the junior members of her household, but at the same time prioritised the happiness of her children – a clever move in the eyes of her relatives. It might be noted here that a woman is maintaining honour through a presentation of control, rather than deference. As the head of the household, this reaffirms the multiple pathways to honour determined by power as well as gender (Abu-Lughod 1988; Jeffery 1979).[8]

Das reports a similar case in which a pre-marital conception was disguised as a premature birth. The parents were privately the subject of gossip and ridicule, but were not insulted by *baraderi* members to their face. She notes that although gossip about girls' moral character is a popular pastime, it is done warily lest the same thing is happening in one's own household (Das 1976: 215). Whilst rumour and derision cannot be escaped, it seems, suspicion alone is not always sufficient to justify the risk of publicly smearing another's honour. This creates a space of ambiguity in which creative solutions to the tension between honour and emotion may be attempted. Similarly, Mody presents a type of case in which the children rather than the parents are the main agents in negotiating the definition of their marriage. In 'love-cum-arranged' marriages, the couple marry in secret and then return to their homes, where over time they bring their parents round to the idea of the match. Second ceremonies are then held, despite the risk of loss of honour to the parents if the origins of the marriage in a love relationship became known (Mody 2002a).

In addition to Das's two forms of Punjabi kinship, the 'social' and the 'natural' emotions, there are other sources of legitimacy to which Pakistanis may appeal if they hope to follow courses of action that might be seen as subversive. Amongst young people trying to make space for alternative views in negotiations over their marriage, the most common of these is religion. So Mina, seeking release from her forced marriage, silenced her mother's objections by pointing out that Islam allows women to ask for a divorce. Divorced Rubina, who now thinks that her best chance of remarriage is a love match, attempted to broaden her opportunities by arguing that Muslims are permitted to marry any other Muslim, and so her parents should not object if she were to marry someone who was not Pakistani – even a black man, despite the widespread bias towards fair skin, and indeed the prejudice against Afro-Caribbeans and other *kala* (a black person) that sometimes exists among Pakistanis in Britain. Meanwhile, a young cousin came to her seeking religious advice on whether Muslims were duty-bound to marry cousins. Rubina assumes that her family have claimed that this is the case, and informed her that cousin-marriage was a matter of tradition rather than religion.

'Tradition' can provide yet another source of legitimacy (Brown 2006). When I accompanied Arifa on a visit to her relatives in another British city, the conversation turned to marriage. Arifa, who does not want to marry a cousin, seemed to attempt a strategic definition of the boundaries of *baraderi* to broaden her choice of marriage partners, whilst maintaining the cultural acceptability of such a marriage. Taking advantage of the expandability and conceptual slipperiness or 'sliding semantic structure' (Alavi 1972) of the concept outlined in Chapter 3, she asserted that people were allowed to marry not just someone with whom a relationship may be traced but any member of the same *zat* (caste), and still maintain *baraderi* endogamy.

Rethinking honour: collapsing categories

In an earlier chapter I suggested that the concept of *rishta* provided a bridge between the issues of strategy and emotion in the analysis of Pakistani marriage choices. In a similar fashion, the concluding section of this chapter will argue for rethinking Pakistani experiences of honour. Das's valuable opposition of the 'natural' and the 'social' forms of Punjabi kinship, I suggest, is nevertheless too rigid. The polarisation of these terms disguises the leakages between honour and emotion, the points at which these categories meet and slip into each other to the extent that it becomes impossible to distinguish them. To elucidate this argument, I will return once more to the issue of 'honour killings', this time to a case that occurred in Bristol some years before my fieldwork.

I have heard several different accounts of the incident, but the gist of the story is that a husband, whose wife was having an affair, killed her and their daughters. One man, asking whether I had heard about the case, explained that the husband was taking revenge for his wife's behaviour which would be felt as a *besti* among the *baraderi*. I discussed the murder with Humera and Bushra, who agreed that the husband was justified in Islamic terms in killing his wife, but that it was terrible that the children had died. In one version I heard of the case, the husband actually surprised his wife with her lover and killed in a rage. Humera, on the other hand, told me that she believed he was a good man, but that his family had put him under incredible pressure as they felt that their honour had been besmirched, and eventually the strain had been such that it 'turned his head' and he committed the killings. Here, the way in which honour makes its demands on the individual is through influence exerted along the bonds of close kinship. Moreover, the requirements of honour are believed to have been perceived as intense emotion to the point of a temporary madness. Evidently, then, Pakistani conceptions of honour do not exclude emotion, but rather emotion is integral to the experience and mechanisms of honour. Honour is maintained by control – both of others and of one's lower, natural self and emotions. A quarrelling family brings dishonour upon itself, but where honour is challenged, a reaction of anger is often expected. Furthermore, these examples suggest that honour is not simply, as Das suggests, a 'mask' presented to the world through the sacrifice of true selves and instinctual bonds, but something that itself can result from seemingly 'natural' reactions to the transgressions of wives, daughters and sisters, or duty towards and pressure from kin. In Jordan, the defence of honour is naturalised to the extent that the killing of a wife by a husband who discovers her adultery is justified in law on the grounds that under such circumstances it is inevitable that the man's 'blood will boil' (Sawalha 2002).

Returning, finally, to Yasmin, who described how her father 'totally flipped out', this chapter has presented two interpretations of his sudden *volte face* in going against the wishes of the *baraderi* to return his son-in-law to Pakistan: that his personal honour as father and head of the household was undermined by the situation in his household, or that his 'natural' instinct to protect his daughter overwhelmed the imperatives of maintaining family honour. In the moment of discovering that someone had been hurting his daughter under his own roof, however, it seems likely that the pain and anger of his damaged honour and the urge to protect his daughter were so inter-linked as to be indistinguishable.

Although Veena Das's (1976: 199) emphasis is on the disjunction and dialectic between the two strata, she acknowledges at the start of her paper that they 'may partially overlap'. The preceding argument has been an attempt to augment this analysis by suggesting that these categories, like so many others encountered in the social sciences, are contextual. These slippages, the collapsing of categories, seem from the material presented above to occur most in times of crisis when the challenge to honour and the attack on the bonds that stem from 'procreation and copulation' (Das 1976: 198) become one. This suggestion may also help disentangle an apparent inconsistency in the elegant metaphor of 'Masks and Faces' which forms the title of Das's paper. Throughout the argument, the 'mask' refers to the system of honour and kinship morality concealing the true 'natural' self with its emotional bonds to close kin, but at the same time a loss or redemption of honour is described as losing or saving 'face'. It is my contention that this seeming duality – the true face behind the mask, as well as that which is at stake in crises of honour – reflects an experiential eliding of *izzat* and emotion under the highly charged conditions in which honour is most threatened.

It might be suggested that the strength of the discourse of fatherly love that encouraged Yasmin's father to act against the interests of the honour of his kin group is at least in part a product of the family's prolonged residence in the UK. In Britain, the priority of emotional ties between members of the nuclear family is often held as self-evident, exemplified by the horror with which exceptions to the rule (such as parents who harm their children) are viewed. Indeed, Das's informants themselves were middle-class urban Punjabis, and historical research has demonstrated that the middle classes under British Indian rule were affected by the colonists' opinions, remodelling representations of religion, gender and kinship as a result (cf. Chatterjee 1989; Mani 1989; Metcalf 1994). One response would be to question the utility or possibility of isolating a 'pure' Pakistani discourse on kinship and emotion in isolation from the influence of Britain and the West. More pertinently, however, recent scholarship has suggested that the very model of a rigid, unemotional South Asian approach to kinship and marriage upon which these criticisms rest is itself more 'our' imagining than either an historical or contemporary reality (Parry 2001). As Mody (2002b) notes, descriptions such as her account of Delhi love marriages, present a marked counter to the common stereotype of South Asian arranged marriage. This exploration of Yasmin's family's highly emotional response to her marital difficulties is another blow to this dominant image.

A further challenge to stereotypes is presented in the next chapter. My discussions of risk have shown how concern over the dangers involved in marriage have focused on women. Brides are considered more vulnerable to mistreatment or unhappiness, thanks in large part to the fact that they normally migrate on marriage to live as an in-comer in their husband's household. As I set out in the Introduction, however, almost half of the spousal immigrants to Britain from Pakistan are now men, so male marriage migration has come to represent a challenge to the norm of the migrant bride. The next chapter will piece together some of the difficulties that men in this position can face, leading to a discussion on masculinity and emotion in which the issues raised here will be revisited.

Notes

1 *Baraderis*, as has been noted, tend to sub-divide into inter-marrying units along socio-economic lines.
2 Saba's mother seems not to have shared her sister's concerns, as this was the young man Saba went on to marry.
3 See: www.guardian.co.uk/uk/2009/may/29/slave-daughters-woman-jailed (accessed 01/02/2012).
4 Public displays of affection between husband and wife are considered shameful (cf. Das 1976).
5 A similar distinction exists in Iraq between *sherat* and *ird* (al-Khayyat 1990: 21).
6 The Human Rights Commission of Pakistan reported 227 such deaths in Pakistani Punjab in 2001, with the real figure likely to be higher (*Dawn* 2002).

7 Other estrangements may last longer: weeks, months or even years.
8 In addition, this woman illustrates one of the possible effects of migration on gendered relations of power, as it may be due to her residence in Britain rather than Pakistan that, as a widow, she is able to act as the head of the household in this way (cf. Rauf 1982 on male migration from Pakistan to the Gulf and 'matrifocal households').

7 Migrant *mangeters*
Masculinity, marriage and migration

> I didn't even cry on my wedding day. Everybody said, 'Why didn't you cry?' I said I was going to come back to England. He should be crying – *he*'s leaving *his* house.

These words belong to Asma, a young woman from Bristol. Her husband was going to leave Pakistan and his natal home to join her in Bristol, whilst she would be staying in the bosom of her family, so she saw no reason to follow convention and grieve at her *rukhsati*. Her statement makes the connection discussed in earlier chapters between marriage, migration and emotional loss. Conventionally, this is the experience of the bride. Here Asma points out that it is her husband Tahir who will suffer the losses of migration. He would not be expected to publicise these 'female' emotions in a show of tears for the wedding guests. Nevertheless, interviewing Tahir in Bristol revealed that his migration had indeed been a traumatic time. This chapter features extended interview excerpts in which Tahir and another migrant husband, Junaid, describe the difficulties they faced.

In the literature on marriage-related migration, female marriage migrants are often considered vulnerable to isolation and abuse (Schlenzka 2006; Wilson 2007). The plight of unhappy South Asian brides has been documented both within the subcontinent (e.g. Jeffery and Jeffery 1996) and in the UK (e.g. Fenton and Sadiq 1993), but less attention has been paid to the experiences of those men who, like Tahir, find adjusting to life in Britain difficult. In this chapter, I explore such men's culturally informed experiences of migration and expressions of emotion. Since I first published on this issue (Charsley 2005), the literature on migration and masculinity has expanded (e.g. Ahmad 2009; Batnitzky *et al.* 2008; Donaldson *et al.* 2009; Gallo 2006), and includes other work exploring the gendered challenges of migration for men (Osella and Osella 2000; Gamburd 2000). Both Gallo (2006) and George (2005), for example, have explored how Keralan husbands of migrant nurses and domestic workers negotiate the feminised position of trailing spouse.

Increased attention has also been paid to the denigration by British Pakistanis of new migrants from Pakistan. Harriss and Shaw (2009) note newly arrived migrants laughingly referred to as clueless 'freshies'.[1] *Mangeter* (groom/fiancé) is another term used to refer to marriage migrants (Ahmad 2008), and images of the transnational *mangeter* have proliferated since my first fieldwork (cf. Kalra 2009: 11). A Pakistani music video by Imran Shaukut, for example, shows an imported groom in the UK working multiple jobs in shops and a sewing workshop only to hand over his wages to his wife (she gives him back just enough to buy a few cigarettes) and then have to cook a meal for his in-laws. I have heard the term *mangeter* used to refer to men long after their marriage and arrival in Britain. It can be read, like the petrification of Thai marriage migrants as eternal 'brides' (Sims 2012), as a denial of both belonging and full adult status. This chapter will examine the experiences of male Pakistani marriage migrants, to show how the combination of the social and economic processes of migration interact with features of Pakistani kinship and masculinity to produce particular challenges for some immigrant husbands. These include problems of employment and downward mobility, loss of social networks, the culturally unusual position of residence in their wife's household, experiences of cultural difference and challenges to *izzat*. In extreme cases, these processes may help to explain the catastrophic ways in which some marriages, presented largely from the perspective of the wives and their families in earlier chapters, have gone wrong. Whilst it is not my intention to suggest that all husbands coming to Britain from Pakistan are in these situations, on my return to Bristol I was saddened to learn of several divorced among those with whom I had worked, including Asma and Tahir. In other cases the experiences explored in this chapter may constitute a phase resolved to a greater or lesser degree with the passage of time. The model can also, however, be useful in understanding the positive experiences of some male marriage migrants, as differences from the archetype of the 'unhappy husband' (Charsley 2005) help account for the ease with which others have adapted to life in Britain.

The exploration will revisit Yasmin's narrative (addressed from the perspective of her father in the preceding chapter), to bring to light the submerged figure of the errant husband. I will suggest that Yasmin's reports of their disagreements and his complaints reveal frustrations with wider relevance for Pakistani immigrant husbands to Britain. In doing so, it becomes possible to address two different masculine responses to a set of events, those of both the father of a bride (in the last chapter), and now from that of the husband. A final interview narrative from Junaid, a migrant husband whose marriage had ended in divorce, allows a return to the issue of *izzat*, and informs a discussion of gender and emotion which will conclude the chapter.

Tahir's marriage migration

Tahir's marriage to his maternal cousin in Bristol was arranged by his parents when he was 20:

> Once I saw her a few times after our engagement it was all right. There are some suspicions in mind obviously, but I think the way their family

behaved and all that – it seemed like it was quite like our own family, so it was all right ... Like, to tell you the truth, a lot of girls [in Britain], even in Asian families over here, they go around with boys and have relationships with other people. And for a boy from there, especially for myself, I would say it's unacceptable, something that really demoralises a person ... There could have been something like that because of the different circumstances prevailing over here, but as we saw the family, how they behaved, I thought it was all right, that she was a nice girl, decent behaviour, so I didn't really mind ... I think what [his parents] saw in her [was] that she was simple, and secondly that she would mix up in the family [i.e. fit in well] ... These days [even girls in Pakistan] don't behave like her, most of them. Some of them are like her – I wouldn't say that she's one in a million – but a lot of them have become a little different in thinking. Family-wise, they want to get married, get separate [i.e. move out of the extended family home].

I came over in April [to Britain from Pakistan] ... The same time, about a week earlier my father went over to *haj* [pilgrimage to Mecca]. A week later I left, so my father he got quite emotional at that time. First time really I saw him emotional ... They do miss me. I miss them too, but it [being settled in Britain] has grown with time, it has gone a little more firm – I have children. But in the long run we have decided to move over there. Maybe next year we might be going over for a couple of years [to Pakistan in order to complete his studies] ... I knew that there would be problems [coming to Britain without finishing his qualification], but what it was – I couldn't stay any longer, she was pregnant at that time. Secondly, financially we were a little bit disturbed at that time so I had to come over immediately, otherwise I might have stayed a little bit longer ... She likes it over there as well. It's a more social life. She's adjusted herself quite well in the family. She didn't have to make any major changes, but still she likes it more over there, so might as well go over there – she gets a little more helping hand with the kids and all that.

... When I came over, when I came off the plane [I thought]: 'All right. New place ... All right, nice place, motorway's nice' ... [Then after a] couple of days, a week – getting more and more annoyed. Because I'd left everything – friends, family. It's a totally new situation, and so [Asma] helped me out a lot. She always used to listen to me, stay close to me, whatever the adjustments were. There are differences in families – the way of thinking, everything, but she always stuck over to my side, more like she was grown up in *my* family! So she's been very helpful for my initial adjustments ... The boys over here, they're just terrible! No respect – nothing! ... A lot of different things I had to adjust on in life over here. I tried to get control, but it took some time before I could. Because I used to get those day nightmares: 'Where am I? What? Can I go home? Let's go!' ... because over there I spent most of the time outside. I was at home at night time and some of the time at dinner time, but most of the time I was outside with friends, or in college, or at the hospital. So total change, like. Go out – just stare about, can't even talk to anybody because if I start talking [the other person will think], 'Oh, what does he want? Who is he?' It's natural, because it takes a whole new time to build up those things that took me about maybe twenty years of my life to build up. So I say it's a zero start. I have to start again ... but it takes me time to make friends. Secondly, I'm very cautious about what kind of friends I make. Over here I have found a few people, but it's just spending time – I haven't got anybody really close. Except Asma. She's the only friend I've managed to get.

For two or three weeks he tried to find medical jobs, but was unsuccessful as his training was not quite complete. He then found work through an agency.

... they were terrible jobs. I had to work in the rain holding things. ... manual jobs. So for the time being it was all right – shook out the rust out of me ... Later on I managed to get another job. It was same type of job, manual job, but a little better ... I worked there for four months. It was a refrigerator – I had to work inside it! But then I found [his current processing job] ... They advertised it, and secondly there are a few people around here that work [in the same place]. Some are our relatives. They told me the address to phone up over here ... It's nice and comfortable, just sitting around. Just have to spend the time ... It's all the same, so it just becomes like a robot or something. So keep on doing it, keep on talking ... In the beginning it was very hard, because I had never thought in my life that I would have done anything like this. Maybe I didn't know what it was like over here, but over there you know most of the students they are leeches on their family, basically. They don't work much. They do some tuition or something sometimes, but work like this – no. So it was quite an extraordinary experience, but later on I realised I had to do it. Got a family to manage. Maybe later on in life when good times come ...

It's been the opposite way round – usually girls make adjustments ... Some things I can't change like certain habits of mine. I've changed most of them – I don't smoke inside, I smoke always outside now ... I think it's more comfortable [since we have moved out of the extended family home]. We have our own privacy. Secondly, the lifestyle we want to develop for our own selves, we can. That's most important to me – I can grow my children the way I want to. Teach them the things I want. Otherwise if I lived in joint family, somebody comes around [and says to his child]: 'What are you doing?' – gives my child a slap [and shouts]: 'Go over there!' It's not right ...

Before they are ten years old, I would like them to go back. Even if I'm here or I'm over there, I would like them to be brought up over there ... After ten they can go either way – they can stay straight, they can go the other way. If after twelve or fourteen I take them over, it wouldn't be right for them because they will be mixed up in a mixture of environments ... Before ten I think they can adjust ... Secondly, they know a little bit about over here as well, they still have quite a memory about over here, so maybe later in life if they come over they won't have such a problem ... Our main aim is to stay together, but the only reason I might be over here after they are ten is for studies in the long run. Otherwise if it's just for gathering a few more rupees – no, I wouldn't do that. I would prefer my own family life ... I think they might turn out well, but there are chances. I don't want to take those chances. There are a lot of children here that go well. Everybody has their own characteristics but, like Asma's family for example, it's very nice, they're nice to their parents and everybody. But if ... my parents had children like Asma's family, there were a lot of things that they couldn't have tolerated. Like if we talk rude to our parents, even in early ages, maybe in later life we can still get beaten! ... And second thing is religion. [That's the] most important thing. Over here they do religion, but to learn something, and to see something, is two different things. Like, it can be in your mind, but if you don't see, if religion isn't around you, you'll certainly say, 'What is this? This is something bookish, or something related to books' ...

In the first year I [kept thinking] ... 'Isn't there any way out? Isn't there any way to go back?' That's sort of a little more, it has cooled down a bit. I think [that's because of] different factors like my children, my wife – we've grown quite close together. My sister's come over, so it's sort of a small family like we have. So I think it's all right – a little bit all right. But I would love to go, we'd all like to live with our parents all together. My father he said, 'All right – I'll grow your children up for you'. I said, 'That's very nice'. Different things we cherish, we can cherish all together [with the family], we do miss over here. I would like those things to be all together, but sometimes I have sort of grown sort of immune to it now. I try to keep those a little back now and see the new world ...

I would say if I'd come over for holiday over here it would have been wonderful, but coming into the circle of a new life, it's difficult to adjust to it ... I think I'm getting used to it now, but life over here is quite stressful. Like jobs, to run about [paying] the bills – mentally you're crowded all the time [thinking]: 'Got to do this, that.' Maybe the job that I'm doing, maybe that's why I have to give more hours. Sometimes, most of the months, I'm working seven days a week. Maybe it's that that I can't really find time for myself to think, sit down ... Because if I just work plain [without overtime] I can just manage, maybe hardly manage the life I'm living with my wife over here. Sometimes I do send money over – every three, four months maybe one hundred, two hundred pounds. That isn't that much, but to manage all that we are affording at the moment, I have to work that much. Because it isn't a very, very well paid job.

Migration and downward mobility: 'starting from scratch again'

In an early contribution to the literature on masculinity and migration, Margold (1995) writes of the 'crisis of masculinity' suffered by Filipino migrants to the Gulf as a result of racism, degrading treatment by employers, and witnessing corporal or capital punishment meted out to fellow migrants. Some joke about escaping the trials of labour migration by offering themselves as 'mail-order bridegrooms' to Filipina-Americans. Tahir's tale, however, reveals how the more mundane challenges and humiliations of life as a migrant husband can cumulatively act to create similar crises of masculine identity.

Pakistan's troubled economy is characterised by high levels of unemployment, and for most men, migration to a more developed country offers opportunities to earn far more than they could have achieved at home. Nevertheless, Pakistani migrants to Britain are not drawn from the poorest sections of their home society (Ballard 1987), and often have relatively comfortable lives before coming to Britain. Migration itself requires a certain level of resources, and remittances from previous migrants in the family have often helped boost the economic standing of those left in Pakistan still further. In Bristol, as is many other British cities, although there are high levels of home ownership, many Pakistanis live in small properties in deprived inner-city areas. The environment in which their British spouse and relatives live often comes as a surprise to new arrivals. Hamid, a recently arrived husband, told me that his expectations of a clean, honest country had been destroyed when he arrived in Bristol and was robbed by a customer while working in a petrol station near his new inner-city home. Ghalib, who came to Britain for marriage in the 1970s, remembered:

> When I came here I had dreams ... A big myth that is in the Third World ... about Europe and England – they think that everything is rosy, the grass is greener on the other side, people live luxuriously. Because they watch the films, the TV and they see all these big houses, cars ... When you come here and reality hits you, it's all shattered, it's all different.

For most Pakistanis, the impression gained through the media of the wealthy West is reinforced by the impressive homes built in Pakistan with money remitted from overseas, and lavish spending by Pakistanis from Europe or America on visits 'back home'. Many migrant husbands expect, if not streets paved with gold, then certainly material advantages to life in the West. Even photographs of British-resident relatives' lifestyles may be misleading when seen through Pakistani eyes. A student in Rawalpindi, for example, showed me pictures of her sister's house in the UK. To me, it seemed a tidy but modest affair, but to her the fitted carpet and kitchen units were indicative of a high standard of living. Such items are usually only found in the more wealthy and 'Westernised' homes in Pakistan and as such are status symbols, so that I found a fully fitted kitchen in the village home of a family with many members living overseas. Their British relative who was showing me around told me that she had advised against it, but that the family remaining in Pakistan had insisted they have one. It then sat unused while the family's cooking was done in the traditional manner at floor-level elsewhere.

When Salma visited Bristol from Pakistan as a girl, she asked where the rest of her aunt Farida's house was, assuming that the small rooms in which they had stayed on their arrival must be an annex of a more substantial property. Since her mother's sister had migrated over 15 years before, the immediate family left in Pakistan had gone up in the world, moving to large properties in good areas of the cities. Whilst much of this was due to their own efforts in education and career building, their upward mobility had been assisted by remittances from abroad. One of Salma's mother's brothers, for example, had built a smart new house in the suburbs from the proceeds of his work in America. It was thus a surprise for Salma to find that her cousins in the countries that are seen as a source of prosperity were existing in relatively meagre circumstances. Her aunt in Bristol is hardly living in poverty, but she and her husband have had to work in low-paid, low-status jobs. Salma's family in Pakistan, on the other hand, had pursued education and moved to more prestigious residential areas.[2]

The Pakistani population in Britain is characterised by high levels of unemployment, large numbers in semi-skilled manual work, and low levels of professionals, managers and employers. Whilst there has been some improvement over recent decades (Modood *et al.* 1997: 342), and greater levels of participation in higher education (Modood 2004) suggest future improvement, low female labour force participation contributes to a depressed socio-economic profile (Peach 2006). It is into this context of low-paid, low-skilled employment that the migrant husbands in this book arrived. Questions of racism in the job market aside, a family in this position were unlikely to be able to offer contacts or advice on more interesting and lucrative opportunities to the new arrival.

The perception amongst my informants in Bristol was that Pakistani qualifications are devalued in the British job market. Shareen, for example, advised her husband to quit his studies in Pakistan and concentrate on learning practical skills while his visa application was being processed, as she felt that his education would count for little once he came to the UK. Many new arrivals are forced to take employment well below their status in Pakistan, let alone their expectations for their new life, and those from relatively high-status families, or who held good jobs or professional qualifications at home, may find themselves, like Tahir, doing repetitive manual labour.

Lack of language skills, resources and knowledge about the new environment mean that husbands have to rely on their wives or in-laws for help with filling in forms, applying for jobs, dealing with bills, for transport and so on. From the wives' and their families' perspectives, such men may seem frustratingly helpless, an impression compounded by the prevalent expectation that their wives will carry out the bulk of domestic tasks. One woman, talking of how much her husband had 'improved' over the years, noted that when he first arrived he was a 'typical Pakistani man – not willing to wipe his own bum'. Husbands' perspective on the frustrations of this dependent status will be explored later in this chapter.

Modood *et al.* (1997) see the high level of self-employment among Pakistani men in Britain as one response to discrimination and lack of opportunity, providing a 'culture of hope' and conferring status within the community. Taxis are a particularly popular enterprise, with one in five Pakistani men in the 1994 PSI survey in transportation, primarily as taxi- and mini-cab drivers (Modood *et al.* 1997: 348). Taxi-driving is potentially highly remunerative, but the poor conditions and low status can be troubling. Driving at night is more lucrative – roads are clear and customers plentiful as pubs and clubs empty onto the streets – but it involves dealing with drunken or troublesome clients. Hence, when Iqbal arrived in Britain and was working two jobs (in a restaurant and a wholesale 'cash and carry') to make ends meet, it took his neighbour repeated attempts to persuade him that the money he could earn from driving taxis was enough to compensate for the occupation's disreputable status. Another immigrant husband told me delightedly of becoming an insurance salesman. The income, he told me, was irregular and much lower than from his taxi work, but it was a good job – a white-collar job.

The Post Office is another popular employer among Pakistanis in Bristol, but Azra complained that there were no jobs available in such reputable places by the time her husband arrived at the start of 2000. So many young men were coming over, she said, that everywhere was fully staffed and employers could pick and choose the cream of the applicants. Moreover, unlike Tahir, she lacked family contacts already in such relatively desirable employment to help her husband find jobs. He eventually started work in a dry-cleaning factory, long known in the city as somewhere that men and women with little English could find employment, but he found the work heavy and demeaning. Azra told me angrily that even toilet breaks were timed, and that the white foreman shouted in Urdu/Punjabi: '*Jaldi karo!*' (the familiar/impolite form of 'do it quickly!').

Because the jobs typically found by migrants are poorly paid, men like Tahir and Azra's husband often have to take the better-paid night shifts and/or lots of overtime, particularly if they want to remit money to family in Pakistan. This can leave them with little spare time to make new social networks to replace the friends and family lost through migration. Some immigrant husbands are lucky enough to have congenial kin of a similar age living locally, but others find that long hours and cultural differences make them very isolated. While Tahir finds the behaviour of young British Pakistanis objectionable, Omar, a Karachi urbanite, has not made friends amongst the Punjabis in his place of work. The fact that others from similar backgrounds are also working long hours in factories, shops and taxis further limits social opportunities. Azra's husband's only social life is gathering at the mosque for prayer, so he was upset when another member of the congregation told him that all husbands from Pakistan ended up working in the dry cleaners. 'Why do they say that – rub it in?' he complained to his wife. Thomas Walle (2007) describes cricket matches as arenas for friendship among Pakistani migrants in Norway, but such activities were not reported by the migrant husbands I interviewed.[3] As a final limitation on the social possibilities for migrant husbands, while many of the pioneering Asian community groups in Bristol were set up by men, during my fieldwork, the sector was dominated by female-run groups serving Asian women, children and the elderly. Tahir's narrative, however, reveals something more than the difficulties of 'starting again'. The boys whose behaviour he criticises are his own brothers-in-law, and his account is punctuated by his rejection of his wife's family lifestyle.

The transnational *ghar damad*: being an imported son-in-law

Pakistani marriages are alliances between families rather than just individuals. Marriage entails new kinship relationships and statuses, not just for the bride and groom, but in the wider field of new affines. In both the academic literature and among those I worked with in the UK and Pakistan, it is the relationships marriage forges between women that are most commonly discussed, with strong stereotypes of the overbearing mother-in-law, jealous sister-in-law and the vulnerable new bride. The reason for this gendered discourse lies in conventional virilocal residence patterns: a bride goes to live in her husband's family home, and so the nature of her relationships with his relatives are of fundamental importance to the quality of her married life. However, the literature on South Asia reveals that some grooms do live with their in-laws – *ghar jamai/ghar jawai*, literally meaning 'house son-in-law'.[4] My informants in Pakistan and Bristol more commonly use the term *ghar damad* (*damad* also meaning son-in-law). Among Muslims in Indian Gujrat, they occur in relatively wealthy families without sons to farm their land (Lambatt 1976: 54–55). In Hindu Bengal, *ghar jamai* are described as a mechanism for parents without sons to keep married daughters living with them, providing someone to inherit their property, and to care for them in old age (Lamb 2002: 58). University students in Pakistan told me that this type of husband is sometimes obtained through promises of money if a wealthy father does not want to send a cherished (and by implication, spoilt) daughter as a bride to another household. In Bangladesh, *ghar jamai* are often landless, lacking an established household to which they could take their wife, but they can also be the result of migration as fathers working overseas leave a son-in-law to look after their womenfolk at home (Gardner 1995: 167). The *ghar jamai/damad* is the subject of negative stereotypes, and is generally considered to be an undesirable position (Gardner 1995; Jeffery *et al.* 1989), with connotations of being, like the conventional daughter-in-law, dependent on and subservient to the in-laws. Displaced from the patrilineal household, they are 'out of place' (Douglas 1966) in kinship terms, and as such are objects of sexualised insult (Chopra 2009).

Most grooms imported from Pakistan to Bristol find themselves, at least initially, living in their wife's family home. Two British Pakistani women did tell me that they viewed the opportunity to stay with their parents as a reason for choosing a husband from Pakistan, but this situation is more often simply a by-product of the economic implications of migration. It is highly unusual for unmarried Pakistani women in Bristol to live apart from the family, and a husband just arrived from Pakistan is unlikely to be able to afford a place of his own. One woman I met in Bristol had managed to save up and buy a house before her husband's arrival, and some families do purchase properties for their children. However, given the often strained family economic circumstances following an expensive marriage, the cost of airfares, the addition of a new member to the household and the economic constraints on new migrants, many will spend at least some time living with the wife's parents.

Despite their dependency, imported husbands living with their in-laws in Bristol were not spoken of as *ghar damad*. Of course, the derogatory connotations mean that people are unlikely to describe themselves or their husband as being in such a position. One young woman who told me I was wrong to use the term of immigrant husbands said that she had heard of the concept from Hindi movies, suggesting that it is not in everyday usage. It may also be that the stigma is avoided or reduced in the context of migration. Travel may in itself be transformative – in the early years of 'pioneer' male migration to Britain, many cultural norms were relaxed. These were often restored once large numbers of women and children started coming to join their husbands and the idea of residence in Britain as merely a sojourn was abandoned (Anwar 1979; Shaw 1988), but it may be that contempt for the *ghar damad* has faded in a diasporic context where uxorilocal grooms are a common feature and so no longer a curiosity. As Chopra writes, 'The knowledge of risks entailed in migration without safety nets reinscribes the transnational *ghar jawai* in a more positive frame, as one of the few legitimate avenues for migration' (Chopra 2009: 101). The often temporary residence against the virilocal norm dwindles in importance in the face of the issues of migration and risk (to migrant and non-migrant spouses) which dominate people's concerns – the fact that the groom lives with his in-laws is simply not considered the defining feature of the marriage. In analytical terms, however, and with apologies to informants who resisted the use of the term *ghar damad*, I would argue that the concept is helpful in understanding elements of many Pakistani men's experience of marriage migration.

The issue of 'missing kin' was raised in a previous chapter, but the pertinent point here is not simply the absence of certain relations, but the unusual presence, or at least proximity, of others. Whilst the groom is in the abnormal position of being the in-comer without family support, and facing a new family's habits and way of life, his wife starts her married life with her parents and siblings close at hand. The loss of social capital in terms of networks of kin and friends normally suffered by brides is reversed in this situation. Even if the couple do not live in the wife's parents' home, the 'boy' may still feel himself lacking support, and under scrutiny from the wife's relatives, as young couples' new residences are often very close to the existing family home. Some families have branches in neighbouring streets, or at least the same area, facilitating frequent visiting and even shared cooking, so that Uzma and Nadir, for example, have moved to a separate house but still eat with her family. This kind of arrangement erodes the distinction between extended family households and couples who live separately. Becoming 'separate' can, however, help ease the husband's discomfort, as was initially the case when Tahir and Asma moved across the road from her parents to a house owned by Asma's father. Nevertheless, the concept of the *ghar damad* will here be extended to husbands who, although living separately, are in structurally similar positions. Thus, one young man living with his wife in a rented flat near his in-laws complained: 'You've got all your family and I have no one.'

The wife's strong ties within the household or neighbourhood in which the husband is an outsider can disrupt conventional power relationships, giving the woman more support in case of conflict. Equally, part of becoming a wife is being a daughter-in-law, and the lack of this position of subordination and training, combined with the husband's want of family support, may alter the dynamics of power between husband and wife. Yasmin, for example, was able to turn to her parents and siblings for support when she and her husband argued, with the eventual result that he was sent back to Pakistan. Thus whilst some British Pakistani men may hope to reassert gendered relations of power in seeking a 'traditional' wife from Pakistan, British Pakistani women's marriages to migrant husbands may undermine the conventional gendered model of domestic power relations (cf. Lievens 1999; Liversage 2012). The 'Lievens hypothesis' that ethnic minority women may seek transnational marriages in the hope of redressing domestic relations of power has been challenged on the basis of data showing transnationally married Turkish German women are not less likely to live with the extended family after marriage (González-Ferrer 2006). However, this latter analysis misses the significance of the details of the family members with whom the couple live: for young women, co-residence with their own natal family rather than their in-laws has very different implications.

The importance of support from the kin group has been discussed in previous chapters, with those without brothers described as 'alone' and so vulnerable to victimisation (Jeffery and Jeffery 1996: 208). A *ghar damad* can be in a similarly weak position, unable to defend himself from criticism. In Bristol, Azra told me that her husband's friend, recently arrived from India, was thinking of returning home and abandoning his marriage. Azra said that she could tell me straight away what the problem was: his wife must be listening to her parents. *Sas* and *sasur* (mother- and father-in-law), she said, are always critical, but the important thing is not to listen to them, and to be loyal to your husband. Her own parents, for example, moan about her husband's difficulties in filling out job applications, but she knows that he works hard and she will not criticise him. Such situations can, however, lead to conflict if the young man tries to assert his authority, or dislikes the family in which he finds himself.

In Yasmin's marriage, it was when her husband started to criticise her family that the serious arguments started. Each of the complaints Yasmin reports her husband as making are significant:

> Your sister's a bad mother. Your mother's cooking's not that nice. Your dad's so forcive [forceful] and he doesn't understand and he doesn't listen. Your brothers have got attitude problems. Your mother hasn't taught you much about marriage and being a wife ...

His criticism of his wife's mother and brother echo Tahir's concern about the ways British Pakistanis are raised, and being able to raise his children according to his own family's practices. With virilocal residence, this type of small-scale cultural reproduction is in effect patrilineal, so Tahir's father offers to 'grow' his son's children, and men are used to the idea that their family's lifestyle will be dominant in the raising of their children. This system relies heavily on the inculcation of the husband's family's habits on the incoming bride by her mother-in-law and other female elders, a training that is absent in the situation of male marriage migration. They therefore risk the end of this micro-cultural lineage, producing sons who may carry on the family name, but behave as foreigners.

The issue of men's expectations of continuity in 'family culture' across their lifecourse is in marked contrast to those of young unmarried women, and is exemplified in the criticism of the wife's mother's cooking. Daughters-in-law are conventionally trained in their new household's style of cooking, so Yasmin's husband's complaint can be seen as symptomatic of the broader adjustments he has to make to his wife's family culture. Interestingly, this complaint was echoed by Sumera's husband, who disliked both his wife's and his mother-in-law's cooking. When his mother visited from Pakistan, Sumera realised that she used far more chilli and green coriander, something that Sumera would have picked up immediately had she gone to live in her husband's home.

In Pakistan, girls are prepared from a young age for marriage. They are told not to get too attached to ways of life because once they arrive in their husband's home they will have to adjust and adopt their in-laws' patterns (Singh and Uberoi 1994). Female children may be chided for being demanding, and told they won't be able to behave like that in their *susral* (in-laws' household). Alternatively, girls who are overly shy may be asked teasingly if they are already in their *susral*. Yasmin's husband, however, complains that this preparation has been neglected. In another interview, Omar and Jamilah debated this point, leading to some interesting observations about gender roles in Britain and Pakistan, and their basis in religion:

OMAR: ... The parents should tell [the girl what marriage will be like].
JAMILAH: Are you complaining? My parents were hunky dory! They're like: 'Woah! She's doing it herself! She's *wanting* to get married at 19! What more can we ask for?'

OMAR: I'm not saying *her* parents. My sister ... my dad since when she was fourteen used to say, 'Look *beti* (daughter), don't do this. When you go to your in-laws it will be changed. Everything will be changed'. They were making her mind to do the things, and this thing is really absolutely classic and absolutely perfect to tell a daughter, to make her mind before it's going to happen.

JAMILAH: This is where the cultural difference comes in again ... My parents never did that because we never expected that to happen, we expected to live an equal life.

OMAR: This is a separate issue, and I'm talking about a separate thing ... She said, 'My parents never told me' ... Tell me, it's an Islamic question ... God has explained everything in Quran, yeah?

JAMILAH: But your interpretation is different from mine. I did read them, I did read them. In there it says everything's equal ... I read about five or six books about women in Islam, women and marriage, women as mothers. I read all of those books and I read them out of interest, rather than [because] I felt I should read them and prepare. It was more out of interest, [to find out] what my role was ... Much before he came, I used to read them all the time ... but from my interpreting those books, I don't see the culture match that he's talking about – that your father starts training you from a young age. They do train you for adulthood, but they don't train you for, you know, 'You mustn't raise your voice', little issues like that ... These things aren't in the book. It's general things like, 'Respect your husband'. He [Omar] puts that slightly higher than where I would put the level, if you know what I mean ... But I think he's improved, he's definitely improved. So all of this is doing something, isn't it? Little things like pushing the pushchair. Like some Asian men think, 'Oh my God, I'm pushing the pushchair, I must be some kind of sissy man', or something like that. In Pakistan, men wouldn't even dream of picking up a child. People used to make fun of him because he was picking up his daughter. They would be like, 'My God he's picking up the baby!' For me, it doesn't say in Islam about ... Your cousin would say, 'What are you holding her for? Give her to your wife' ... It was offending to me.

This discourse of cultural difference, the 'culture clash' discussed in Chapter 3, is a common one, and interacts with the powerlessness of the *ghar damad* position. Shaw (2000b) suggests that young women like Jamilah raised in Britain may have very different expectations of domestic relations of authority from those of their Pakistani husbands, and that these views are influenced by their mothers, the wives of pioneer migrants to Britain, who also found themselves living outside their mother-in-law's household, and so with greater levels of autonomy.

Some migrant husbands' parents do attempt to prepare their sons to enter a new household. One young woman engaged to a cousin in Pakistan told me about his visit to stay with them in Bristol, explicitly comparing the preparation for marriage given to daughters and the instruction given to her fiancé by his mother:

The mothers tell the girls, 'When you go to a household, you adjust totally with what they do, with their ways of living, with their friends, how they talk to their friends, their relatives. You just go along with what they do – no ifs, no buts, no questions ... ' Whereas the boys – I think it's because the girls go to the boy's house, that's why – but I think when the boys do come to the girl's house, I'm sure they're told by their mothers more. You know, 'When you go to their house be polite, don't be silly', sort of thing, 'Don't do anything stupid', because I think I remember Asif said, 'Mum told me so many things. Mum said, "Don't do this, don't do that. If you want some water, you get it yourself. If you want something, you do it yourself – get up"'. And he said, 'My mum told me all these things before I came', and he was saying, 'Oh God, I felt like a two year old when she was telling me all these things!'

The (rare) opportunity to visit Britain also serves as a kind of preparation. Tahir, for example, brought his sister to Bristol to toughen her up before marriage, and in one very successful marriage, both the husband and wife had spent extended periods in each other's countries: he lived in Pakistan as a child and she came for a six-month visit before they were engaged. Other men were warned by friends or relatives that they would have to work much harder in Bristol than in Pakistan. Nonetheless, it is clear that most men are not prepared, or culturally pre-disposed, to 'adjust' as girls are traditionally trained to do, in order to reduce conflict within the new household.

Marriage, migration and masculinity

Your dad's so forcive [forceful] and he doesn't understand and he doesn't listen.

Yasmin's husband's final accusation speaks of the frustration of the *ghar damad*'s weak position in the household structures of power. While his father-in-law is forceful in support of his daughter, there is no senior member of the family to whom the *ghar damad* can appeal for help with his complaints. Globalisation, writes Kimmel, 'disrupts and reconfigures traditional, neo-colonial, or other national, regional or local economic, political and cultural arrangements. In so doing, globalisation transforms local articulations of both domestic and public patriarchy' (Kimmel 2001: 24). In transnational Pakistani marriages, male migration creates new domestic power relationships. These have been seen from two perspectives: that of the father dealing with the behaviour of an immigrant *ghar damad*, and now from the viewpoint of the migrant husband who finds himself living under the scrutiny of his father-in-law.

Osella, Osella and Chopra (2004) note that:

Compared to the multiplicities of femininity in South Asian studies, men emerge in a lesser and often two-dimensional range. Commonly they are householders; sometimes priests or renouncers; workers – be they landlord-farmers or landless labourers; patrons or clients – and always almost everywhere 'patriarchs'. Too often men become mere ciphers ... brothers-in-law who exchange women in order to maintain relationships whose affective or gendered content is rarely written about.

(Osella *et al.* 2004: 2–3)

In women's narratives of failed transnational marriages, men do at times appear as somewhat two-dimensional villains. However, the approach I have taken here is to use these tales in combination with interview material from men, and other discourses on immigrant husbands, to start to build a more complex picture of Pakistani masculinity in the context of transnational marriage.

Residing in his father-in-law's household can undermine the migrant husband's ability to act in accordance with Pakistani ideals of masculinity. These 'hegemonic masculinities' 'define successful ways of "being a man"', and so consequently 'define other masculine styles as inadequate or inferior'. The *ghar damad* represents one of these other, 'subordinate variants' (Cornwall and Lindisfarne 1994: 3) of Pakistani and north Indian masculinity, and as such may be perceived as emasculating or infantilising by men aspiring to a hegemonic masculine role. So Asif, the visiting fiancé, describes being made to feel like a child when his mother gave him the kind of instructions usually given to young women to prepare them for life in their marital home. Tahir, it will be remembered, wanted to take his children to Pakistan while they were young enough to 'adjust'. While women and children are expected to adapt themselves to new environments, men emphatically are not.

My examination of Yasmin's father's behaviour on behalf of his daughter centred on what might be thought of as a central feature of hegemonic Pakistani masculinity, that of honour based on control. For Yasmin's father, however, honour was not only problematic in the accepted sense of competition with other men, but was seen at times to create internal conflict, bound up with bonds between kin, and experienced as strong emotion. As Osella *et al.* (2004: 14) astutely observe, men can appear as 'especially fragile persons who insist on especially powerful personae'. Break beyond this front and masculinity is, not only for the subaltern but also for the apparent patriarch, 'an ambivalent complex of weakness and strength'.[5]

As has often been noted of women, men are not simply men, and masculinity is braided with other identities. Tahir's wish to control the way his children were raised, for example, was not simply a drive to assert his masculine authority in the matter, but a heartfelt concern over the future loss of Pakistani, Islamic and his individual family's cultural identity. Although it has been suggested that South Asian men's positions vary less than those of women across their life course (Mines and Lamb 2002), ideals concerning manhood change as a man ages and takes on different roles in relation to others. A son should respect his parents, and provide for them when they are older. As a husband

and father, a man should both provide for his family and, as outlined in the previous chapter, be able to exert a certain level of control over his wife (or wives) and children. Marriage migration can limit a man's ability to fulfil several of these roles. In a virilocal context, the son would contribute to the household budget, which is normally controlled by his parents, thus fulfilling his duties to both his parents and his wife and children. After migration, however, this becomes a 'double responsibility' to provide for his dependants in Britain, and to contribute financially to his family in Pakistan. This burden may be particularly onerous for the elder brother after his father has died, when he becomes responsible not only for the day-to-day expenses, but for the marriages of any unmarried siblings. In some low-income households in Bristol, the husband's desire to remit money to Pakistan from an already stretched family budget can become a point of tension between husband and wife. Having accepted a *rishta* from a financially stable family in the hope that funds would not be drained by the need to support her husband's relatives, Azra says her husband has only mentioned the matter of remittances once, and does not dare repeat the suggestion as he knows it will make her angry.

The 'new economics of labour migration' views emigration in search of opportunities as part of collective processes of family 'survival strategies' (Castles 2002; Massey *et al.* 1997). A Pakistani man's migration, whether to Britain or to the Gulf states, is often motivated by a desire to contribute to family finances. Although poverty makes the need more urgent, even the better-off are likely to share the general aspiration to fulfil this important part of a son's duties. It is ironic that in marrying into Britain, the effort to fulfil the masculine role of provider may impose on a migrant groom the emasculating experiences of the *ghar damad*. Moreover, in Azra's husband's case, his weak position in the household has denied the migrant husband the ability to remit money at all.

Living in the father-in-law's home can also undermine a man's authority over his wife and children. Yasmin, as we heard, was largely able to deny her husband sexual access to her by staying up late with her sisters, or turning to her father for support. In this, the young man's autonomy as a husband was constrained when he came into conflict with the more senior male in the household's fatherly duties to protect his daughter. These cumulative pressures may help in understanding the more extreme actions of some imported Pakistani husbands. As in other chapters, my suggestion is that the emotional response highlighted by an exploration of cultural models provides more nuanced insights into motivations for behaviour. I have already argued that Yasmin's husband's anger can be understood by his position as a *ghar damad*. After Tahir and Asma's marriage ended in violence, one of her friends suggested that the pressure of his 'double responsibilities' (which later included financing his sisters' weddings) may have played a role in his deteriorating behaviour – maybe he just 'couldn't cope'. Sumera, whose husband liked more chilli and coriander in his food, said that small arguments like these built up gradually to his violence, and taking a second wife in Pakistan (cf. Charsley and

Liversage 2012a). While not excusing his actions, it is interesting to note that he was under several of the other forms of pressure described in this chapter: having given up what he described as an 'executive job' with a foreign firm in Pakistan, he found himself doing long night shifts of repetitive low-status work; having married outside the family, he had a complete lack of kinship networks for support in Bristol; his wife, although highly religious, is confident and assertive; and he feels he has suffered racism in his workplace.

It is not my intention to suggest that all or even the majority of incoming Pakistani husbands are unhappy class casualties and *ghar damad*s. As Cornwall and Lindisfarne make clear, 'hegemonic forms [of masculinity] are never totally comprehensive, nor do they ever completely control subordinates. That is, there is always some space for subordinate versions of masculinity – as alternative gendered identities which validate self-worth and encourage resistance' (Cornwall and Lindisfarne 1994: 5). It is possible for the *ghar damad* to find subtle ways of re-defining his position, as Ghalib, who came to Britain in the 1970s, clearly demonstrates:

> It was very difficult. But I remember one thing my father said to me, like they say to girls: 'When you go from here, he is your father, and she is your mother, and you respect her.' They say to the girl, you know … 'Your in-laws are your father and mother and you should respect them'. In my case, my father said a similar thing, he said, 'We are your parents, but now you are going to live with them. They will be like your father and mother, do not disobey them'. That's what my father given me – the last lesson, in airport. And believe you me, I'm not saying trying to blow my own trumpet, as they say in England, [but] if my father-in-law comes here and you ask him, 'How do you find Ghalib here as [son-]in-law?' he will say, 'I personally think he's not my in-law, he's my son'. And that's the way he treated me, all the way. He was there for me financially, physically – in every way and I admire him … He says to me, 'Daytime is night', I say, 'Yes, it is night', even [though] I knew it is daytime and I can say to him, 'It's wrong, it's daytime' – I never say to him. At that time, I agree, but then quietly, politely, I say to him, 'What do you think if we just go outside and see if it's day or night?' Then he say, 'Yeah, yeah'. So that's why I think we had a relationship between ourselves very successful. I'm never, never outspoken in front of them. That's the key for success I think.[6]

Instead of railing against the new structures of authority in which he found himself, Ghalib paints a picture of a young man fulfilling the role of a good son by obeying his father's instructions to regard his father-in-law as his father. His deference to his wife's father can then be understood at one level as fulfilling kinship obligations, but at another he makes clear that it was in fact he who, by his tactful cunning, had the upper hand in the relationship, allowing him to emerge from a potentially weak position with his masculine authority unscathed.

For those with good relations with their in-laws, the home environment can be welcoming and supportive for a new immigrant. For Omar, life got worse when, after he had been in the country a year, they moved out of his wife's family home. Where before he had had money left over for travel, leisure and remittances, he now finds it difficult to afford the expenses of independent living. Nevertheless, as demonstrated above, some aspects of the *ghar damad* model are useful in understanding his experience of marriage migration, and this may be the case for the majority of husbands. Hamid, for example, is happy in his new life. Of course, a host of personal attributes may have contributed to his success: he is adaptable, well-liked, is eager to improve his already competent English, and as tall and fair-skinned as his British relatives, blending in unremarked at social occasions. However, this lack of conflict can also be partially understood in relation to the *ghar damad* model. First, he has a good relationship with both his wife and mother-in-law. One imported wife with in-law troubles told me that if the husband and wife's relationship is good then it doesn't matter if the rest of the family are hostile, and the same may be true for imported husbands. Tahir, it will be remembered, initially found sanctuary from the rest of the family in his wife's friendship. In addition, far from being unsupported, Hamid has several male relatives of his own age whom he had met in Pakistan and with whom he socialises regularly. He has been given a relatively interesting job in a firm owned by a kinsman, and he has been able to send money back to his family in Pakistan. Moreover, his wife's father died before the marriage, and her only adult brother lives outside the family home, so Hamid also did not come into conflict with established structures of male authority in the household.

Some unhappy husbands may continue to argue with their wives, and resent the Britishness of their children. For Humera, the conflict that has been a feature of her marriage from the start, when her husband was shocked at his outspoken and outgoing British bride, emerged again as her eldest daughter approached marriageable age. After Humera's own experience of 'culture clash', she and her daughter wanted to find a husband of similar 'understanding' in Britain. When her mother-in-law declared pointedly that she knew where her granddaughter would be married, implying that the decision had been made, Humera asserted that, on the contrary, she would not be marrying anyone from her father's family. Humera's husband was furious both at his wife's independent decision about the marriage, and that she had dared to argue with his mother, and serious arguments ensued.

It is likely that many husbands eventually adjust to their changed circumstances, and that their circumstances and relations with their in-laws alter over the years. Migration is a process that extends well beyond the physical relocation (Werbner 1990). As years go by and the couple perhaps move to their own home, the husband becomes head of his own household, develops more social networks and maybe climbs the employment ladder, the causes of friction may decrease. The stigma associated with their position may also reduce, as Chopra (2009: 102–3) notes of the migrants who later develop an alternative identity as enablers of the migration of other male members of their patrilineage. Tahir's family did relocate to Pakistan for a while, but others who plan to take their family back to Pakistan to escape the indignities of life in Britain may find (like an earlier generation) that they give up on their plan to return as their lives become entwined in their new country through their children, homes, businesses and relationships. Some 18, 20 or more years later, a new generation of fathers may be hoping to take the opportunity of their children's marriages to reaffirm and strengthen ties with the Pakistan to which they have returned only as visitors. Whether such hopes will be realised is another matter: when I asked Iqbal about his hopes for his son's *rishte*, he replied that they would have a more peaceful life if they married a girl from Pakistan, but that he didn't think they would listen to his opinions.

Divorce, masculinity and *izzat*

Some marriages do not last under the type of pressures outlined above. In his first statement to me about his marriage, Junaid (a divorced former migrant husband and father of three) said he did not understand why his wife had been unhappy in the marriage. How could one man, he asked, make her that unhappy? His clear implication is that women married to migrant husbands should view themselves as fortunate to be relieved of the conventional pressure of living with in-laws. His narrative, told to me in a later interview, brings together many of the themes of the last two chapters, and paves the way for a discussion of the gendering of emotion.

> She went there to Pakistan, we met before marriage, we see each other, we talk to each other, she stays in my house couple of days ... Obviously it's her *mamu*'s (mother's brother) house, her uncle's home ... So basically stayed there for a couple of days, it was all 'yes', and that was it. After a few days later, we went into her village, where her father is, and we get married. That was 1993. Then she came here, we applied for the visa, she went back for the interview, we both went to the embassy, and we got the visa, we came back here and start living as a happy family. I rent a house, she never ever worked, I was the one who was working, so I was the one who was provider.
>
> Basically it was all demands. My point of view it was always living under the thumb – too much expectation ... And basically careless – no more care of the husband. I think if they're [a couple] both working, I understand. Because I drive taxi. If husband and wife work, both share mortgage, house and all that. But I was the one who was working and provider. When I go home, I should be looked after ...
>
> And then it always comes into my conversation – my mother-in-law, my brother-in-law, father-in-law. They overrule everything ... how come she's not asking me [the] question – it's my father-in-law and brother-in-law come into my home and they're asking me ... 'Why did you send that

money to Pakistan?' Hang on a minute ... the things will be provided, the mortgage paid, everything I'm working hard for that. I'm not sending *your* money, I'm not sending your daughter's money! Why would they ask me that? That's the problem, that's annoying me ... I would say – any marriage ... when the in-laws interfere, overrule their daughter, overrule their son-in-law, it doesn't work.

My daughter went into private school. I was a taxi-driver, she never worked. Where does the money come from? ... I never left my children to cry for something and I sent money to my parents. Absolutely not.

My brother-in-law even come and shout at me at home. My father-in-law even comes at home and shout at me few times. But it was never reason of money. OK – we got small land in Pakistan. Because they are brother and sister – my grandfather died, he left some land [to the male heir only]. If she wants that land, it's got nothing to do with me. I told her a few times, 'Look – whatever you need, go to Pakistan, deal with it. Don't tell me. Before even I [was] born, he was your brother – OK. So whatever between you – don't involve us' ... Now you know: I cannot fulfil the demands ... At the same time, I was the provider – I sent my daughter to tuition, I bought for my daughter a computer, I bought for my daughters toys, I bought for my daughters birthday present. I bought for my sons. I bought for my wife gold, jewellery, 24 carats. Who was the provider? Where does it come from?

I was working at my brother-in-law's shop ... Obviously people come to me and say hello to me. One day, people buy chapatti flour, onions, spices, vegetable oil, such as they ask – can I put them in the car boot. Lady came, she asked [for] something, I put it in her car. I still remember, in front of the garage, the lady ask – 'Are they related to you?' I say 'Yes, she is my father's sister'. That's all ... What I found out about that five years later – my brother-in-law went in to my wife, tell her I was talking to this lady ... Why would they go to my wife to influence: 'he's talking to those girls'? What is the outcome? How ... they wash their brains. OK, I become a taxi-driver. Sometimes you pay more attention on the road, you are happy, you talk to your customer, you don't pay any attention to who is going past by you. My brother-in-law passed by me. He called my wife and tell her 'He was talking to a white girl, she was sitting right in the front seat. And he ignored me'. I understand, but somehow ...

My brother-in-law went into my home. He said, 'Oh – other taxi-driver coming to my home and they telling me they're making £1,000 a week' ... And if I answer him there is a fight. So I didn't answer him back, and I'm still thinking today ... If that person earning thousand pound a week ten years 1998 to 2008, that person should be multimillionaire! ... I give you my hand – take me to any taxi-driver who is working last ten years and is multimillionaire ... To earn a thousand pounds at least you need £200 to £250 petrol or diesel. You sleep in the car? Where's your wife, where's your children, where's your life? ... I don't do that. I want my wife to be, my children to be known – I am their father, I am their husband. I want to take care of them. If I earn my money, I have to spend my money. Life is one – you have to live for it ... but at the same time I do work hard ... sixty seventy [hours] a week, any time, weekend nights, during the week days. Ah, also – I always pick up my daughter and drop my daughter to school.

... I took her [wife] to Pakistan, OK. We lived there two and a half months. When I came back, I was working, I came home – she never said that to me before – she said, 'You are not a man enough'. I said 'What happened?' She argue, I left the house, I came back after a couple of hours and she said, 'Why don't you divorce me and fuck off!' I was shocked ... Next morning I sat with her in the kitchen, make a tea, same as we are sitting. I said, 'Look, I want to know why did you ask divorce from me'. 'Oh, I was angry, it was yesterday.' I said 'OK, I need some explanation'. She didn't explain, she avoid that, she went out. I was thinking, 'Hang on a minute, what kind of nonsense is this?' Two hours later the phone rings, 'Come back from the work'. My mother-in-law, my brother-in-law, my father-in-law was there. My mother-in-law swear at me, she said, 'Divorce my daughter and bugger off'. [KC: Why?] I still want to know ... If she told me, if there is a problem from my side, I was willing to fix that – which I always did. If there is any way problem, from the bill, from the money, I bought the car for her even, from the push-chair, buggy, feed, feeder, pins to needles – whatever it was needed [or] from that house becomes a problem, I was fixer. I always fix it ... I have only one reason for divorce, she asked me divorce, so I gave her. Nothing more to do.

Eventually, he gave her a three-*talaq* divorce.

I couldn't sleep for three weeks. I used to cry. I miss my daughter, I miss my son. Anyway, it's life. I still miss my children. She never let me to see them. I still want to know why. How she slept with me, she give me three children, and she was divorced from me ... I didn't come in this country for this ...

I even gave her my whole house. [Now he is renting a room in a house shared with other Pakistani men.] Know why I signed that house to her? I love her ... also she is the mother of my three children. I left the roof for my children at the same time for my wife. Children can grow up, maybe they get educated, they can work hard, they can have their house, they can have their happy life, yeah?

When the case went to court, he was denied access to his children. It has been five years since he has seen them.

People think I'm very happy. Whenever my colleagues, when I talk to them, because I don't show them my personal – inside me – they think

I'm very happy. And I'm not ... I don't know what she's drawing the picture of me to my children. But one day, pray to the god, one day, once, they will come to me ... I paid so much money to barristers, to court and all that, to get access to my children. The system will not allow me ...

That's the allegation she made – that I will kill her and kill my children and fly to Pakistan ... I was saying to the court, 'Keep my passport. OK? Keep my passport and give me access to my children. I don't care what the other people did'. I say to even police, I say to even judge, I say to everybody, 'If you think I will fly back to Pakistan, I need a passport. I give you my passport, all the details. You give me access to my children'.

The one thing I don't understand – the person who worked hard, the person who was the provider, the woman who she never ever work, and court still listen to her, and not to me – because I'm from outside ... Where does the children come from? If I'm not here, the children won't be here ... I love my children but I couldn't get through anywhere. You need a lot of money to do that ... At the moment I am stopped because I have no money. I want my life as well ...

I'm renting the car [for his taxi-driving]. No money. I'm paying whenever I can. But soon as I get something I will go back to court again. I need a roof on my head now. When I have my roof on my head, the children – I will apply to them. If I have my wife again [i.e. after his planned marriage in Pakistan, when he has brought his second wife to Britain], I will take her to see the court – look I'm a married man. Look at my wife, let's see where we go from there. I haven't given up on them, but time is running so fast.

Even if I go there [to Pakistan] now, there is nothing to do. Kids are here, my loyalties here, I may one day have access to them. My parents are old now. Say for another five years they will be dead, or two years, or tomorrow they died. Who am I going to see there? ... So brothers are married, they are all home. They have their own lives. My priority is, even if I get married again, I still like to see my children ...

One thing you just mentioned – can I ask you a question: How does a man go to extreme and kill his wife and children? [KC: I don't know.] Same here. I never see in front of my eyes in my life, my grandfather beating my grandmother, my uncle (*taya*, *chacha*) beating my uncles, aunties, my father beating my mum – I never see that. I never grew up in that atmosphere back in Pakistan ...

What does it mean *izzat*, honour? ... My personal opinion *izzat* – you respect yourself, watch your tongue, watch you eyes, watch your thingibob [sex organ]. That's your *izzat*. Don't think your eye's not your *izzat*, your tongue's not your *izzat*, your thingibob is not your *izzat*. If you go and sleep with other women, is that your *izzat*? Look dirty on other women, is that your *izzat*? You can abuse verbally, by tongue, whatever it is, is that your *izzat*?

... OK, he killed his wife, he killed his children. He's in prison now. Is that *izzat*, is that what you telling me? ... Does it say in the books to kill your wife and all that to go to prison, does it? ... *Izzat* is you have to be gentle, you have to be humble, you shouldn't abuse with your tongue to anybody, you shouldn't touch with horrible hands to anybody, you should respect your thingibob, you should respect other women as you respect your own women. You should the same way respect your daughter, the other women. That's *izzat*.

I don't care what other people think, my dear. I won't go into that. If somebody has two million ... He doesn't pay my mortgage. He doesn't pay my rent, my bill. So if he wants respect from me, for me he's a normal person. I can respect him as a human, but I don't respect his wealth ... Let me give you another example. It's a *chaudhry*, it's a land owner, blah, blah, living in Pakistan, Muslim. His daughter has a boyfriend, she has intercourse before marriage. Is that *izzat*? Everybody knows in the whole village what *chaudhry*'s daughter doing, but only *chaudhry* doesn't know what his daughter is doing. Is that *izzat*? OK. I divorce my wife. My mother-in-law asked me for divorce, my wife asked me from divorce. Is that *izzat* now?

For you I think I was a stranger, but ... Thank you – you didn't look at me the way other people thinks. The way people look at me – as you mentioned, community and all that. You didn't look at me that way, and I'm proud of that. But today you talked to me, you know who I am ...

Where is the ground? Where is the love? Where is the passion? What has she done for me? [If] I done something nasty to her OK, where is my forgiveness, my ground, who am I? Do you think I don't need nobody?

[KC: Do you have friends you can talk to?] Yes, but I don't talk them these personal things. I talked to you first time in my life my personal things. But I never talked this very personal things to anybody ... You just mentioned in my interview – concept [of] *izzat*. [KC: So people will think that you have no *izzat* if you ...] Thank you very much ... That *izzat* does not pay my bills! It's very hard to find the good people. Very hard to find the good friends.

He talks to his family in Pakistan every day, but has not talked about his problems.

My mum will cry, my father will cry, my sister will cry. What's the point to telling them there, when they don't know the system or anything. Apart from crying, what they can I do? OK, say for example I tell them, 'Father – your sister done this to me, your brother done this to me, your niece ... ' Apart from being nasty, outcome is zero. They will be nasty to them ... What would I do that for? [To] hurt my children? I'm not that kind of person. I have no time for it.

Because I'm suffering and struggling with my personal things, good things, bad things, nasty things – I don't do nights [i.e. he doesn't drive taxis the more lucrative but troublesome night shift, when drivers have to deal with drunken and aggressive behaviour]. I don't want to go into that part of it ... Money's not everything.

You know funny thing about what we just said – arranged marriage, arranged divorce, *izzat* – in her statement, in her statement [to the court] she said that exactly same thing what you say. 'If I divorce or if I do something I will be bringing embarrass[ment] to my family.' She said that, and she's doing it! It's in her statement, it's in writing. I just click[ed]. She write that – family pressure to stay with me.

Izzat is – this is what I'm coming to – *izzat* is if I still respect that lady who was the mother of my three children. If I'm still good to her. If I'm nasty to her, that's not *izzat*. That's what I thought. If I give her house, that is *izzat* – roof on her head. I can live on the street, you live – that is the *izzat* to me.

As a husband and wife, whatever you do behind the door ... nobody knows apart from God. Why does your parents, family, and all of them know what happens behind the door? Second question: When you do something behind the door. As a woman, as a man, as a woman, as a man, boyfriend or girlfriend, husband and wife, you didn't like what you did behind the door – anybody else has to know outside? Family? It should stay private ... You don't like, man or a woman, to be talked about outside. Is that your *izzat*?

In his narrative, Junaid illustrates several of the dynamics discussed in the preceding chapters. His frustration at his weak position vis-à-vis his in-laws is evident. His repeated refrain that he was 'the provider' for his marital family is both a defence against criticism of his remitting money to Pakistan, and an assertion against the denigration he feels he has suffered, that he was in fact capable of fulfilling the role of a good husband (cf. Charsley and Liversage 2012b).[7] In this case, it seems to have been the wife and her parents who pushed for a divorce. Although Junaid says he does not know why they were unhappy with him, differing interests and the multiple motivations for close kin marriage appear to have played a role, as Junaid was unable or unwilling to fulfil his mother-in-law's hopes of access to her father's estate in Pakistan. Fear of causing conflict within the kin group prevents him from seeking support in his troubles from his natal family.

Junaid's narrative is notable for its musings on the multiple meanings of *izzat*. Denying the validity of acts of honour violence, and denigrating the importance of honour as prestige or status, he stresses private morality as the core of *izzat*. Adding another layer to the discussion of corporate and personal honour from the previous chapter, this stress on personal morality and comportment echoes the observation by Hannah Siddiqui of the campaigning group Southhall Black Sisters (SBS) that:

> For some sections within minority communities, however, notions of 'honour' may have more positive connotations, and are not about social

control, but about respecting a sense of 'personal honour', dignity and integrity.

(Siddiqui 2005: 260)

Whilst SBS has employed this 'subversion' of 'traditional' notions of shame and honour in its campaigns against 'honour crime' (e.g. the slogan 'There is no "honour" in domestic violence'),[8] Junaid's account of personal morality as the true sense of *izzat* helps his narrative reconstruction (Williams 1984) of an identity as an honourable man worthy of respect. Writing of Turkish migrants to Sweden, Apkinar (2003: 435) suggests that immigrant men may emphasise control over women to compensate for powerlessness in the job market or in terms of control over children raised in the country of settlement. Junaid, however, lacking the ability to achieve *izzat* by the accumulation of assets, or control over others, emphasizes honour achieved by control over one's self – the victory of the 'higher self' over animal human nature described by Das (1976), providing an alternative to the reactionary patriarchal behaviour suggested by Apkinar.

Despite his positive personal reinterpretation of the meaning of honour, Junaid felt inhibited from discussing his problems by the fear of being judged against an understanding of *izzat* as reputation. Junaid is unlikely to be alone in this inhibition. A recent BBC news story (Buttoo 2009) on domestic violence against South Asian male marriage migrants reported that 9% of calls to the National Men's Advice Line were from South Asian migrants to Britain. The article carried an interview with a Pakistani man accusing his wife's family of keeping him in Britain, beating him, forcing him to work, and depriving him of contact with other relatives. Concerns of honour loom large in the piece. 'I know many other Asian men who are suffering,' the interviewee is reported as saying, 'but how can we just leave and go back home, it would be so shameful for us and our families.' A National Men's Advice Line representative suggested that such men were 'under cultural pressures not to admit they have a problem', whilst a spokesperson for Karma Nirvana (an organisation campaigning on honour-based violence) gave the opinion that those seeking help were the tip of an iceberg: 'Men would feel embarrassed to admit that they were having problems and choose to suffer in silence for the sake of respect.'

The model of *izzat* as public 'face' which may be damaged by the revelation of lack of control in one's private life (Das 1976), is of course the very form of 'honour' charged with underlying the honour-based violence that Junaid repudiates. However, the two forms of *izzat* (public and private) can also be seen as intimately interconnected, as Junaid illustrates when he argues that part of this personal honourable behaviour is not to tell others about what happens 'behind the door'. *Izzat* thus emerges as a complex, multifaceted concept, with multiple connotations allowing room for manoeuvre in the presentation of self, but where individual assertions of honourability are constrained by others' assessments (actual or imagined) of actions and

182 *Migrant* mangeters

achievements. The more public aspect of *izzat* remains part of a hegemonic masculine model which, as Connell (2002: 143) notes, comes at a price. In these cases, men who may not reap a 'patriarchal dividend' (Connell 2002: 143) in terms of domestic control, nevertheless carry the cost of bearing their subordination in silence.

Notes

1 See Mawaan Rizwan's spoof pop video 'Being a Freshie is Cool', www.youtube.com/watch?v=d6WNfVuRGb4 (accessed 16/07/12).
2 Farida was, however, very proud of the fact that her father's sister's daughter, who was born in Britain and gained professional qualifications, is sending her child to a private school. Given the imbalance in residential status between the two transnationally separated sections of this kin group, it is interesting that Farida's family later sold their two inner-city properties to move to a more prestigious area.
3 One man who arrived on a work permit rather than through marriage described playing sport once a fortnight with other work permit holders, and remarked that he was afraid to speak to British-born Pakistanis who he said did not understand his speech, and viewed him as a 'typical Paki'.
4 See Chopra 2009 on why 'househusband' may be viewed as a mistranslation.
5 See Alter (2002) for an interesting account of the 'degenerative, nerve-wracking, biomoral dis-ease' of masculinity in the context of Indian wrestling.
6 Interestingly, this formulation is sometimes given as advice to women as to how wives can influence their husbands (P. Jeffery, personal communication).
7 A phrase also used by Iqbal, another migrant husband, to justify his sending of remittances.
8 Cf. the Swedish 'Sharaf Heroes' project (Thapar-Björkert 2009).

8 Gender, emotion and balancing the picture

This concluding chapter will draw together the themes of gender and emotion present in the pages of this book, consider the significance of incorporating emotion into understandings of transnational marriage, and attempt to rebalance the focus on negative emotions with some closing examples of successful transnational unions.

Gendered emotion

We have heard connections made between transnational marriage, and indeed many of the central events of a woman's life – her own marriage, and those of her sisters and daughters – and sadness, loss, separation and risk. Women are seen as vulnerable; as potential victims. Descriptions of men, on the other hand, have concerned honour and control. Challenges to *izzat* or other masculine forms may lead to frustration, anger and even violence. These have emerged as publicly recognised discourses on male and female emotion in response to the problems faced by men and women.[1] 'Honour killings', for example, are sometimes explained as a natural male emotional response to threats to their *izzat*. These gendered discourses on emotion were reflected in the different ways men and women presented their marriages to me. Whilst women talked of love and loss, men tended to stress duty and the proper Islamic practices, showing themselves as controlled, honourable men.

The differing ways in which men and women recounted their experiences of transnational marriage during this research strongly echo the gendered narratives found by Katy Gardner in her work with Bangladeshi elders in London, where the identities constructed in interviews were also linked to lifestage. While the men stressed their active roles as migrants and workers in earlier years, but now as religiously knowledgeable elders, the women she spoke to narrated their lives as concerned with caring and suffering (Gardner 2002b). Narrating the bearing of suffering, as Grima (2002) has suggested of *Puxtun* women in Pakistan, may be one way in which women demonstrate their own honour. For some Pakistani marriage migrants to Britain described in this book, these differing gendered tropes – the silently suffering woman and the controlled honourable man – may have the same end result in inhibiting them from seeking support for the difficulties they face in their married lives in Britain.

Yet apart from honour and suffering, as Das (1976) shows in the context of kinship codes, there are other discourses on emotion and behaviour. The cross-sex relationships explored in this book demonstrate how men and women participate in both 'sets' of emotions in their intimate relationships. A father's honour is intertwined with protectiveness for a beloved daughter, and some husbands experience the 'female' role of marriage migration. Tahir experiences this as loss, loneliness and bewilderment, whilst others seem to react with frustration and anger. Azra is seen wanting to control the household income to which she contributes more than her recently arrived husband, by preventing him from sending money to his parents in Pakistan. Azra describes herself as getting angry in this situation, and says she actually enjoys these arguments with her husband. The influence of seniority also mediates gender, producing less acknowledged emotional models such as the frustration of the young man, or the power of a mother-in-law. Even in the most extreme examples of 'female' and 'male' patterns of emotion, both genders are visible, so that Rukhsana Naz's mother took an active part in the 'honour killing' of her daughter. In Asma and Tahir's accounts, the archetypal image of the new bride and her female relatives crying at her *rukhsati* is replaced by that of a just-married son leaving his weeping father at the airport as he boards a plane to join his wife in Britain. In these examples, men are transformed from two-dimensional patriarchal villains to people with comprehensible emotional lives, and women redeemed from the image of passive victimhood. These stereotypes are, of course, perpetuated not only by the popular orientalist imagination, but in part by the discourses of self-representation of Pakistani men and women themselves. Nevertheless, as social scientists have long been aware, what people say is not necessarily the same as what they do, and behaviour is subject to context. Pakistani discourses on gender and emotion thus belie a more complex behavioural reality.

Incorporating emotion into understandings of transnational marriage

For the French anthropologist Lévi-Strauss, the exchange of women between groups through marriage is the foundation of society. Weddings usually involve not just the exchange of women – the gift of the bride – but substantial additional gifting, often between a large number of people. Even the wedding itself can be seen as a gift, in the same way as we talk about 'giving a party' in English. Given the prevalence of unions between close kin in the transnational marriages described here, marriage often does not *start* a relationship, as the families involved tend to be related or at least known to each other before, but Pakistani marriages are often motivated by a desire to *strengthen* relationships between kin. However, as has been seen, they carry the danger of having the opposite effect if things go wrong.

Women, Lévi-Strauss (1969) suggests, are just one among the gifts that maintain social relations, albeit the most important – the 'supreme gift'. South Asian arranged marriages might seem to provide an archetypal instance in which this model of marriage can be applied. In north India, after all, the bride is explicitly talked of as a gift (*kanya-dan* – the gift of a virgin), and the importance of gifting is of enduring importance in Pakistani weddings. Much of the existing literature on Pakistani marriage practices has focused on strategy, or a Lévi-Straussian duty of exchange with kin. Anti-immigration discourses on transnational marriage replicate this approach in their focus on corporate strategies of continued immigration (sometimes at the expense of the wishes of young people coerced into sponsoring the migration of spouses).

My own work, by contrast, highlights the importance of emotional ties. These are, however, not only between women, but are found even in the heart of masculine *izzat*. In arranging transnational marriages to relatives, British parents have been shown as seeking both to protect their children, and to renew their emotional linkages with much-missed kin in Pakistan. Two young women mentioned in this study even saw such marriages as a way of avoiding migration on marriage, thus preserving the close relationship with their parents, something which conventionally suffers through marriage. Matters of group interest certainly do influence Pakistani transnational marriage, but here relationships between individuals have also emerged as crucially important. These are not necessarily between the couple getting married, although ethnography has been presented here that supports the view that romance is not incompatible with arranged marriage. Indeed, the imagery and narration of weddings is often richly romantic. Instances of great affection between husband and wife, which appear in contrast to stereotypes of such relations, have also been reported in these pages. However, the emotional relationships that have come to the fore as explanatory factors for both transnational and close kin marriage among Pakistanis in Bristol, are those between members of the natal family: parents and their distant siblings, and parents and the children about whose futures they care deeply.

An understanding of the intensity with which transnational marriages are bound up not just with migration strategies, but with emotional relationships, is vital in the contexts of increasing attempts to restrict marriage-related migration witnessed in Britain, as well as elsewhere in Europe. These marriages are often between individuals who may not have developed a romantic relationship before their engagement, but they reach to the heart of bonds between parents and children, and migrants and distant siblings, and have implications for the harmony of much wider kin relations. Many attempts to limit marriage-related migration have been justified as responses to threats to (predominantly) women brought up in Britain – being forced into a transnational marriage, or being abandoned by a spouse sponsored from overseas who turns out to have little commitment to the marriage once settlement rights are obtained (Home Office 2007; UKBA 2011; cf. Jørgensen 2012 on Danish policy discourses). These issues are matters of concern to those with whom I have worked, but must be balanced against the harm and distress caused by preventing such marriages.

Underlying governmental discourses of forced and bogus marriages are implicit unfavourable and homogenising portrayals of male marriage migrants. These stand in urgent need of interrogation. At the time of writing, for example, the British government has proposed that where someone who has gained settlement through marriage themselves sponsors a spouse from overseas (within five years of settlement), this should be taken as evidence that their intentions in contracting the first transnational marriage were not genuine. As the probationary period before settlement was recently increased to five years, this presents remarriage within a decade of a first unsuccessful union as inherently suspicious (UKBA 2011). Whilst expressed in gender-neutral terms, this proposal is clearly primarily aimed at migrant husbands, long suspected of having primarily economic motivations for marriage (Wray 2011). The case of Asma and Tahir, however, demonstrates that the later failure of a marriage cannot be taken to indicate that it was not entered into with genuine commitment on both sides. An understanding of the potential stresses of transnational marriage migration for both men and women may make space for more sympathetic interpretations of marital and migration histories. It could, furthermore, inform the provision of more appropriate forms of support to such couples.

Balancing the picture

One fear in writing this book was that in exploring fears surrounding marriages, and the emotional fallout from conflict surrounding marriage, I might inadvertently pathologise the very marriages I hoped to rescue from stereotypical problematisation. It is probably true that a disproportionate amount of the material presented in this book concerns examples of marriages going badly. With the exception of the caring attachments between kin, spouses and friends, the emotions discussed in these chapters are often negative ones: risk, fear, loss, loneliness, frustration and anger.

One defence of this focus on the worries and distress surrounding troubled marriages is, of course, that these are also the preoccupations of my informants. Whilst successful marriages are talked about, they do not provide the rich source of fascination and gossip of those that go wrong. As Junaid complained after our interview, wives may more rarely talk with others about the mundane private acts of love within their marriage than complain about perceived injustices. In a context in which many are considering marriage choices for themselves, their children or siblings, instances of marital conflict or failure provide a vehicle both for examining risk and for justifying decisions. In addition, the majority of my conversations on these matters have been with women, and (as noted above) there may be a tendency among Pakistani women to dwell on the negative as part of narrations of an honourable, forbearing self (cf. Grima 2002; Gardner 2002b). In other cases, interviews and conversations with me may have provided opportunities to discuss problems and unhappiness with an 'outsider' without fear of repercussion or stigma. One young woman who described her difficult marriage at length ended by comparing our interview to therapy, whilst Junaid expressed his gratitude for the ability to discuss his experiences without fear of loss of *izzat*. My own engagement with the topic may also have helped steer the research in this direction. In the proposal for my initial fieldwork, I outlined the cases of three women who had inspired the project: one whose husband had abandoned her soon after she arrived in Britain, another who told me she had wanted a husband from Pakistan so that she would be able to tell him how things worked here and so have more control in the marriage, and a third who valued the religious commitment she felt she shared with her Pakistani husband. Part of the initial motivation for my research was to counteract the overwhelmingly negative popular portrayal of transnational marriages, in which women are portrayed as at best passive recipients of parental direction, or mere pawns in their relatives' plans for the migration of family members, and at worst the victims of coercion and sometimes violence. Two of the three women were very happy with their marriages at the time I first met them, and both British-born wives had actively decided on the choice of a spouse from Pakistan. When I revisited these two women during the course of my research, however, I found their lives had changed. The feisty young wife who told me that she would work for several years before having children, in order to put her husband through courses of study, was now a contented mother. However, I was shocked to hear that the last couple, whose religiously inspired match had seemed so encouraging, had split up amid rumours of domestic violence. When I met up with the young woman again, now with two children, she told me a story of great unhappiness. The first woman I mentioned, who had migrated to Bristol through marriage, remained in a similar position to when we first met, living alone with her child and hoping that her husband would eventually return to her. The balance in the cases on which I had initially chosen to focus had thus shifted from a positive to a negative majority. Of course, this was an arbitrary and tiny sample, but it is conceivable that this sad encounter early on in my research with the failure of what had seemed a promising marriage may have influenced the focus of later discussions. In returning to Bristol for my second period of fieldwork, I heard that other marriages that I had thought promising, such as that between Asma and Tahir, had also run into difficulty – although this of course is not surprising given that 10% of UK marriages end in divorce within the first five years alone (UKBA 2011: 27). The failure of some transnational marriages does not therefore necessarily suggest that they should be regarded as particularly problematic. Indeed, many work well, and even those with rocky beginnings can develop into caring and positive unions.

Nevertheless, as Mitchell notes, ethnographic researchers:

> ... are not just learners. We are also rememberers. We talk to people, watch them and make notes – elaborating our notes later on, on the basis

of our memories. Even if we record our informants on audio or video tape, we still rely on our memories for context. Our memories, or 'head notes', as Ottenberg (1990: 144) first called them, give us the overall feel for the ethnographic situation that leads us, almost instinctively, to 'make sense' of what we experience in the field. They are the raw materials with which we make our interpretations of particular situations, and from which we create our representations of those interpretations: the ethnographic text.

(Mitchell 1997: 91–92)

He goes on:

But the memories of fieldwork do not exist in a social vacuum. Because we learn in a social setting, our memories of that setting are also social. Our memories as ethnographers are bound up in the memories of our informants, whose semiotic, practical and emotional knowledge is bound up in ours.

(Mitchell 1997: 92)

The orientation of this research towards exploring the problems encountered in some transnational marriages is therefore likely to result from a blending of my own experiences with the preoccupations of those with whom I worked.

This book has been an attempt to 'balance the picture' in several ways: in filling in a gap in the literature on contemporary Pakistani diasporic kinship practices; introducing emotion into a predominantly strategic view of marriage, and the voices of women into arrangements sometimes presented as controlled by men; and documenting the experiences of men migrating through marriage. Here, I would like to balance the picture in one final way, by presenting two contrasting vignettes of successful transnational marriages.

The first vignette is the story of what was, in many ways, a rather 'traditional' transnational arranged marriage between a young woman raised in Britain and a cousin from rural Pakistan. Parveen led a rather sheltered life in Bristol. When she left school, her parents didn't want her to pursue further education or go out to work, preferring to guard her reputation until a future husband took responsibility for deciding on the appropriateness of such activities for his wife. Parveen had grown up knowing that her *rishta* had been arranged with a cousin 10 years her senior in Pakistan, but this knowledge made the pair shy around each other when the family visited the subcontinent, so she hadn't spoken to her fiancé. She was happy to go along with her parent's plans, and married when she was 16, staying in Pakistan for several months before returning to Bristol to arrange for her husband to join her in Britain. Now safely married, she was permitted to take a supermarket job in order to demonstrate to the immigration authorities her ability to support her husband. The visa application was initially refused, Parveen's youth having triggered suspicion of forced marriage. Seeing that their daughter was missing her husband, Parveen's parents sent her back to Pakistan where she spent a happy year and a half living with her in-laws in their village, cooking for the family over an open fire. When the visa finally came through, the couple moved back to Bristol, living with Parveen's family until they were expecting their first child, when her husband decided they should get their own place and 'stand on their own two feet'. Her husband had limited education, and has rejected the more lucrative option of taxi driving as disreputable, so his earnings (from part-time shop work) are low. With his permission, however, Parveen later obtained a child-care qualification and started a new career. The couple, who live in one of Bristol's 'Asian' neighbourhoods, have enjoyed what Parveen describes as 20 years of happily married life, and are now saving to contribute towards the marriage expenses of his sister's daughters in Pakistan.

The second of the two closing vignettes provides a contrasting account of 'modern', urban young people behaving in non-'traditional' ways, suggesting the variety of experiences of transnational marriage. This final brief portrait ends with the cinematic cliché of a young couple walking off into the sunset: On a visit to Bristol during the writing up of my initial fieldwork, I attended an open-air music event in the city centre one evening, where I met up with Tariq and Miriyam. He is a Bristolian young professional. Miriyam, his educated and beautiful wife from a prestigious area of Lahore, was wearing flowing Western clothes. I introduced them to the white friends I was with, and we enjoyed a pleasant chat about my research, during which their affection for each other was obvious. I noticed that she frequently touched her husband as we talked, and I joked with the couple about the disapproval such behaviour would attract in Pakistan. Miriyam told me about the part-time job that she enjoyed, and how nice it was that her sister was also married in Bristol and lived locally. When they left, hand in hand, to attend a dinner engagement with relatives, one of my companions looked after them with envy, not believing that such a happy outcome could be the product of an arranged marriage between two people who were relatives, but who barely knew each other when they married.

Note

1 Cf. Boehm's (2011) account of gendered emotions among Mexican couples separated by migration to the USA. Whilst women feared desertion, men carried the burden of breadwinner expectations. Migration in this case again has the potential to reinforce or undermine conventional gender norms.

Bibliography

Abu-Lughod, L. (1988) *Veiled Sentiments: Honor and Poetry in a Bedouin Society*, Berkeley: University of California Press.
Adams, J. (1995) *Risk*, London: UCL Press.
Ahmad, A.N. (2008) 'Gender and Generation in Pakistani Migration: A Critical Study of Masculinity', in L. Ryan and W. Webster (eds) *Gendering Migration: Masculinity, Femininity and Ethnicity in Post-war Britain*, Aldershot: Ashgate, 155–70.
——(2009) 'The Myth of Arrival: Pakistanis in Italy', in V.S. Kalra (ed.) *Pakistani Diasporas*, Oxford: Oxford University Press, 63–82.
——(2011) *Masculinity, Sexuality and Illegal Migration*, London: Ashgate.
Ahmad, F. (2001) 'Modern Traditions? British Muslim Women and Academic Achievement', *Gender and Education* 13(2): 137–52.
Ahmad, I. (ed.) (1978a) *Caste and Social Stratification among Muslims in India*, Delhi: Manohar.
——(1978b) 'Endogamy and Status Mobility among the Siddiqui Sheikhs of Allahabad, Uttar Pradesh', in I. Ahmad (ed.) *Caste and Social Stratification among Muslims in India*, Delhi: Manohar.
Akhtar, P. (forthcoming) 'British Muslim Participation: After Bradford', *Political Quarterly*.
Alavi, H. (1972) 'Kinship in West Punjabi villages', *Contributions to Indian Sociology* 14(6): 1–27.
Alibhai-Brown, Y. (1998a) 'A Hard Lesson for the Asian Community to Learn', *The Independent*, 8 June.
——(1998b) 'A New Age for Asian Women', *The Independent*, 17 July.
——(1998c) 'God's Own Vigilantes', *The Independent*, 12 October.
——(1999) 'A Sari Doesn't Make Us Fair Game', *The Independent*, 3 June.
al-Khayyat, S. (1990) *Honor and Shame: Women in Modern Iraq*, London: Saqi Books.
Alter, J. (2002) 'Nervous Masculinity: Consumption and the Production of Embodied Gender in Indian Wrestling', in D. Mines and S. Lamb (eds) *Everyday Life in South Asia*, Bloomington: Indiana University Press, 132–45.
Altorki, S. and C.F. el-Sohl (1988) *Arab Women in the Field: Studying your Own Society*, Syracuse: Syracuse University Press.
Anderson, B. (1983) *Imagined Communities: Reflections on the Origin and Spread of Nationalism*, London: Verso.
Anthias, F. (1998) 'Evaluating "Diaspora": Beyond Ethnicity?' *Sociology* 32(3): 557–80.
Anwar, M. (1979) *The Myth of Return: Pakistanis in Britain*, London: Heineman.

Apkinar, A. (2003) 'The Honour/Shame Complex Revisited: Violence Against Women in the Migration Context', *Women's Studies International Forum* 26(5): 425–42.

Appadurai, A. (1990) 'Disjuncture and Difference in the Global Cultural Economy', *Theory, Culture and Society* 7: 295–310.

Ardener, E. (1975) 'Belief and the Problem of Women', in S. Ardener (ed.) *Perceiving Women*, London: Malaby Press.

Austen, J. (1994 [1881]) *Persuasion*, London: Penguin.

Azam, F. (1995) 'Emigration Dynamics in Pakistan', *International Migration Review* 31: 729–65.

Baldassar, L. (2007) 'Transnational Families and the Provision of Moral and Emotional Support', *Identities* 14(4): 385–409

Ballard, R. (1987) 'The Political Economy of Migration: Pakistan, Britain, and the Middle East', in J. Eade (ed.) *Migrants, Workers, and the Social Order*, London: Tavistock.

——(1990) 'Migration and Kinship: The Differential Effect of Marriage Rules on the Processes of Punjabi Migration to Britain', in C. Clarke, C. Peach and S. Vertovec (eds) *South Asians Overseas*, Cambridge: Cambridge University Press, 219–50.

——(1994) *Desh Pardesh: The South Asian Presence in Britain*, London: Hirst.

Ballard, R. and K. Gardner (n.d.) *Kinship, Entrepreneurship and the Transnational Circulation of Assets*, www.casas.org.uk/presentations/kinship/Kinship%20and%20entrepreneurship_files/frame.htm.

Barbalet, J.M. (1998) *Emotion, Social Theory, and Social Structure*, Cambridge: Cambridge University Press.

——(ed.) (2002) *Emotions and Sociology*, Oxford: Blackwell.

Barnard, A. and A. Good (1984) *Research Practices in the Study of Kinship*, London: Academic Press.

Basch, L., N. Glick Schiller and C. Szanton Blanc (1994) *Nations Unbound: Transnational Projects, Postcolonial Predicaments, and Deterritorialized Nation-states*, London: Routledge.

Bates, C. (ed.) (2001) *Community, Empire and Migration*, Houndmills: Palgrave.

Batnitzky, A., L. McDowell and S. Dyer (2008) 'A Middle-class Global Mobility? The Working Lives of Indian Men in a West London Hotel', *Global Networks* 8(1): 51–70.

Baumann, G. (1995) 'Managing a Polyethnic Milieu: Kinship and Interaction in a London Suburb', *Journal of the Royal Anthropological Institute* (n.s.) 1: 725–41.

——(1996) *Contesting Culture: Discourses of Identity in Multi-ethnic London*, Cambridge: Cambridge University Press.

Beck, U. (1992) *Risk Society: Towards a New Modernity*, London: Sage.

Beck-Gernsheim, E. (2007) 'Transnational Lives, Transnational Marriages: A Review of the Evidence from Migrant Communities in Europe', *Global Networks* 7(3): 271–88.

——(2011) 'The Marriage Route to Migration: Of Border Artistes, Transnational Matchmaking and Imported Spouses', *Nordic Journal of Migration Research* 1(2): 60–68.

Bhachu, P. (1986) *Twice Migrants*, London: Tavistock.

Bloch, M. (1992) *Prey into Hunter*, Cambridge: Cambridge University Press.

Boddy, J. (2003) 'Alliance and Endogamy: Dynamics of Relatedness in Riverine Northern Sudan', paper presented to the Department of Social Anthropology, University of Edinburgh, February.

Boehm, D.A. (2011) '*Deseos y Delores*: Mapping Desire, Suffering and (Dis)loyalty within Transnational Partnerships', *International Migration* 49(6): 95–106.

Boehm, D.A. and H. Swank (2011) 'Affecting Global Movement: The Emotional Terrain of Transnationality', *International Migration* 49(6): 1–6.

Boggan, S. (1999) 'Shame', *The Independent*, 27 May.

Bolognani, M. (2007) 'The Myth of Return: Dismissal, Revival or Survival?' *Journal of Ethnic and Migration Studies* 31(1): 59–76.

——(2009a) '"These Girls Want to Get Married as Well": Normality, Double Deviance, and Reintegration amongst British Pakistani Women', in V.S. Kalra (ed.) *Pakistani Diasporas: Culture, Conflict and Change*, Oxford: Oxford University Press, 150–66.

——(2009b) *Crime and Muslim Britain: Race, Culture and the Politics of Criminology*, London: I.B. Tauris and Co.

Bonjour, S. (2010) 'Between Integration Provision and Selection Mechanism: Party Politics, Judicial Constraints, and the Making of French and Dutch Policies of Civic Integration Abroad', *European Journal of Migration and Law* 12: 299–318.

Bourdieu, P. (1977) *Outline of a Theory of Practice*, Cambridge: Cambridge University Press.

——(1990) *The Logic of Practice*, London: Polity Press.

Bowen, J. (2004) 'Beyond Migration: Islam as a Transnational Public Space', *Journal of Ethnic and Migration Studies* 30(5): 879–94.

Bradby, H. (2000) 'Locality, Loyalty and Identity: Experiences of Travel and Marriage Among Young Punjabi Women in Glasgow', in S. Clift and S. Carter (eds) *Tourism and Sex: Culture, Commerce and Coercion*, London: Pinter, 236–49.

Bredal, A. (2005) 'Tackling Forced Marriage in the Nordic Countries: Between Women's Rights and Immigration Control', in L. Welchman and S. Hossain (eds) *Honour*, London and New York: Zed Books, 332–53.

Brettell, C. (2003) *Anthropology and Migration*, Walnut Creek: Altamira.

Brown, K. (2006) 'Realising Muslim Women's Rights: The Role of Islamic Identity Among British Muslim Women', *Women's Studies International Forum* 29(4): 417–30.

Brubaker, R. (2002) 'Ethnicity Without Groups', *Archives Européennes de Sociologie* XLIII(2): 163–89.

Bryceson, D.F. and U. Vuorela (eds) (2002) *The Transnational Family: New European Frontiers and Global Networks*, Oxford: Berg.

Bujra, J. (2000) 'Risk and Trust: Unsafe Sex, Gender and AIDS in Tanzania', in P. Caplan (ed.) *Risk Revisited*, London: Pluto Press.

Burki, S.J. (1988) *Pakistan Under Bhutto 1971–77*, London: Macmillan.

Buttoo, S. (2009) 'Abused Asian Men's Lives "Living Hell"', news.bbc.co.uk/1/hi/uk/8286744.stm (accessed 30/10/2012).

Callaway, H. (1992) 'Ethnography and Experience', in J. Oakley and H. Callaway (eds) *Anthropology and Autobiography*, London: Routledge.

Campbell, J.K. (1964) *Honour, Family and Patronage*, New York: Oxford University Press.

Caplan, P. (1992) 'Spirits and Sex: A Swahili Informant and his Diary', in J. Okely and H. Callaway (eds) *Anthropology and Autobiography*, London: Routledge, 64–81.

——(2000) 'Introduction', in P. Caplan (ed.) *Risk Revisited*, London: Pluto Press.

Carling, J. (n.d.) Theorising Risk, Money and Moralities in Migration (TRiMM), www.prio.no/Research-and-Publications/Project/?oid=102106 (accessed 30/01/2012).

——(2008) 'The Human Dynamics of Migrant Transnationalism', *Ethnic and Racial Studies* 31(8): 1452–77.

Carling, J. and M. Hernández Carretero (2008) 'Kamikaze Migrants? Understanding and Tackling High-risk Migration from Africa', paper presented at Sussex Centre for Migration Research, University of Sussex, September.

Carsten, J. (1997) *The Heat of the Hearth: The Process of Kinship in a Malay Fishing Community*, Oxford: Clarendon.
Castles, S. (2002) 'Globalisation and Migration', seminar presented to the School of Social and Political Studies, University of Edinburgh, May.
Chamberlain, M. and S. Leydesdorff (2004) 'Transnational Families: Memories and Narratives', *Special Issue of Global Networks* 4(3).
Chantler, K., G. Gangoli and M. Hester (2009) 'Forced Marriage in the UK: Religious, Cultural, Economic or State Violence?' *Critical Social Policy* 29(4): 587–612.
Charsley, K. (2005) 'Unhappy Husbands: Masculinity and Migration in Transnational Pakistani Marriages', *Journal of the Royal Anthropological Institute* (n.s.) 11: 85–105.
——(2012) *Transnational Marriage: New Perspectives from Europe and Beyond*, London: Routledge.
Charsley, K. and M. Benson (2012) 'Marriages of Convenience and Inconvenient Marriages: Regulating Spousal Migration to Britain', *Journal of Immigration, Asylum and Nationality Law* 26(1): 10–26.
Charsley, K. and A. Liversage (2012a) 'Transforming Polygamy: Migration, Transnationalism and Multiple Marriage Among Muslim Minorities', *Global Networks* [early view online].
——(2012b) 'Silenced Muslim Men: Marriage Migration and Masculinity', paper presented to The Invisible (Migrant) Man workshop, Middlesex University, January.
Charsley, K. and A. Shaw (2006) 'Introduction: South Asian Transnational Marriages in Comparative Perspective', *Global Networks* 6(4): 331–44.
Charsley, K., N. van Hear, M. Benson and B. Storer (2012) 'Marriage-related Migration to the UK', *International Migration Review* 46(4): 861–90.
Chatterjee, P. (1989) 'Colonialism, Nationalism and the Colonized Woman', *American Ethnologist* 16(4): 622–33.
Chopra, R. (2009) '*Ghar Jawai* (Househusband): A Note on Mis-translation', *Culture, Society and Masculinities* 1(1): 96–105.
Clarke, C., C. Peach and S. Vertovec (eds) (1990a) *South Asians Overseas*, Cambridge: Cambridge University Press.
——(1990b) 'Introduction: Themes in the Study of the South Asian Diaspora', in C. Clarke, C. Peach and S. Vertovec (eds) *South Asians Overseas*, Cambridge: Cambridge University Press.
Cohen, A. (1985) *The Symbolic Construction of Community*, London: Tavistock.
Connell, R.W. (2002) *Gender*, Cambridge: Polity Press.
Constable, N. (ed.) (2005) *Cross-Border Marriages: Gender and Mobility in Transnational Asia*, Philadelphia: University of Pennsylvania Press.
Cornwall, A. and N. Lindisfarne (eds) (1994) *Dislocating Masculinity: Comparative Ethnographies*, London: Routledge.
Crick, M. (1992) 'Ali and Me: An Essay in Street-corner Anthropology', in J. Okely and H. Callaway (eds) *Anthropology and Autobiography*, London: Routledge, 174–92.
Dale, A. (2008) 'Migration, Marriage and Employment Amongst Indian, Pakistani and Bangladeshi Residents in the UK', University of Manchester: CCSR Working Paper 2008-02.
Das, V. (1973) 'The Structure of Marriage Preferences: An Account from Pakistani Fiction', *Man* 8(1): 30–45.
——(1976) 'Masks and Faces: An Essay on Punjabi Kinship', *Contributions to Indian Sociology* 10(1): 1–30; reprinted in P. Uberoi (ed.) (1994) *Family, Kinship and Marriage in India*, Delhi: Oxford University Press.

194 Bibliography

Davison, C., S. Frankel and G. Davey-Smith (1989) 'Inheriting Heart Trouble: The Relevance of Common-sense Ideas to Preventive Measures', *Health Education Research* 4: 329–40.

Dawn (2002) 'Women Fight Honour Killing', 25 November.

Delaney, C. (1987) 'Seeds of Honor, Fields of Shame', in D. Gilmore (ed.) *Honour and Shame and the Unity of the Mediterranean*, Washington: American Anthropological Association.

di Leonardo, M. (1987) 'The Female World of Cards and Holidays: Women, Families, and the Work of Kinship', *Signs* 12(3): 440–53.

Donaldson, M., R. Hibbins, R. Howson and B. Pease (eds) (2009) *Migrant Men*, London: Routledge.

Donnan, H. (1988) *Marriage Among Muslims: Preference and Choice in Northern Pakistan*, Delhi: Hindustan Publishing Corporation.

——(1994) 'Marriage Preferences Among the Dhund of Northern Pakistan', in P. Uberoi (ed.) *Family, Kinship and Marriage in India*, Delhi: Oxford University Press.

Donnovan, J. (1986) *We Don't Buy Sickness, it Just Comes*, Aldershot: Ashgate.

Douglas, M. (1966) *Purity and Danger*, London: Routledge and Kegan Paul.

——(1992) *Risk and Blame*, London: Routledge.

Douglas, M. and A. Wildavsky (1983) *Risk and Culture*, Berkeley: University of California Press.

Edwards, J. and M. Strathern (2000) 'Including Our Own', in J. Carsten (ed.) *Cultures of Relatedness: New Approaches to the Study of Kinship*, Cambridge: Cambridge University Press, 149–66.

Eglar, Z.S. (1960) *A Punjabi Village in Pakistan*, New York: Columbia University Press.

Elliot, M. (2002) 'The Nation's Non-formal Classroom: Education in the Indian Museum, Calcutta', paper presented to South Asian Anthropologists Group, University of Edinburgh, September.

Erdal, M.B. (2011) '"A Place to Stay in Pakistan": Why Migrants Build Houses in their Country of Origin', *Population, Place and Space*, 18(5): 629–641.

Espin, O.M. (1997) 'The Role of Gender and Emotion in Women's Experiences of Migration', *Innovation: the European Journal of Social Science Research* 10(4): 445–55.

Fenton, S. and A. Sadiq (1993) *Sorrow in my Heart … Sixteen Asian Women Speak About Depression*, London: CRE.

Fischer, M. (1991) 'Marriage and Power: Tradition and Transition in an Urban Punjabi Community', in H. Donnan and P. Werbner (eds) *Economy and Culture in Pakistan: Migrants and Cities in a Muslim Society*, Basingstoke: Macmillan.

Fischer, M. and W. Lyon (2000) 'Marriage Strategies in Lahore: Projections of a Model Marriage on Social Practice', in M. Böck and A. Rao (eds) *Culture, Creation and Procreation: Concepts of Kinship in South Asian Practice*, Oxford: Berghahn Books, 297–322.

Fournier, P. (2010) *Muslim Marriage in Western Courts*, London: Ashgate.

Fouron, G.E. and N. Glick Schiller (2002) 'The Generation of Identity: Redefining the Second Generation within a Transnational Social Field', in P. Levitt and M.C. Waters (eds) *The Changing Face of Home: The Transnational Lives of the Second Generation*, New York: Russell Sage Foundation, 168–210.

Franks, M. (2000) 'Crossing the Borders of Whiteness? White Women who Wear the Hijab in Britain Today', *Ethnic and Racial Studies* 23(5): 917–29.

Friedman, J. (2002) 'From Roots to Routes: Tropes for Trippers', *Anthropological Theory* 2(1): 21–36.

Fruzzetti, L.M. (1982) *The Gift of a Virgin: Women, Marriage and Ritual in Bengali Society*, New Delhi: Oxford University Press.

Fuller, C. (1994) 'Legal Anthropology, Legal Pluralism and Legal Thought', *Anthropology Today* 10(3): 9–12.

Gallo, E. (2006) 'Italy is not a Good Place for Men: Narratives of Places, Marriage and Masculinity among Malyali Migrants', *Global Networks* 6(4): 357–72.

Gamburd, M.R. (2000) *The Kitchen Spoon's Handle: Transnationalism and Sri Lanka's Migrant Housemaids*, Ithaca: Cornell University Press.

Gardner, K. (1993) 'Desh-Bidesh: Sylhetti Images of Home and Away', *Man* (n.s.) 28: 1–15.

——(1995) *Global Migrants, Local Lives*, Oxford: Clarendon Press.

——(2002a) 'Death of a Migrant: Transnational Death Rituals and Gender among British Sylhetis', *Global Networks* 2(3): 191–204.

——(2002b) *Age, Narrative and Migration: The Life Course and Life Histories of Bengali Elders in London*, London: Berg.

——(2006) 'The Transnational Work of Kinship and Caring: Bengali–British Marriages in Historical Perspective', *Global Networks* 6(4): 373–87.

Gardner, K. and R. Grillo (2002) 'Transnational Households and Ritual', *Global Networks* 2(3): 179–90.

Gardner, K. and A. Shukur (1994) 'I'm Bengali, I'm Asian and I'm Living Here', in R. Ballard (ed.) *Desh Pardesh: The South Asian Presence in Britain*, London: Hurst.

Gedalof, I. (2007) 'Unhomely Homes: Women, Family and Belonging in UK Discourses of Migration and Asylum', *Journal of Ethnic and Migration Studies* 33(1): 77–94.

George, S.M. (2005) *When Women Come First: Gender and Class in Transnational Migration*, Berkeley: California University Press.

Georgiadis, A. and A. Manning (2011) 'Change and Continuity Among Minority Communities in Britain', *Journal of Population Economics* 24: 541–68.

Giddens, A. (1991) *Modernity and Self-Identity: Self and Society in the Late Modern Age*, Cambridge: Cambridge University Press.

Gilmore, D. (ed.) (1987) *Honour and Shame and the Unity of the Mediterranean*, Washington: American Anthropological Association.

Glick Schiller, N. (2008) 'Beyond Methodological Ethnicity: Local and Translocal Pathways of Immigrant Incorporation', Willy Brandt Series of Working Papers, Malmö: Malmö Institute for Studies of Migration, Diversity and Welfare, and Department of International Migration and Ethnic Relations.

Glick Schiller, N., A. Cağlar and T. Guldbrandsen (2006) 'Beyond the Ethnic Lens: Locality, Globality and Born-again Incorporation', *American Ethnologist* 33(4): 612–33.

González-Ferrer, A. (2006) 'Who do Immigrants Marry? Partner Choice Among Single Immigrants in Germany', *European Sociological Review* 22(2): 171–85.

Grima, B. (2002) 'The Role of Suffering in Women's Performance of *Paxto*', in D. Mines and S. Lamb (eds) *Everyday Life in South Asia*, Bloomington: Indiana University Press, 48–55.

Grover, S. (2009) 'Lived Experiences: Marriage, Notions of Love and Kinship Support Among Poor Women in Delhi', *Contributions to Indian Sociology* 43(1): 1–33.

The Guardian (1999) 'The Case of the Reluctant Brides', 15 January.

Guibernau, M. and J. Rex (1997) 'Introduction', in M. Guibernau and J. Rex (eds) *The Ethnicity Reader: Nationalism, Multiculturalism and Migration*, Cambridge: Polity Press, 1–10.

Bibliography

Hall, K. (2002) 'British Sikh Lives, Lived in Translation', in D. Mines and S. Lamb (eds) *Everyday Life in South Asia*, Bloomington: Indiana University Press, 412–24.

Hannerz, U. (1980) *Exploring the City: Inquiries Towards an Urban Anthropology*, New York: Columbia University Press.

Harriss, J. (2003) 'Widening the Radius of Trust: Globalisation and Family Business in India', paper presented to the Centre for South Asian Studies, University of Edinburgh, May.

Harriss, K. and A. Shaw (2009) 'Kinship Obligations, Gender and the Life Course: Re-writing Migration from Pakistan to Britain', in V.S. Kalra (ed.) *Pakistani Diasporas: Culture, Conflict and Change*, Oxford: Oxford University Press, 105–28.

Haw, K. (2010) 'Being, Becoming and Belonging: Young Muslim Women in Contemporary Britain', *Journal of Intercultural Studies* 31(4): 345–61.

Herzfeld, M. (1980) 'Honour and Shame: Problems in the Comparative Analysis of Moral Systems', *Man* 15: 339–51.

——(1984) 'The Horns of the Mediterraneanist Dilemma', *American Ethnologist* 11: 439–54.

——(1987) '"As in Your Own House": Hospitality, Ethnography and the Stereotype of Mediterranean Society', in D. Gilmore (ed.) *Honour and Shame and the Unity of the Mediterranean*, Washington: American Anthropological Association, 75–89.

Hirsch, J.S. (1999) 'En el Norte la Mujer Manda: Gender, Generation and Geography in a Mexican Transnational Community', *American Behavioural Scientist* 429: 1332–49.

Hochschild, A.R. (1983) *The Managed Heart*, Berkeley: University of California Press.

Home Office (1999) *Control of Immigration: Statistics United Kingdom, first half 1999*, London: Home Office Research Development and Statistics Directorate.

——(2000) *A Choice by Right: Report of the Working Group of Forced Marriage*, UK: Home Office Publications.

——(2001) *Control of Immigration: Statistics United Kingdom 2000*, UK: The Stationery Office.

——(2002) *Secure Borders, Safe Haven: Integration with Diversity in Modern Britain*, UK: The Stationery Office.

——(2007) *Marriage to Partners from Overseas: A Consultation Paper*, London, UK: The Stationery Office.

——(2011) *Family Migration: Evidence and Analysis*, Home Office Research Report 94, www.homeoffice.gov.uk/publications/science-research-statistics/research-statistics/immigration-asylum-research/occ94/occ94?view=Binary (accessed 07/03/2011).

Hussain, M. (2001) 'Mapping Minorities and their Media', paper presented to the European Media, Technology and Everyday Life Conference, London School of Economics.

Inden, R.B. and R.W. Nicholas (1977) *Kinship in Bengali Culture*, Chicago: University of Chicago Press.

Jaeger, D.A., T. Dohmen, A. Falk, D. Huffman, U. Sunde and H. Bonin (2010) 'Direct Evidence on Risk Attitudes and Migration', *The Review of Economics and Statistics* 92(3): 684–89.

Jeffery, P. (1976a) *Migrants and Refugees: Muslim and Christian Pakistani Families in Bristol*, Cambridge: Cambridge University Press.

——(1976b) 'Can you Tell *dalda* from *ghee*? Rhetorics of Spouse Selection among the Pirzadas of Hazrat Nizamuddin', paper presented to the Social Anthropology Department, University of Edinburgh, November.

——(1979) *Frogs in a Well: Indian Women in Purdah*, London: Zed Books.
——(2001) 'A Uniform Customary Code? Marital Breakdown and Women's Economic Entitlements in Rural Bijnor', *Contributions to Indian Sociology* 35(1): 1–32.
Jeffery, P. and R. Jeffery (1996) *Don't Marry Me to a Plowman!* Oxford: Westview.
Jeffery, P., R. Jeffery and C. Jeffrey (2004) 'Islamisation, Gentrification, and Domestication: An "Islamic Course for Girls" and Rural Muslims in Bijnor, Uttar Pradesh', *Modern Asian Studies* 38(1): 1–54.
Jeffery, P., R. Jeffery and A. Lyon (1989) *Labour Pains and Labour Power: Women and Childbearing in India*, London: Zed Books.
Jha, S. and M. Adelman (2009) 'Looking for Love in All the White Places: A Study of Skin-colour Preferences on Indian Matrimonial and Mate-seeking Websites', *Studies in South Asian Film and Media* 1(1): 65–83.
Johnson-Hanks, J. (2002) 'On the Limits of Life Stages in Ethnography: Toward a Theory of Vital Conjunctures', *American Anthropologist* 104(3): 865–80.
Jørgensen, M.B. (2012) 'Danish Regulations on Marriage Migration', in K. Charsley (ed.) *Transnational Marriage: New Perspectives from Europe and Beyond*, London: Routledge, 60–80.
Kalra, V.S. (2009) 'Introduction', in V.S. Kalra (ed.) *Pakistani Diasporas*, Oxford: Oxford University Press, 1–14.
Kelly, E. (1990) 'Transcontinental Families: Gujarat and Lancashire', in C. Clarke, C. Peach and S. Vertovec (eds) *South Asians Overseas*, Cambridge: Cambridge University Press, 251–68.
Kenna, M.E. (1992) 'Changing Places and Cultured Perspectives: Research on a Greek Island in the 1960s and in the 1980s', in J. Okely and H. Callaway (eds) *Anthropology and Autobiography*, London: Routledge, 147–62.
Kimmel, M.S. (2001) 'Global Masculinities', in B. Pease and K. Pringle (eds) *A Man's World?* London: Zed Books.
Kofman, E. (2004) 'Family-related Migration: A Critical Review of European Studies', *Journal of Ethnic and Migration Studies* 30: 243–62.
Kohn, T. (1998) 'The Seduction of the Exotic: Notes on Mixed Marriage in East Nepal', in R. Breger and R. Hill (eds) *Cross-Cultural Marriage: Identity and Choice*, Oxford: Berg, 67–83.
Korteweg, A. and G. Yurdakul (2009) 'Islam, Gender, and Immigrant Integration: Boundary Drawing in Discourses on Honour Killing in the Netherlands and Germany', *Ethnic and Racial Studies* 32(2): 218–38.
Krimsley, S. and D. Golding (eds) (1992) *Social Theories of Risk*, Westport: Praeger.
Kurin, R. (1984) 'Morality, Personhood and the Exemplary Life', in B.D. Metcalf (ed.) *Moral Conduct and Authority: The Place of Adab in South Asian Islam*, Berkeley: University of California Press, 196–20.
——(1988) 'The Culture of Ethnicity in Pakistan', in K.P. Ewing (ed.) *Shari'at and Ambiguity in South Asian Islam*, Berkeley: University of California Press.
Kurtz, S. (2007a) 'Marriage and the Terror War (Part I and II)', *National Review Online*, www.nationalreview.com/articles/219989/marriage-and-terror-war/stanley-kurtz, www.nationalreview.com/articles/220002/marriage-and-terror-war-part-ii/stanley-kurtz# (accessed 30/10/2012).
——(2007b) 'Assimilation Studies', *National Review Online*, www.nationalreview.com/articles/220338/assimilation-studies/stanley-kurtz (accessed 30/10/2012).
Lamb, S. (2002) 'Love and Ageing in Bengali Families', in D. Mines (eds) *Everyday Life in South Asia*, Bloomington: Indiana University Press, 62–74.

Lambatt, I.A. (1976) 'Marriage among the Sunni Surati Vohras of South Gujerat', in I. Ahmad (ed.) *Family, Kinship and Marriage among Muslims in India*, Delhi: Manohar.

Lambert, H. (2000a) 'Sentiment and Substance in North Indian forms of Relatedness', in J. Carsten (ed.) *Cultures of Relatedness: New Approaches to the Study of Kinship*, Cambridge: Cambridge University Press, 73–89.

——(2000b) 'Village Bodies? Reflections on Locality, Constitution, and Affect in Rajasthani Kinship', in M. Böck and A. Rao (eds) *Culture, Creation and Procreation: Concepts of Kinship in South Asian Practice*, Oxford: Berghahn Books, 81–100.

Lefebvre, A. (1999) *Kinship, Honour and Money in Rural Pakistan*, Richmond: Curzon.

Lever, A. (1986) 'Honour as a Red Herring', *Cultural Anthropology* 1(2): 83–106.

Lévi-Strauss, C. (1969) *The Elementary Structures of Kinship*, London: Tavistock.

Levitt, P. (2001a) 'Transnational Migration: Taking Stock and Future Directions', *Global Networks* 1(3): 195–216.

——(2001b) *The Transnational Villagers*, Berkeley: University of California Press.

——(2002) 'The Ties that Change: Relations to the Ancestral Home over the Life Cycle', in P. Levitt and M.C. Waters (eds) *The Changing Face of Home: The Transnational Lives of the Second Generation*, New York: Russell Sage Foundation, 123–44.

Levitt, P. and N. Glick Schiller (2004) 'Conceptualizing Simultaneity: A Transnational Social Field Perspective on Society', *International Migration Review* 38(3): 595–62.

Levitt, P. and M.C. Waters (eds) (2002) *The Changing Face of Home: The Transnational Lives of the Second Generation*, New York: Russell Sage Foundation.

Lievens, J. (1999) 'Family-Forming Migration from Turkey and Morocco to Belgium: The Demand for Marriage Partners from the Countries of Origin', *International Migration Review* 33(3): 717–44.

Liversage, A. (2012) 'Transnational Families Breaking Up – Divorce among Turkish Immigrants in Denmark', in K. Charsley (ed.) *Transnational Marriage: New Perspectives from Europe and Beyond*, London: Routledge, 145–60.

Lutz, C. and G.M. White (1986) 'The Anthropology of the Emotions', *Annual Review of Anthropology* 15: 405–36.

Lutz, C. and L. Abu-Lughod (1990) *Language and the Politics of Emotion*, Cambridge: Cambridge University Press.

Lyon, M. (1995) 'Missing Emotion', *Cultural Anthropology* 10(2): 244–63.

Mand, K. (2002) 'Place, Gender and Power in Transnational Sikh Marriages', *Global Networks* 2(3): 233–48.

——(2003) 'Gendered Places, Transnational Lives', unpublished PhD thesis, University of Sussex.

——(2012) 'Capturing and Reproducing Marriages: Transnationalism, Materiality and the Wedding Video', in K. Charsley (ed.) *Transnational Marriages: New Perspectives from Europe and Beyond*, London: Routledge, 175–88.

Mani, L. (1989) 'Contentious Traditions: The Debate on Sati', in K. Sangari and S. Vaid (eds) *Recasting Women*, New Delhi: Kali for Women, 88–126.

Marcus, G. (1995) 'Ethnography in/of the World System: The Emergence of Multi-sited Ethnography', *Annual Review of Anthropology* 24: 95–117.

Margold, J.A. (1995) 'Narratives of Masculinity and Transnational Migration: Filipino Workers in the Middle East', in A. Ong and M.G. Peletz (eds) *Bewitching Women, Pious Men: Gender and Body Politics in Southeast Asia*, Berkeley: University of California Press, 247–98.

Maschio, T. (1998) 'The Narrative and Counter-Narrative of the Gift: Emotional Dimensions of Ceremonial Exchange in South Western New Britain', *Journal of the Royal Anthropological Institute* (n.s.) 4: 83–100.

Massey, D.S., J. Arango, G. Hugo, A. Kouaouci, A. Pellegrino and J.E. Taylor (1997) 'Causes of Migration', in M. Guibernau and J. Rex (eds) *The Ethnicity Reader: Nationalism, Multiculturalism and Migration*, Cambridge: Polity Press, 310–20.

Maududi, S. Abul A'la (1939 [1983]) *Purdah and the Status of Woman in Islam*, Lahore: Islamic Publications.

Mauss, M. (1924 [1990]) *The Gift*, London: Routledge.

Menski, W. (ed.) (1988) 'English Family Law and Ethnic Laws in Britain', *Kerela Law Times* 1: 56–66.

——(1998) *South Asians and the Dowry Problem*, Delhi: Vistaar.

——(1999) 'South Asian Women in Britain, Family Integrity and the Primary Purpose Rule', in R. Barot, H. Bradley and S. Fenton (eds) *Ethnicity, Gender and Social Change*, London: MacMillan, 81–98.

Metcalf, B. (1984) 'Islamic Reform and Islamic Women', in B. Metcalf (ed.) *Moral Conduct and Authority: The Place of Adab in South Asian Islam*, Berkeley: University of California Press, 184–95.

——(1994) 'Reading and Writing about Muslim Women in British India', in Z. Hasan (ed.) *Forging Identities*, New Delhi: Kali for Women, 1–21.

Migration Watch UK (2004) 'Immigration and Marriage: The Problem of Continuous Migration', Briefing Paper 10.8, www.migrationwatchuk.com/Briefingpapers/other/Immigration_Marriage.asp (accessed 28/02/2009).

——(2005) 'Transnational Marriage and the Formation of Ghettoes', Briefing Paper 10.12, www.migrationwatchuk.com/Briefingpapers/other/transnational_marriage.asp (accessed 28/02/2009).

Milewski, N. and C. Hamel (2010) 'Union Formation and Partner Choice in a Transnational Context: The Case of Descendants of Turkish Immigrants in France', *International Migration Review* 44(3): 615–58.

Mines, D. and S. Lamb (2002) *Everyday Life in South Asia*, Bloomington: Indiana University Press.

Mines, M. (1978) 'Social Stratification among Muslim Tamils in Tamil Nadu, South India', in I. Ahmad (ed.) *Caste and Social Stratification among Muslims in India*, Delhi: Manohar.

Mitchell, J.P. (1997) 'A Moment with Christ: The Importance of Feelings in the Analysis of Belief', *Journal of the Royal Anthropological Institute* 3: 79–94.

Mittman, K. and Z. Ihsan (1991) *Culture Shock! Pakistan*, Singapore: Times Books International.

Modood, T. (2004) 'Capitals, Ethnic Identity and Educational Qualifications', *Cultural Trends* 13(2): 87–105.

Modood, T., R. Berthoud, J. Lakey, J. Nazroo, P. Smith, S. Virdee and S. Beishon (1997) *Ethnic Minorities in Britain: Diversity and Disadvantage*, London: PSI.

Mody, P. (2002a) 'Love and the Law: Love-Marriage in Delhi', *Modern Asian Studies* 36: 223–56.

——(2002b) 'Kidnapping and Abduction: Love-Marriage in Delhi', paper presented to the Department of Social Anthropology, University of Edinburgh, February.

Moor, A. (1991) 'Gender, Property and Power: *Mahr* and Marriage in a Palestinian Village', in K. Davis, M. Leijenaar and J. Oldersma (eds) *The Gender of Power*, London: Sage.

Narayan, K. (2002) 'Placing Lives through Stories: Second-Generation South Asian Americans', in D. Mines and S. Lamb (eds) *Everyday Life in South Asia*, Bloomington: Indiana University Press, 472–86.
Nazroo, J. (1997) *The Health of Britain's Ethnic Minorities*, London: PSI.
Noman, O. (1990) *Pakistan: Political and Economic History since 1947*, London: Kegan Paul.
ONS (Office for National Statistics) (1998) *International Migration: United Kingdom, England and Wales*, London: The Stationery Office.
OPF (Overseas Pakistanis Foundation) (n.d.) *Pakistani Migrant Workers: An Overview*, Islamabad: OPF.
Osella, F. and C. Osella (2000) 'Migration, Money and Masculinity in Kerala', *Journal of the Royal Anthropological Institute* 6: 117–33.
Osella, F., C. Osella, and R. Chopra (2004) 'Introduction', in R. Chopra, C. Osella and F. Osella (eds) *South Asian Masculinities*, New Delhi: Kali for Women, 1–35.
Papanek, H. (1964) 'The Woman Fieldworker in Purdah Society', *Human Organisation* 23(2): 160–63.
Parkes, P. (2000) 'Kinship as "Anger": Relations of Resentment in Kalasha Divination', in M. Böck and A. Rao (eds) *Culture, Creation and Procreation: Concepts of Kinship in South Asian Practice*, Oxford: Berghahn Books, 271–96.
Parreñas, R.S. (2005) *Children of Global Migration: Transnational Families and Gendered Woes*, California, USA: Stanford University Press.
Parry, J. (1986) '"The Gift", the Indian Gift and the "Indian Gift"', *Man* (n.s.) 21: 453–573.
——(2001) 'Anakalu's Errant Wife: Sex, Marriage and Industry in Contemporary Chhattisgarh', *Modern Asian Studies* 35(4): 783–820.
Passaro, J. (1997) '"You Can't Take the Subway to the Field!": "Village" Epistemologies in the Global Village', in A. Gupta and J. Ferguson (eds) *Anthropological Locations: Boundaries and Grounds of a Field Science*, Berkeley and Los Angeles: University of California Press, 147–62.
Pastner, C.M. (1982) 'Rethinking the Role of the Woman Fieldworker in Purdah Societies', *Human Organization* 41(5): 262–64.
Pastner, S. (1988) 'Sardar, Hakom, Pir: Leadership Among the Pakistani Baluch', in K.P. Ewing (ed.) *Shari'at and Ambiguity in South Asian Islam*, Berkeley: University of California Press.
Peach, C. (2006) 'Muslims in the 2001 Census of England and Wales: Gender and Economic Disadvantage', *Ethnic and Racial Studies* 29(4): 629–55.
Peristiany, J.G. (ed.) (1965) *Honour and Shame*, London: Weidenfeld and Nicolson.
Pitt-Rivers, J.A. (1965) 'Honour and Social Status', in J.G. Peristiany (ed.) *Honour and Shame*, London: Weidenfeld and Nicolson.
Platts, J.T. (2000 [1884]) *A Dictionary of Urdu, Classical Hindi and English*, Delhi: Munshiram Maroharlal.
Portes, A. (1998) 'Globalisation from Below: The Rise of Transnational Communities', *Transnational Communities Working Paper Series*, Oxford.
Qureshi, K., K. Charsley and A. Shaw (2012) 'Marital Instability Among British Pakistanis: Transnationality, Conjugalities and Islam', *Ethnic and Racial Studies* [early view online].
Raheja, G. (1988) *Poison in the Gift: Ritual, Prestation, and the Dominant Caste in a North Indian Village*, Chicago: University of Chicago Press.
Raheja, G. and A. Gold (1994) *Listen to the Heron's Words: Reimagining Gender and Kinship in North India*, Berkeley and Los Angeles: University of California Press.

Ramji, H. (2006) 'British Indians Returning Home: An Exploration of Transnational Belonging', *Sociology* 40(4): 645–62.
Rana, J. (2009) 'Controlling Diaspora: Illegality, 9/11, and Pakistani Labour Migration', in V.S. Kalra (ed.) *Pakistani Diasporas*, Oxford: Oxford University Press, 43–62.
Rauf, M.A. (1982) 'Labour Emigration and the Changing Trend of Family Life in a Pakistani Village', in S. Pastner and L. Flan (eds) *Anthropology in Pakistan*, Cornell: Cornell University, South Asia Occasional Papers and Theses.
Rayner, S. (1992) 'Cultural Theory and Risk Analysis', in S. Krimsley and D. Golding (eds) *Social Theories of Risk*, Westport: Praeger, 54–82.
Rex, J. (1997) 'The Concept of a Multicultural Society', in M. Guibernau and J. Rex (eds) *The Ethnicity Reader: Nationalism, Multiculturalism and Migration*, Cambridge: Polity Press, 217–29.
Rose, H. (2000) 'Risk, Trust and Scepticism', in B. Adam, U. Beck and J. van Loon (eds) *The Risk Society and Beyond*, London: Sage, 63–77.
Rytter, M. (2011) 'Semi-legal Family Life: Pakistani Couples in the Borderlands of Denmark and Sweden', *Global Networks* 12(1): 91–108.
——(2012) 'Between Preferences: Marriage and Mobility among Danish Pakistani Youth', *Journal of the Royal Anthropological Institute* 18(3): 572–90.
Sagan, S.D. (1993) *The Limits of Safety: Organizations, Accidents and Nuclear Weapons*, Princeton: Princeton University Press.
Salih, R. (2002) 'Reformulating Tradition and Modernity: Moroccan Migrant Women and the Transnational Division of Space', *Global Networks* 2(3): 219–32.
——(2003) *Gender in Transnationalism: Home, Longing and Belonging among Moroccan Migrant Women*, London: Routledge.
Samad, Y. (2010) 'Forced Marriage among Men: An Unrecognized Problem', *Critical Social Policy* 30(2): 189–207.
Samad, Y. and J. Eade (2002) *Community Perceptions of Forced Marriage*, Community Liaison Unit, Foreign and Commonwealth Office.
Sawalha, L. (2002) 'Crimes of Honour in Jordan', paper presented to the Department of Social Anthropology, University of Edinburgh, 1 November.
Schlenzka, N. (ed.) (2006) *Female Marriage Migrants: Awareness Raising and Violence Prevention*, Berlin: Edition Parabolis.
Schmidt, G. (2002) 'Dialectics of Authenticity: Examples of Ethnification of Islam Among Young Muslims in Sweden and the United States', *The Muslim World* 92: 1–17.
——(2011) 'Law and Identity: Transnational Arranged Marriages and the Boundaries of Danishness', *Journal of Ethnic and Migration Studies* 37(2): 257–75.
Schmidt, G., B.K. Graversen, V. Jakobsen, T.G. Jensen and A. Liversage (2009) 'New Regulations on Family Reunification', Copenhagen: SFI, www.sfi.dk/publications-4844.aspx?Action=1andNewsId=2362andPID=10056 (accessed 20/02/2012).
Scott, J.C. (1985) *Weapons of the Weak*, Yale University Press.
Shah, P. (2008) 'Attitudes to Polygamy in English Law', *International and Comparative Law Quarterly* 52: 369–400.
Shah-Kazemi, S.N. (2001) *Untying the Knot: Muslim Women, Divorce and the Shariah*, London: Nuffield Foundation.
Sharma, U. (1984) 'Dowry in North India: Its Consequences for Women', in R. Hirschon (ed.) *Women and Property, Women as Property*, London: Croom Helm, 62–74.
Shaw, A. (1988) *A Pakistani Community in Britain*, Oxford: Basil Blackwell.

—— (1994) 'The Pakistani Community in Oxford', in R. Ballard (ed.) *Desh Pardesh: The South Asian Presence in Britain*, London: Hirst, 35–57.

—— (2000a) *Kinship and Continuity: Pakistani Families in Britain*, Amsterdam: Harwood.

—— (2000b) 'Conflicting Models of Risk: Clinical Genetics and British Pakistanis', in P. Caplan (ed.) *Risk Revisited*, London: Pluto Press, 85–107.

—— (2001) 'Kinship, Cultural Preference and Immigration: Consanguineous Marriage among British Pakistanis', *Journal of the Royal Anthropological Institute* (n.s.) 7: 315–34.

—— (2005) 'Attitudes to Genetic Diagnosis and to the use of Medical Technologies in Pregnancy: Some British Pakistani Perspectives', in Maya Unnithan-Kumar (ed.) *Reproductive Agency, Medicine and the State*, Berghahn Books.

—— (2009) *Negotiating Risk: British Pakistani Experiences of Genetics*, Oxford: Berghahn.

Shaw, A. and K. Charsley (2006) 'Rishtas: Adding Emotion to Strategy in Understanding Pakistani Transnational Marriages', *Global Networks* 6(4): 405–21.

Sheridan, L. (2009) *I know it's Dangerous: Why Mexicans Risk their Lives to Cross the Border*, Arizona: University of Arizona Press.

Siddiqui, H. (2005) '"There is no 'Honour' in Domestic Violence, Only Shame!" Women's Struggles against Honour Crimes in the UK', in L. Welchman and S. Hossain (eds) *Honour*, London and New York: Zed Books, 263–81.

Sims, J. (2012) 'Beyond the Stereotype of the "Thai Bride"', in K. Charsley (ed.) *Transnational Marriages: New Perspectives from Europe and Beyond*, London: Routledge, 161–74.

Singh, A.T. and P. Uberoi (1994) '"Learning to Adjust": Conjugal Relations in Indian Popular Fiction', *Indian Journal of Gender Studies* 1(1): 93–120.

Skrbiš, Z. (2008) 'Transnational Families: Theorising Migration, Emotions and Belonging', *Journal of Intercultural Studies* 29(3): 231–46.

Slovic, P., M.L. Finucane, E. Peters, D.G. MacGregor (2004) 'Risk as Analysis and Risk as Feelings', *Risk Analysis* 24(2): 311–22.

Smith, R.C. (2002) 'Life Course, Generation, and Social Location as Factors Shaping Second-Generation Transnational Life', in P. Levitt and M.C. Waters (eds) *The Changing Face of Home: The Transnational Lives of the Second Generation*, New York: Russell Sage Foundation, 145–67.

Smith, S. (1989) *The Politics of 'Race' and Residence*, Oxford: Blackwell.

Srinivas, M.N. (1984) *Some Reflections on Dowry*, Delhi: Oxford University Press.

Stark, O. and D. Levhari (1982) 'On Migration and Risk in LDCs', *Economic Development and Cultural Change* 31(1): 151–56.

Svašek, M. (2008) 'Who Cares? Families and Feelings in Movement', *Journal of Intercultural Studies* 29(3): 213–30.

—— (2010) 'On the Move: Emotions and Human Mobility', *Journal of Intercultural Studies* 36(6): 865–86.

Swalha, L. (2002) 'Crimes of Honour in Jordan', paper presented at the University of Edinburgh, November.

Tarlo, E. (2007) 'Hijab in London: Metamorphosis, Resonance and Effects', *Journal of Material Culture* 12(2): 131–56.

Taylor-Gooby, D. and J.O. Zinn (2006) 'Current Directions in Risk Research: New Developments in Psychology and Sociology', *Risk Analysis* 26(2): 397–411.

Thapar-Björkert, S. (2009) 'Conversations across Borders: Men and Honour Related Violence in U.K. and Sweden', *Norma: Nordic Journal for Masculinity Studies* 4(1): 46–65.

Tilly, C. (2007) 'Trust Networks in Transnational Migration', *Sociological Forum* 22(1): 3–24.

Trawick, M. (1990) *Notes on Love in a Tamil Family*, Berkeley: University of California Press.

Tugby, D.J. (1959) 'The Social Function of Mahr in Upper Mandailing, Sumatra', *American Anthropologist* 61: 631–46.

Turton, D. (2003) 'Conceptualising Forced Migration', RSC Working Paper No. 12, Oxford: Refugee Studies Centre.

UKBA (UK Borders Agency) (2011) *Family Migration: A Consultation*, London: UK Borders Agency.

Usmain, S.K. (1991) 'Islam and the Muslim Family in India', in M. Singh Das (ed.) *The Family in the Muslim World*, New Delhi: M.D. Publications.

Vatuk, S. (1972) *Kinship and Urbanization: White Collar Migrations in North India*, Berkeley: University of California Press.

Velayutham, S. and A. Wise (2005) 'Moral Economies of a Translocal Village: Obligation and Shame Among South Indian Transnational Migrants', *Global Networks* 5(1): 27–47.

Wakil, S.P. (1991) 'Marriage and the Family in Pakistan', in M. Singh Das (ed.) *The Family in the Muslim World*, New Delhi: M.D. Publications.

Walle, T.M. (2007) 'Making Places of Intimacy – Ethnicity, Friendship, and Masculinities in Oslo', *NORA – Nordic Journal of Feminist and Gender Research* 15(2–3): 144–57.

Watson, H. (1994) 'Women and the Veil: Personal Responses to Global Process', in A.S. Ahmed and H. Donnan (eds) *Islam, Globalization and Postmodernity*, London: Routledge, 141–59.

Watson, J. (1977) *Between Two Cultures*, Oxford: Blackwell.

Weiss, A.M. (1994) 'Challenges from Muslim Women in a Postmodern World', in A.S. Ahmed and H. Donnan (eds) *Islam, Globalization and Postmodernity*, London: Routledge, 127–40.

Werbner, P. (1987) 'Enclave Economies and Family Firms: Pakistani Traders in a British City', in J.S. Eade (ed.) *Migrants, Workers and the Social Order*, London: Tavistock, 213–33.

——(1990) *The Migration Process: Capital, Gifts and Offerings among British Pakistanis*, Oxford: Berg.

——(1994) 'Diaspora and Millennium: British Pakistani Global-local Fabulations of the Gulf War', in A.S. Ahmed and H. Donnan (eds) *Islam, Globalization and Postmodernity*, London: Routledge, 213–36.

——(1996) 'Fun Spaces: On Identity and Social Empowerment among British Pakistanis', *Theory, Culture and Society* 13: 53–79.

——(1997) 'Introduction: The Dialectics of Cultural Hybridity', in P. Werbner and T. Modood (eds) *Debating Cultural Hybridity: Multi-cultural Identities and the Politics of Anti-racism*, London: Zed Books, 1–23.

——(2002a) 'The Place which is Diaspora: Citizenship, Religion and Gender in the Making of Choardic Transnationalism', *Journal of Ethnic and Migration Studies* 28(1): 119–33.

——(2002b) *Imagined Diasporas among Manchester Muslims*, Oxford: James Currey.

Williams, G. (1984) 'The Genesis of Chronic Illness: Narrative Reconstruction', *Sociology of Health and Illness* 6(2): 175–200.

Williams, R., W. Wright and K. Hunt (1998) 'Social Class and Health: The Puzzling Counter-example of British South Asians', *Social Science and Medicine* 47(9): 1277–88.

Wilson, A. (2007) 'The Forced Marriage Debate and the British State', *Race and Class* 49(1): 25–38.

Wimmer, A. (2004) 'Does Ethnicity Matter? Everyday Group Formation in Three Swiss Immigrant Neighbourhoods', *Ethnic and Racial Studies* 27(1): 1–36.

——(2007) *How (Not) to Think about Ethnicity in Immigrant Societies: A Boundary Making Perspective*, Oxford: COMPAS.

Wimmer, A. and N. Glick Schiller (2002) 'Methodological Nationalism and Beyond: Nation–State Building, Migration and the Social Sciences', *Global Networks* 2(4): 301–34.

——(2003) 'Methodological Nationalism, the Social Sciences, and the Study of Migration: An Essay in Historical Epistemology', *International Migration Review* 37(3): 576–610.

Winkvist, A. and H.Z. Akhtar (2000) 'God Should give Daughters to Rich Families Only: Attitudes Towards Childbearing Among Low-income Women in Punjab, Pakistan', *Social Science and Medicine* 51(1): 73–81.

Wray, H. (2011) *Regulating Marriage Migration into the UK: A Stranger in the Home*, Farnham: Ashgate.

——(2006a) 'An Ideal Husband? Marriages of Convenience, Moral Gate-keeping and Immigration to the UK', *European Journal of Migration and Law* 8: 303–20.

——(2006b) 'Guiding the Gatekeepers: Entry Clearance for Settlement on the Indian Subcontinent', *Immigration, Asylum and Nationality Law* 20(2): 112–29.

——(2006c) 'Hidden Purpose: Ethnic Minority International Marriages and "Intention to Live Together"', in P. Shah and W. Menski (eds) *Migration, Diasporas and Legal Systems in Europe*, London and New York: Routledge-Cavendish, 163–84.

Yamani, M. (1998) 'Cross Cultural Marriage within Islam: Ideals and Reality', in R. Breger and R. Hill (eds) *Cross-Cultural Marriage: Identity and Choice*, Oxford: Berg, 153–70.

Yilmaz, I. (2002) 'The Challenge of Post-modern Legality and Muslim Legal Pluralism in England', *Journal of Ethnic and Migration Studies* 28(2): 343–54.

Index

9/11 events 18–19

Abu-Luhgod, L. 4, 20, 125, 146–47, 150, 152
afsos (condolence) 78
'Angrezi Sharia' (English Islamic law) 115
'aql (reasoned discrimination) 148
'arranged' marriages: British Pakistanis 79; *izzat* and emotion 148: 'love marriage 75–76; transnationalism 188–89; *see also rishta*

'backdrop of globalisation' 58
bahar se (outside the kin group) 145
Ballard, Roger 54, 162
bap ki taraf (father's side) marriages 89
baraderi (patrilineage/kin group): *besti* 153; class/residential lines 81; concept 88–89; definition 89; endogamy 61, 153; 'ex-communication' 102; good relationships and matches 142; gossip 152; honour 149; *izzat* and emotion 150–51, 153; kinship 83; marriage partners 60, 102; obligations and assets 91, 93; Pakistan 60; Pakistanis in Oxford 89; power 83; pre-marital conception 152; pressure and female education 84; marriage 150; 'process of inship' 100; reducing risk – knowledge and nature 100; *rishta* 77, 90; *rishte* 79; 'sliding semantic structure' 89, 153; Tamil Muslims 100; transnational *rishte* 79; Yasmin 154; *see also zat*
baraderi/zat 89
barat (fêting of groom's party) 25, 32, 34–35, 43, 118, 120
Baumann, G. 102, 106

bawan (power within the extended family) 93
be-izzati see besti
beards (men) 59
besti (inglorious disesteem, dishonour, disgrace, ignominy) 146, 151, 153
Between Two Cultures 54
bhai (brother/sister/cousin) 106–7
'bogus' transnational marriages 87–88
Bollywood movies 29
book summary 22–23
Born In Bradford survey 89
Bristol: ethnic geography 12–14; 'money business' 36
Britain: marriage and immigration policy 2; marriage migration 7–9; Pakistani migration 12–17
British Pakistanis: arranged marriages 79; behaviour 164; betrayals 103; cross-border connections 69–60; cousin marriage 89, 107; decadent West influence 99; genetic testing 89; interviews 19, 73; marital practices and risk 88; marriage to Pakistani nationals 2, 7; matches/mis-matches 66, 69, 104; obligation to family in Pakistan 91; Pakistanis spouses 112; perceptions 18; privileging religious marriages 116; raising children 168; *rishta* 82; self-employment 164; term 17; 'uncle' term 45; visiting Pakistan 81; weddings 22, 25, 39–41
British Pakistanis and transnationalism: ethnic groups and transnational boundaries 48–50; 'just *miling* everybody': language, culture and code-switching 54–60; transnational engagements 50–54

burri gifts (groom's family to bride) 33, 35, 129, 135, 140

Caplan, Pat 87
Carsten, J. 99, 104, 108
Certificates of Approval Scheme 11
chand-rat (moon night) 28
'classic' legal pluralism 117
close kin marriage: conclusions 111–12; continua and relatedness 100–108; endogamy, cousin marriage and genetic risk 88–90; obligations and assets 90–94; reducing risk: knowledge and nature 98–100; reproducing risk – danger of the double-*rishta* 108–11, 112; risk, society and migration 86–88; Shareen's cousin marriage 94–98; transnational marriage 99, 112
'Community' term 14
conflicting interests: concealment, hope and fear in marriages of Pakistani women to British men 143–46; *izzat* and emotion 146–53; rethinking honour: collapsing categories 153–55; taking sides – rifts in the family 141–43; Yasmin's marriage 134–41
connections: British Pakistanis 59–60; *see also zarurat rishta*
cousin marriage 88–90, 107–8
'culture clash' 17, 67, 169

Daily Jang 62
dan (gift) 35
'Danish Pakistanis' 52
Das, Veena 83, 89, 99, 101, 106, 111, 123, 145, 147–48, 150–55, 181, 184
delayed *rukhsati* 121–24, 132, 134
Desh Pardesh 54
dholki (drum) 27
'doing *rishte*' (suggesting matches) 68–75
Donnan, Hastings 64, 80, 83, 88, 90–91, 101, 129
'double-*rishta*' 109–11, 112, 143
Douglas, Mary 86
dupatta (scarves) 27, 56

East is East (film) 67
emotion: *izzat* 146–53; gender 184–86, 186–89; gendered 183–84; migration and transnationals 2–4; *rishta* 83–84; transnational marriage 184–86

endogamy (marriage within kin group) 2, 4, 61, 88–90, 100, 103, 153
entry clearance officer (ECO) 10
ethnographic researchers 187–88
European Convention on Human Rights 1

forced marriages (*zabardasti ki shadi, marzi ke bagair*) 10, 11, 75, 113, 145, 152, 188
France marriage and immigration policy 2
'friendship-cum-kinship network' 101
'fun space' 30

Gardner, Katy 50, 56, 63, 87, 183–84, 186
gender, emotion and balancing the picture 186–89; emotion and transnational marriage 184–86; gendered emotion 183–84
gender issues (fieldwork) 20–22
'generation' term 17
genetic issues 88–90
ghar damad (house son-in-law) 23, 165–70, 171–74
ghar jamai/ghar jawai (house son-in-law) 165–66
ghar jamail/damad (undesirable position like daughter-in-law) 165
ghar (house) 101
Giddens, A. 86
gore log (white people) 13, 19
gori (white woman/ girl) 19
Greek Sarakatsani people 147, 149
gurudwara (Sikh place of worship) 79

halal meat 14
hath (hand) system of assessing power in kin groups 142
hijab (women) 31, 58–59, 106
Hindus: marriages in North India 103; relationships 101; wedding traditions 31
honour *see izzat*
'honour killings' 150–51, 183, 184
'human dynamics of transnationalism' 103

Immigration and Nationality Directorate 125
Iram (bride): *mehndi* 26–28, 56–57; *walima* 37, 43, 46, 54
Islam: *Angrezia Sharia* 115; close kin marriage 100; endogamy 88; identities

48, 58–59; Islamophobia 6, 58; laws 102; *shari mahr* 129; weddings 26, 31, 36, 38–39, 41; the 'West' 144; women and divorce 153; women's rights 129, *see also mahr*; *nikah*
Islamabad British High Commission 9–10
istikhara (prayer) 74
izzat (honour): concept 23, 147, 181–82; divorce and masculinity 175–82; emotion 146–53; gender and emotion 158; land ownership 147; masculine 183, 185, 187; public and private 181

'*Jaldi karo!* '(do it quickly!) 164
jahez (dowry) 25, 29, 35, 42
jangli (wild, uncultivated) 15
Jeffery, Patricia 18, 34, 48–49, 98, 147, 152
Johnson-Hanks, Jennifer 51, 59
Jullunduri Sikh populations 50
'just *baraderi*' (distant relationship) 101
jute (shoes) 34

kala (black person) 153
kameti (rotating credit schemes) 102
kammi (artisan) caste 88
Kanya dan (gift of a virgin) 35, 185
Karma Nirvana organisation 181
kashmiri chai (tea) 37
kin relationship, immediacy of (*qarib rishte-dar*) 80

lalchi (greedy) 127
larka and *larki* (boy and girl) 75
legal pluralism: 'classic' 117; concept 115; *mehndi* 114; multiplication of marriage rituals 114–18; new 117
lehnga (skirt with tunic top) 32–33, 42, 56
Lévi-Strauss, C. 35, 184–85
Levitt, Peggy 51
Londoni (someone settled in UK) 63
'love marriage' 151

mahaul (environment) 144
mahr (Islamic payment to bride) 115, 128–31, 132
majbur (helpless, oppressed, in need) 99
mamu (maternal uncles) 80, 101
man ki taraf (mother's side) marriages 89
mangeter (grooms/fiancés) term 158

marriage: cousin 88–90. 107–8; failed 126; Hindu 103; immigration policy 1; migration 104; Muslim 103–4; *qismat ki bat* 74; Shareen's cousin 94–98; *watta-satta* 110–11, 141; *see also* 'arranged' marriages; close kin marriage
married but not married (divisibility of weddings and protection of women): conclusions 131–32; delayed *rukhsati* 121–24; divisible wedding 118–20; fears for British Pakistani women 124–28; legal pluralism and multiplication of marriage rituals 114–18; *mahr*: Islam's protection of women in marriage 115, 128–31, 132; separate *nikah* 120–21
'Masks and Faces' metaphor 154
'matchmaker' term 65
mehndi (henna) celebration: British behaviour 56; cash 41; divisible wedding 118; female space 45; Iram's wedding 26–28, 56–57; legal pluralism 114; reducing risk: knowledge and nature 98; religion and tradition 30–31; seating 43; term 25; traditions of opposition 34; wedding styles 37–38, 42
migrant *mangeters* (grooms/fiancés – masculinity, marriage and migration): divorce, masculinity and *izzat* 175–82; introduction 157–58; masculinity, marriage and migration 170–75; migration and downward mobility: 'starting from scratch again' 162–65; Tahir's marriage migration 158–61; transnational *ghar damad* – being an imported son-in-law 165–70
migration: marriage migration to Britain 7–12; emotion and transnationalism 2–4; marriage 104; Pakistani 4–7, 157–58;
milna (to meet) 54
Mines, M. 100
Ministry of Overseas Pakistanis 6
Mirpuris 14–15, 39
'missing kin' 166–67
mithai (sweetmeats) 27
Mody, Perveez 29, 148, 151–52, 155
money *har* (garlands) 41
Muharram (mourning month) 72
munh-dikhai custom 44, 130
'Muslim law' 115

208   *Index*

Muslims: marriages in North India 103–4; Tamil 100

nafs (animal self) 148, 150
National Men's Advice Line 181
Naz, Rukhsana 150, 184
New Labour Government 9
New Laddism 56
'new' legal pluralism 117
nikah (Islamic marriage ceremony) 31, 114, 117, 118, 120–21, 124, 131
nikah-nama (Islamic marriage contract) 114, 120

'one does not share bread, but one shares the blame' (Punjabi proverb) 149
'outside' *rishte* 70

Pakistan: economy 162–63
Pakistanis: British community 12–17; British Pakistanis distinction; 16–17; home ownership 162; honour concept 149–50, 153–54; kinship and emotion 155; language skills 163; migration 4–7, 157–58; term 17
pindu (from village) term 15–16
'points of tension' (social structure) 94
polygamy 115, 131
polygny 125
Post Office (employment in Bristol) 164
Primary Purpose Rule (PRP) 9, 125
'process of kinship' in Malaysia 100
'Prophet's *mahr*' 129
Punjab Marriage Functions Act 36
Punjabi language 19
Punjabi-*bolnewale* (speaking) 52
Puxtun women in Pakistan 183

qarib rishte-dar (close relatives) 80
qarib (spatial nearness) 80
qaum see zat
qismat (fate) 73–74
qismat ki bat (a thing of fate) 74
Quran 53

Ramazan fasting 27, 28, 72, 135
rasm (custom) 39
rasuli mahr see 'Prophet's *Mahr*'
'rationalisations' (close kin marriage) 111
Rayner, S. 102–3

regions of origin for Pakistanis in Britain 14–15
'religious' weddings 38
research methods 17–22
rishta (proposal/relationship): acceptance 74; arranged 188; *baraderi* 77; British Pakistanis 82; close kin marriage 104–6; concept 84, 153; failure 109; Islamic behaviour 105; love match 152; proposal 86; relationship 86; relatives 143; religious commitment 106; reproducing risk 109; rethinking honour – collapsing categories 153; separate *nikah* 120; Shareen's cousin marriage 95; term 61, see also 'double-*rishta*'; *zarurat rishta*
rishte (proposals/relationships): early childhood 69; failed marriages 126; family visiste 143; kinship and affinity 149; 'outside' 70; outside of family 99; reducing risk: knowledge and nature 99; relatives 143; taking sides – rifts in the family 141–42; term 61; transnational 78–83, see also 'doing *rishte*'
rishte-dar (relatives) 77–78
risk: *baraderi* 100; close kin marriage 103; genetic 88–90; marital practices and British Pakistanis 88; reducing risk – knowledge and nature 98–100; reproducing risk – danger of the 'double-*Rishta*' 108–11, 112; risk, society and migration 86–88
Risk and Blame 86
Risk and Culture 86
Risk Revisited 87
rukhsati (bride going to in-laws) 36, 114, 118–19, 121–24, 132, 157, 184

salami (money gifts) 40–41
Secure Borders, Safe Haven White Paper 9
self-employment in Bristol 164
separate *nikah* 120–21
shadi wedding halls 30, 36–37, 39–40
shalwar qamis (clothes) 21, 26, 38, 56, 81
shamiana (decorated marquees) 33
Shuakut, Imran 158
Shaw, Alison. 6, 14, 88–89, 91, 101, 103, 107, 111, 129
Siddiqui, Hannah 180
'simple' brides 105–6
'sliding semantic structure' (*baraderi*) 89, 153

Southall Black Sisters (SBS) 181–82
sunnat (sayings of the prophet) 31, 39
susral (in-law's household) 168
'symbolic nobility' 52

talaq (religious divorce) 126, 129
Tamil Muslims 100
tang karna (verbal abuse) 145
taxi/minicab driving (self-employment in Bristol) 164, 189
tel-rite (oil is poured into hair of bride/groom) 28
tel-mehndi 28
The Guardian 10
The News 62
The World 64
'Tradition' 153
'transcontinental families' term 49
'transnational communities' 49
transnationalism: arranged marriage 188–89; 'bogus' marriages 87–88; emotion and marriage 184–86; emotion and migration 2–4; *ghar damad* 165–70; 'love-marriage' 75–77; marriages 1, 61, 108; *rishta* 65; *rishte* 72–73, 78–83; *see also* British Pakistanis; close kin marriage

ubtan (turmeric paste) 26, 28, 56
'Uncle Norman' stories 90
United Kingdom (UK): immigration regulations 116
United States (US): Muslims 59
Urdu language 2, 17, 19, 52

videos of weddings 37–38, 45
'vital conjunctures' concept 51–53
vurri gifts (groom's family to bride) 33

walima (groom's celebration): divisible wedding 118–19; Iram 37, 43, 46, 54; legal pluralism and marriage rituals 114, 117; religion and tradition 31; weddings 25, 34, 46
Walle, Thomas 165
Watson, James 54

watta-satta marriage (opposite/same-sex siblings) 110–11, 141
'wedding culture' 30
wedding (Iram's): before wedding 25–26; *mehndi* 26–28, 56–57; transnationalism 53–54; *walima* 37, 43, 46; wedding day 32–33
weddings: British Pakistanis 22, 25, 39–41; community development 49; conflicts 134–35, 140–42, 145, 151; 'culture' 51; divisible 118–20; emotion and transnational marriage 184–85; English language 54; Hinduism and tradition 31; making the bride beautiful 28–30; meal 36–37; *nikah* 131; political economy of British Pakistani wedding styles 39–41; religion and tradition 30–32; 'religious' 38; *rishta* 62; seeing the bride 43–46; styles 37–38, 41–43; traditions of opposition 33–36; *shadi* 30, 36–37, 39–40; videos 37–38, 45; *walima* 25, 34, 46; *see also* Islam; married but not married; *zarurat rishta*
'when the fence is old, it is your duty to put new wood in it' (Punjabi proverb) 78
Werbner, P. 13, 28, 30, 34–35, 41, 48–49, 51, 55, 78, 80, 88, 100–102, 146, 174
'Western' influence: clothes 53, 55; Islamic values 144
Wildavsky, Aaron 86–87
word, giving one's (*zaban dena*) 70

zarurat plat (house plot wanted) 61
zarurat rishta (connections/proposal wanted): advertisements 62, 64; proposal wanted 61–65; *rishta*: strategy and emotion 83–84; *rishta* transnational 'love marriage' 75–77; *rishta* as connection 77–78; *rishta* as match 65–68; *rishte* 68–75; transnational *rishte* 78–83
zat (caste) 62, 88–89, 90, 102, 153

Taylor & Francis
eBooks
FOR LIBRARIES

ORDER YOUR FREE 30 DAY INSTITUTIONAL TRIAL TODAY!

Over 23,000 eBook titles in the Humanities, Social Sciences, STM and Law from some of the world's leading imprints.

Choose from a range of subject packages or create your own!

Benefits for you
- Free MARC records
- COUNTER-compliant usage statistics
- Flexible purchase and pricing options

Benefits for your user
- Off-site, anytime access via Athens or referring URL
- Print or copy pages or chapters
- Full content search
- Bookmark, highlight and annotate text
- Access to thousands of pages of quality research at the click of a button

For more information, pricing enquiries or to order a free trial, contact your local online sales team.

UK and Rest of World: **online.sales@tandf.co.uk**
US, Canada and Latin America:
e-reference@taylorandfrancis.com

www.ebooksubscriptions.com

Taylor & Francis eBooks
Taylor & Francis Group

A flexible and dynamic resource for teaching, learning and research.